Jeremiah and Lamentations

THE
CROSSWAY CLASSIC
COMMENTARIES

Jeremiah and Lamentations

JOHN CALVIN

SERIES EDITORS

ALISTER MCGRATH

J. I. PACKER

WHEATON, ILLINOIS

Jeremiah and Lamentations

Copyright © 2000 by Watermark

Published by Crossway
      1300 Crescent Street
      Wheaton, Illinois 60187

First printing, 2000

Printed in the United States of America

Library of Congress Cataloging-in-Publication Data
Calvin, Jean, 1509-1564.
  Jeremiah and Lamentations / by John Calvin.
    p. cm. — (Crossway classic commentaries)
    ISBN 13: 978-1-58134-157-7 (alk. paper)
    ISBN 10: 1-58134-157-1
    1. Bible. O.T. Jeremiah—Commentaries. 2. Bible. O.T. Lamentations—
Commentaries. I. Title. II. Series.
  BS1525.3.C35 2000
  224'.2077—dc20   99-053548

5L		31	30	29	28	27	26	25	24	23	22

First British edition 2000

Production and Printing in the United States of America for
CROSSWAY
Norton Street, Nottingham, England NG7 3HR

ISBN 1-85684-196-0

Contents

Jeremiah

Lamentations

Series Preface

The purpose of the Crossway Classic Commentaries is to make some of the most valuable commentaries on the books of the Bible, by some of the greatest Bible teachers and theologians in the last 500 years, available to a new generation. These books will help today's readers learn truth, wisdom, and devotion from such authors as J. C. Ryle, Martin Luther, John Calvin, J. B. Lightfoot, John Owen, Charles Spurgeon, Charles Hodge, and Matthew Henry.

We do not apologize for the age of some of the items chosen. In the realm of practical exposition promoting godliness, the old is often better than the new. Spiritual vision and authority, based on an accurate handling of the biblical text, are the qualities that have been primarily sought in deciding what to include.

So far as is possible, everything is tailored to the needs and enrichment of thoughtful readers—lay Christians, students, and those in the ministry. The originals, some of which were written at a high technical level, have been abridged as needed, simplified stylistically, and unburdened of foreign words. However, the intention of this series is never to change any thoughts of the original authors, but to faithfully convey them in an understandable fashion.

The publishers are grateful to Dr. Alister McGrath of Wycliffe Hall, Oxford, Dr. J. I. Packer of Regent College, Vancouver, and Watermark of Norfolk, England, for the work of selecting and editing that now brings this project to fruition.

THE PUBLISHERS
Crossway Books
Wheaton, Illinois

Introduction

Calvin on Jeremiah began as 193 hour-long classroom lectures, given near the end of Calvin's life at the rate of three a week extemporarily in Latin to a mixed bag of senior schoolboys, pastors, and ministerial students from all over Europe in the Geneva Academy. The work as published was corrected but unadorned transcripts of these lectures, which he had created off the cuff with only an unmarked Hebrew Bible in front of him, and which faithful friends in his small audience had been able to take down word for word (Calvin spoke steadily but slowly).

In his dedication in the original edition Calvin apologizes for the lack of literary airs and graces but covers himself by saying, "I would by no means have allowed this book to go forth to the public had I not thought it would be useful and profitable to the church of God." And he further declares: "If Jeremiah himself were now alive on earth, he would, if I am not mistaken, add his own recommendation; for he would acknowledge that his prophecies have been explained by me not less honestly than reverently; and further, that they have been usefully accommodated to present circumstances." Latter-day readers, with four more centuries of publication and study of commentaries behind them, can only agree. Calvin is still up with the leaders, and as the 1850 translator stated: "Though the lectures were extemporaneously delivered, there is yet so much order preserved, and such brevity, clearness, and suitableness of diction are found in them, that in these respects they nearly equal the most finished compositions of Calvin." This is true. Calvin was amazing.

Though the exposition is, as we would say, strictly grammatical and historical, in the way that once led a critic, used to reading Christ into the Old Testament, to speak of *Calvinus Judaizans* (Calvin acting the Jew), there are plenty of applicatory comments relating sin and grace in Jeremiah to sin and grace in Calvin's western Europe, and by extension to sin and grace in the modern world. Calvin's regular prayer at the start of each lecture was: "May the Lord grant that we shall engage in contemplating the mysteries of his heavenly wisdom with truly growing devotion, to his glory and our own edification." Readers will find that Calvin's text gives much help in this.

Few, I think, would nominate Jeremiah as their favorite Bible book. His language is vivid, his sense of Judah's spiritual tragedy is strong, and the poignancy of his prophecies can be soul-shaking. He has the poet's power to catch the imagination in a way that pierces the heart. But his book is long, and his constant focus on his people's hardness of heart, and the pain and grief that his ministry of recall from perversity and realism about coming judgment brought him, may seem oppressive. Calvin keeps step with Jeremiah, and his commentary is correspondingly lengthy (five volumes in the 1850 translation, including Lamentations); so the present abridgment renders us good service.

Calvin's extempore prayers rounding off each lecture were recorded, and that which closed the second of these may well be our own prayer as we turn to his elucidation of the word of the Lord to and through Jeremiah.

> Grant, Almighty God, that since you are pleased kindly to invite us to yourself, and have consecrated your word for our salvation, O grant that we may willingly and from the heart obey you, and become so teachable that what you have designed for our salvation may not turn to our perdition; but may that incorruptible seed by which you regenerate us into a hope of the celestial life so drive its roots into our hearts and bring forth fruit that your name may be glorified; and may we be so planted in the courts of your house that we may grow and flourish, and that fruit may appear through the whole course of our life, until we shall at length enjoy that blessed life which is laid up for us in heaven; through Jesus Christ our Lord. Amen.

J. I. PACKER

Jeremiah

Introduction to Jeremiah

By John Calvin

Jeremiah started his work as a prophet under Josiah, in the thirteenth year of his reign. Josiah was a sincere servant of God, and he reigned during very confused times. The book of the law was unknown, so that everyone indulged in evil forms of worship. It is recorded in sacred history: "In the eighteenth year of Josiah's reign, to purify the land and the temple, he sent Shaphan son of Azaliah and Maaseiah the ruler of the city, with Joah son of Joahaz, the recorder, to repair the temple of the Lord his God. . . . Hilkiah said to Shaphan the secretary, 'I have found the Book of the law in the temple of the Lord.' He gave it to Shaphan" (2 Chronicles 34:8, 15).

The first thing to be observed is the time when Jeremiah began to teach. Religion was then so corrupt, with everyone inventing errors to suit their own ends, that Jeremiah's work must have been hard and arduous. The end of his work must be noted. He says that he did his work until the deportation; so his work lasted for forty years. We must observe that after the city of Jerusalem was cut off, and its inhabitants were taken as captives into Babylon, Jeremiah continued with his work. He was taken off to Egypt, as we learn from the end of his book (see especially chapter 44). He was taken there by force, while he still pronounced a curse on all the Jews who tried to find hiding places in Egypt.

So, after the destruction of Jerusalem, Jeremiah carried on his work. It may be that he carried on his work for another ten years. It is said that he was stoned to death, and this is not unlikely, for he was just as severe in his criticism of the Jews who had fled into Egypt as he was against the city of Jerusalem while it stood. It is probable that they killed the holy prophet.

I come now to the contents of the book. As Isaiah and the other prophets had spent their labor almost in vain, nothing remained for Jeremiah to do but to briefly announce sentence. In summary, this was: "There is now no pardon; it is the time of extreme vengeance, for they have abused

God's forbearance for too long. He bore with them, was kind to them, exhorted them to repent, and said he would be propitious if they returned to the right way. But God's kindness has been despised by them." So Jeremiah had to speak against them as people in a lost and hopeless state of perverseness. The main thing in this teaching was: "The kingdom and the priesthood are finished. The Jews have so often and in so many ways and for so long provoked God's wrath and rejected the pious warnings of his servants."

Isaiah, in his day, also uttered warnings, but whenever he spoke severely, he added some hope of pardon, to mitigate what was terrible. But after the ten tribes had been carried into exile, and various calamities had come upon the kingdom, the Jews were still impenitent, hardening themselves more and more under God's scourges. So he had to deal with them more severely. God had contended with them through Isaiah and the other prophets. He showed that they were guilty and pronounced on them the sentence of condemnation through Jeremiah and Ezekiel.

Also, in order that Jeremiah's teaching might be complete, God made him the herald of his grace and of the salvation of the promised Christ. However, we must bear in mind that he offered them no hope of mercy until they had suffered the punishment that their sins deserved.

Jeremiah was sent by God to proclaim to the people their last calamity. But he also told them of their future redemption and at the same time reminded them of the intervening seventy years in exile.

Jeremiah
Chapter 1

1. The words of Jeremiah son of Hilkiah, one of the priests at Anathoth in the territory of Benjamin. It is not for nothing that the start of Jeremiah's work as a prophet in God's church is stated. It began when the people were in a very corrupt state, with all their religion vitiated, because the book of the law had been lost. Nowhere else can we find the correct way to worship God. At this time, when impiety had long been the prevailing custom among the Jews, Jeremiah suddenly appeared.

The heaviest of burdens was placed on Jeremiah's shoulders. Most people were trampling underfoot the pure doctrine of the law, and he was trying to bring them back to it; but many people opposed him.

Son of Hilkiah. Jeremiah does not say that Hilkiah was the high priest. On the contrary, he adds, **one of the priests at Anathoth in the territory of Benjamin.** We know that Anathoth was an insignificant village, not far from Jerusalem. And Jeremiah says that it was **in the territory of Benjamin.** Its closeness to Jerusalem may be gathered from the words of Isaiah who says that poor Anathoth was terrified (see Isaiah 10:30ff.).

Jeremiah also says that Hilkiah was **one of the priests.** Hence Jeremiah was more suited to the prophetic office than many of the other prophets, such as Amos and Isaiah. God took Isaiah from the court (he was a member of the royal family) and made him a prophet. Amos had a different background: he was a shepherd.

2. The word of the LORD came to him in the thirteenth year of the reign of Josiah son of Amon king of Judah. Jeremiah explains in this second verse that he brought nothing to the people that he had not received from God; he faithfully declared what God had commanded him. The word of the Lord was given to him.

3. And through the reign of Jehoiakim son of Josiah king of Judah, down to the fifth month of the eleventh year of Zedekiah son of Josiah king of Judah, when the people of Jerusalem went into exile. In my introduction I have shown why Jeremiah says that he had been chosen as a prophet in the thirteenth year of Josiah's reign and that he continued until **the eleventh year of Zedekiah.**

4. The word of the LORD came to me, saying . . . Jeremiah introduces God as the speaker in order to lend more weight to what he says.

5. "Before I formed you in the womb I knew you, before you were born I set you apart; I appointed you as a prophet to the nations." God declares that he **knew** Jeremiah before he **formed** him **in the womb.** This is not said especially of the prophet, as if other people are unknown to God; it refers to the prophetic office. It is like saying, "Before I formed you in the womb, I destined you for this work, so that you may undertake the burden of being a teacher among these people. I formed you in the womb and at the same time appointed you for a special work. And it was not your power that qualified you for this office, for I created not only a man, but a prophet."

It may seem strange that Jeremiah should be called **a prophet to the nations.** God designated him to be the minister of his church. He did not go to the Ninevites, as Jonah did (see Jonah 3:3), nor did he travel into other countries but spent all his time working among the tribe of Judah. So why was he called **a prophet to the nations?** The answer is that although God appointed him especially for his church, his teaching belonged to other nations as well.

6-7. "Ah, Sovereign LORD," I said, **"I do not know how to speak; I am only a child." But the LORD said to me, "Do not say, 'I am only a child.' You must go to everyone I send you to and say whatever I command you."** Here God not only predicts what the prophet was going to do but also declares what he appointed him to do, as if he had said, "It is your duty to obey because I have the right to command. You must, therefore, go wherever I send you, and you must proclaim whatever I tell you." Through these words God reminds Jeremiah that he was his servant and that there was no reason why a sense of his own weakness should make him afraid. It should have been enough for him to simply obey God's command.

It is very important that we know this teaching, for we should not do anything without thinking in whose strength we will accomplish the task. So when God asks us to do anything, we should immediately obey his Word, as it were, with closed eyes. When God calls we should not say, "I am only a child." It is as if God has said, "Although you think you have no talents at all and are fully conscious of your weakness, you should still go wherever I send you." God requires people to obey his commands, even if they think they lack the necessary qualifications.

8. "Do not be afraid of them, for I am with you and will rescue you," declares the LORD. From this verse we learn that Jeremiah was greatly upset when he saw the hard conflicts that faced him. He saw that he had to deal with a people who had almost completely wandered away from God's law. They had shaken off this yoke for many years, and now it was difficult to bring them back into the paths of obedience. It seems that Jeremiah was so overcome by the difficulty of the work that he did not want to undertake the office of prophet. But God provided a suitable remedy for his fear. What does he say? **"Do not be afraid of them."** God, who penetrates into the hearts of people and knows their hidden feelings and motives, heals Jeremiah's timidity by saying, **"Do not be afraid of them."**

The reason God gives for saying that Jeremiah should be bold should also be noted: **"For I am with you and will rescue you."** God reminds the prophet through these words that his divine power would be enough to protect him, so that he did not need to dread the anger of his own nation. It was at first a formidable undertaking when Jeremiah saw that he had to fight not against a few people, but against all of the people. But God sets himself against everybody and says, **"Do not be afraid of them."**

9-10. Then the LORD reached out his hand and touched my mouth and said to me, "Now, I have put my words in your mouth. See, today I appoint you over nations and kingdoms to uproot and tear down, to destroy and overthrow, to build and to plant." Jeremiah speaks again about his calling. He does not want his teaching to be despised, as if it came from a private individual. Therefore he witnesses again that he does not come on his own accord but was sent from above and was invested with the authority of a prophet. This is why he says that God put his words in his mouth.

This passage should be carefully noted, for Jeremiah describes how a true call can be ascertained when one undertakes the office of a teacher in the church. It is discovered in this way: Nothing of one's own is brought (see 1 Peter 4:11).

A visible symbol was added in order to confirm Jeremiah's call. But there is no reason to make this a general rule, as if it were necessary that the tongues of all teachers should be touched by God's hand. There are two things to note here. First, there is the thing itself. All of God's servants are told they should not bring their own ideas but simply deliver, as from one hand to the next hand, what they have received from God. Second, there was something special for Jeremiah: God, by stretching out his hand, touched his mouth. This was to show in a visible way that his mouth was consecrated to God.

"See, today I appoint you over nations and kingdoms." God shows that he wants his Word to be received reverently, even when it is conveyed by frail mortals. We should note the authority that God ascribes to his own Word. God here sets his prophet above the whole world, even above kings. So whoever claims this power must bring forth God's Word and really prove that he is a prophet.

"To uproot and tear down, to destroy and overthrow, to build and to plant." Here Jeremiah puts ruin and destruction before building and planting. This seems to be inconsistent, but we must always bear in mind the condition of this people. Impiety, perverseness, and hardened sin had prevailed for so long that it was necessary to begin with ruin and eradication. Jeremiah could not have planted or have built God's temple unless he first destroyed, pulled down, and laid waste.

God says that he gave authority to his servant, not just over Judea, but over the whole world. It was like saying, "You are but a small part of mankind. So do not lift up your horns against my servant, for you will not be able to do this. He will exercise power not only over Judea but also over all nations, and even over kings, for the teaching I have deposited with him is so powerful that it will stand above all mortals and over much more than a single nation."

11-12. The word of the LORD came to me: "What do you see, Jeremiah?" "I see the branch of an almond tree," I replied. The LORD said to me, "You have seen correctly, for I am watching to see that my word is fulfilled." God confirms in this passage what he had just said about the power of his Word. God made his servant see **the branch of an almond tree.** Why? The answer is supplied: **"You have seen correctly, for I am watching to see that my word is fulfilled."** God is extolling his Word here. It is as if he announced that what his servants said would not vanish into the earth—his power would accomplish everything, just as he had said. "As the rain and the snow come down from heaven, and do not return to it without watering the earth and making it bud and flourish, so that it yields seed for the sower and bread for the eater, so is my word that goes out from my mouth: It will not return to me empty, but will accomplish what I desire and achieve the purpose for which I sent it" (Isaiah 55:10-11).

"Watching to see that my word is fulfilled." It is as if God said, "As they speak from my mouth, I am present with my prophets to fulfill whatever I command them." God ascribes nothing to Jeremiah's power but only to the power of his own Word. It is as if he said, "Provided that you are a faithful minister, I will not frustrate your hope, nor the hope of those who will obey you. For I will fulfill whatever you and they may rightly hope for. Those who resist you will not escape from being punished. For in due time I will bring on them the punishment they deserve."

13-14. The word of the LORD came to me again: "What do you see?" "I see a boiling pot, tilting away from the north," I answered. The LORD said to me, "From the north disaster will be poured out on all who live in the land." Jeremiah now starts to address the people he has been sent to as a prophet. He accommodates his teaching to the people. Hence he says that he had a vision and saw **a boiling pot.** This means that the Chaldeans would come to overthrow Jerusalem, to take away all the honor and dignity both of the kingdom and of the priesthood. The **pot** stands for the nation of the Jews. They are likened to **a boiling pot** because the Lord, as it were, boiled them until they were reduced to almost nothing.

"From the north disaster will be poured out on all who live in the land." Judea is **the land.** In these words God declares that the Chaldeans and the Assyrians had already lit the fire by which he would, as it were, boil his people like meat and eventually consume them.

15. This verse explains the previous one. God explains more clearly that evil will come from the north. He says he will send this evil and speaks of it in this way: **"I am about to summon all the peoples of the northern kingdoms."** The prediction would not have been so effective had he not added that the Chaldeans would come by God's authority, for people always ascribe to fortune whatever takes place (see Lamentations 3:37-38). So God rebukes the Jews sharply because they were so blind in this matter and did not acknowledge God's judgments.

"Their kings will come and set up their thrones in the entrance of the gates of Jerusalem; they will come against all her surrounding walls and against all the towns of Judah." The power of the Chaldeans would be so great that they would boldly pitch their tents in front of the gates.

16. God now explains why he had resolved to deal so severely with the Jews. They had to be taught two things. First, the Chaldeans would not attack them on their own authority but on God's, who would arm them; and second, God would not be cruel to them or forget his covenant, though he would be angry because of the extreme wickedness of the Jews. God had to break them down—moderate corrections had no effect.

"I will pronounce my judgments on my people because of their wickedness." This is like saying, "Until now I have waived my rights and waited for them to return to me. They have not returned and are so depraved that they add evil to evil; so I will take up my office of judge."

"In forsaking me, in burning incense to other gods and in worshiping what their hands have made." This is like saying, "They have completely denied me. I do not say that one of them is a thief, another an adulterer, and another a drunkard. For they have all become apostates. They have all broken the covenant. Thus I am wholly forsaken by them, and they are in every way alienated from me."

17. "Get yourself ready!" (KJV, "Gird up thy loins"). This refers to the clothes Orientals used to wear. When they wanted to start some manual work or go on a journey, they hitched up their long clothes.

"Stand up and say to them whatever I command you." In short, God says he does not want to go to extreme lengths until he has made sure there is no hope of the people repenting. He knew they were irreclaimable, but he intended to find out more fully their perverseness. He would command Jeremiah, finally, to pronounce the extreme sentence of condemnation.

"Do not be terrified by them, or I will terrify you before them." This is like saying, "Take heart, do not be afraid of them, for that would mean you are unworthy of being supported by the strength of my Spirit." From this we learn that God's servants will not lack strength as long as they derive courage from the conviction that God himself is the author of their calling. God will give them strength so that they will be formidable to the whole world.

18. **"Today I have made you a fortified city, an iron pillar and a bronze wall to stand against the whole land—against the kings of Judah, its officials, its priests and the people of the land."** Nobody cared about religion or heavenly truth, and Jeremiah was so diffident that he could not shoulder such a heavy burden without God's supporting hand. So God declares that he will make him like **"a fortified city."** It might seem enough to call Jeremiah **"a fortified city,"** but the Lord also compares him to **"an iron pillar and a bronze wall."** This repetition serves to confirm that Jeremiah will be victorious. Even though Satan will attack him, Jeremiah will win the battle, for he is fighting under God's protection.

"Against the whole land." God is not speaking about the whole world but about the land of Judah. Jeremiah was chosen to work among the chosen people; so it says he will be a conqueror of the whole of Judea. So it follows that he would be successful **"against the kings of Judah."** God encourages this prophet to be firm and to persevere, as though the battle would be long, so that he would not faint from being tired. The prophet would not have to contend with one king only, but as soon as one died, another would rise up and replace him. From this Jeremiah saw there would be no hope of rest until the time that God had appointed arrived.

19. **"They will fight against you but will not overcome you, for I am with you and will rescue you," declares the LORD.** This is like saying, "Be prepared to suffer. If I did not deliver you, you would be finished and defeated a hundred times over. But there is no reason for you to be afraid in the midst of a thousand deaths, since I am with you to deliver you."

Jeremiah
Chapter 2

1-2. The word of the LORD came to me: "Go and proclaim in the hearing of Jerusalem . . . God now tells his servant what message he is to deliver to the kings and priests and to all of the people of Jerusalem. **In the hearing of Jerusalem** refers to all its inhabitants.

"I remember the devotion of your youth, how as a bride you loved me." By these words the Lord shows that he did not act as the Jews deserved, nor did he see them as in any way worthy of his salvation. He tried to bring them back to the right way through the efforts of his prophet, even though this would be ascribed to God's previous benefits. It is as if he said, "It is a testimony to you of my paternal care that I send a prophet to give you hope of pardon, if you return to the right way and are reconciled to me. Since you have forgotten me and have completely neglected my law, why do I still show concern for you? It is because I want to continue to extend my favors to you."

Notice the metaphor used here. God compares himself to a young bridegroom who marries a young bride in the flower of her youth and at her most beautiful. This way of speaking is often used by the prophets. As God had married the people of Israel when he redeemed them and brought them out of Egypt, he now says that he remembers the people because of that love and kindness.

"And followed me through the desert, through a land not sown." We know that the people did not obey God even after they had been redeemed. So God is not here commending any merits of the people, but rather he is confirming that he could not disown them. He has adopted them and led them through the desert so that they might be separate from the rest of the world.

3. "Israel was holy to the LORD, the firstfruits of his harvest; all who devoured her were held guilty, and disaster overtook them," declares the LORD. God rebukes the people for their ingratitude. First, he lists his favors through which he had bound the people to himself forever.

Second, he shows the dreadful response the people made to the many blessings they had received.

In saying that Israel was **"holy,"** he does not intend to praise them. It was in itself an eminent testimony of how God had consecrated them to himself that he designated them **"the firstfruits of his harvest."** Under the law, God had commanded that the firstfruits should be offered to him and then given to the priests. Here he says that in accordance with that rite, Israel was **"the firstfruits of his harvest."**

He then adds, **"all who devoured her were held guilty, and disaster overtook them."** This is like saying, "The profane who devour the first-fruits that have to be dedicated to me will not go unpunished." For if any-one had stolen the firstfruits, God would have punished such sacrilege.

4-5. Jeremiah seeks to gain the attention of the people by saying, **Hear the word of the LORD, O house of Jacob, all you clans of the house of Israel.** It is as if he said, "I come boldly in the name of God, for I do not fear that you can offer any defense against God's justly reproving you. I confidently wait to hear what you may say, knowing that you will be silent. I then declare with the voice of the trumpet that I have come to condemn you. You are free to make any reply. But the truth will make you mute, for your guilt is so odious." In this way he urged them to listen attentively to him.

"What fault did your fathers find in me, that they strayed so far from me? They followed worthless idols and became worthless them-selves." God through Jeremiah accuses the people of two sins: they had departed from the true God, and they had become vain in their behavior. In other words, they had become apostates for no reason. Their sin was made worse because they had no reason to forsake God and to alienate themselves from him.

6-7. **"They did not ask, 'Where is the LORD, who brought us up out of Egypt and led us through the barren wilderness, through a land of deserts and rifts, a land of drought and darkness, a land where no one travels and no one lives?' I brought you into a fertile land to eat its fruit and rich produce. But you came and defiled my land and made my inheritance detestable."** The prophet continues with the same theme. God accuses his people of no small sin, for they have buried his favors in oblivion. We understand what the prophet means when he says, **"They did not ask";** God is sharply reproving the Jews for their stupidity. They did not think they were permanently indebted to God for his great kind-ness in delivering them so wonderfully from Egypt. By saying, **"They did not ask, 'Where is the LORD . . . ?'"** God implies that he was present with them and close to them, but they were blind and had no excuse for their ignorance. If only they had recalled, "Did not God once redeem us?" they would not have lived their vain way of life.

"'Who brought us up out of Egypt and led us through the barren

wilderness, through a land of deserts and rifts.'" He could not have said
that about all nations. These words especially applied to the Jews who had
clearly witnessed God's power. The only way they could have sinned was
by a deliberate and willful act against God. Here the prophet makes their
guilt even worse by citing certain circumstances. He says that the Lord
not only brought them out of Egypt but had been their constant guide for
forty years. (This time is suggested by the word **wilderness**. This story
was so well known that a mere allusion was sufficient.) By mentioning the
wilderness, Jeremiah also extols the glory of God.

"'A land of drought and darkness, a land where no one travels and
no one lives.'" This is like saying that the people had been preserved in
the midst of death, indeed in the midst of many deaths. "When," he asks
in effect, "did you receive salvation? In what circumstances did you experience God's deliverance? Was it not when you were surrounded on all
sides by death itself? Since God was able to bring you out of Egypt by
his incredible power, then fed you in a supernatural way for forty years,
what excuse do you now have for acting in such a mad way that you are
deserting God?"

"I brought you into a fertile land to eat its fruit and rich produce."
That is, "I wanted you to enjoy the large and rich produce of the land."
God intimates that the Israelites ought to have served him after receiving
such blessings. So God adds, "But you came and defiled my land and
made my inheritance detestable." It is as if he said, "This is how my
bounty toward you has been rewarded. I did indeed give you this land,
but on this condition, that you serve me faithfully in it. But you have
polluted it." God calls it his own land, as though he is saying that he still
remained their landlord, even though he had allowed them to occupy the
land.

8. "The priests did not ask, 'Where is the LORD?' Those who deal
with the law did not know me; the leaders rebelled against me." God
singles out the teachers and rulers in this verse. It often happens that ordinary people fall away, while some integrity remains in the rulers. But he
shows here that such was the falling away of the whole community that
priests as well as prophets, and all the leaders, had departed from the true
worship of God and from all uprightness.

"The prophets prophesied by Baal, following worthless idols." The
name of a prophet is sacred. But Jeremiah here, and in other places, calls
people **prophets** (contrary to the real fact), though they were nothing
but impostors. For God had taken from them the light of divine truth.
When the prophet says here that the prophets were ministers of Baal, he
contrasts this name with the only true God. It is as though he said that the
truth was corrupted by them because they had overstepped their limits
and did not obey the pure teaching of the law. They corrupted it from

23

many quarters, even through the many gods that heathen nations had invented for themselves.

9. "Therefore I bring charges against you again," declares the LORD. "And I will bring charges against your children's children." This is like saying, "Do not be under the illusion that you have suffered all your punishment, even though I have punished your fathers severely for their wickedness and obstinacy. Since you follow in their footsteps and show no bounds to your sins, I will punish you and your children and all succeeding generations."

10-11. "Cross over to the coasts of Kittim and look, send to Kedar and observe closely." God uses a metaphor here to expose the wickedness and ingratitude of his own nation. For he says that all nations that believe in one religion practice it as it is handed down to them from their forebears. So why was the God of Israel rejected and repudiated by his own people?

"See if there has ever been anything like this." That is, such a monstrous and execrable thing cannot be found anywhere.

"Has a nation ever changed its gods? (Yet they are not gods at all.) But my people have exchanged their Glory for worthless idols." We should understand these two verses as follows: "Although no nation worships the true God, yet religion remains unchanged among them. Yet you have perfidiously forsaken me, and you have not forsaken a mere phantom, but your 'Glory.'"

12. "Be appalled at this, O heavens, and shudder with great horror," declares the LORD. When the prophet saw he had to deal with people who were practically devoid of all reason, he turned to speak to the heavens. This was a way of speaking that was common among the prophets. They address heaven and earth, which have no understanding; only people are endued with reason and knowledge. They did this in hopeless situations when they found that nobody wanted to learn. So the prophet now asks the heavens to "be appalled" and to "shudder with great horror." It is as if he said, "This is a wonder that almost confounds the whole order of nature. It is as if we were to see heaven and earth mixed together."

13. "My people have committed two sins: They have forsaken me, the spring of living water, and have dug their own cisterns, broken cisterns that cannot hold water." The Lord through Jeremiah says they had "committed two sins." The first was that they had forsaken God, and the other, that they had followed false and imaginary gods. To highlight their sin Jeremiah uses a metaphor and says God is a "spring of living water." He compares idols to broken cisterns that cannot hold water. When one leaves a gushing spring and looks for a cistern, it is evidence of great folly, for cisterns remain dry unless water is poured into them, but springs have their own supplies of water.

14-17. Jeremiah, as if he were astonished by something new and

24

strange, now asks the question, **"Is Israel a servant?"** Israel was more free than all of the other nations. She was God's firstborn child. So we have to ask why she was so miserable. He goes on to say that **"lions have roared; they have growled at him."** He says that their **"towns are burned and deserted."** He says that their land was reduced to desolation. At last he asks, **"Have you not brought this on yourselves by forsaking the LORD your God when he led you in the way?"** This is again put as a question, but it is doubly affirmative, for it removes all doubt: "Why are you so miserable? For everyone is against you, and you are exposed to all kinds of evil deeds. How can you explain this, except to say that it comes as a result of all your wickedness?" Now we see what the prophet means. It is as if he said, "God did not deceive you when he promised to be bountiful to you. His adoption is not deceptive or in vain. For you would have been happier than all the other nations if your own wickedness had not made you miserable."

"Lions have roared; they have growled at him [Israel]." Jeremiah declares that Israel had been deprived of God's protection; otherwise she would not have been exposed to the caprice of her enemies. The prophet seems not simply to compare Israel's enemies to **lions** on account of their cruelty, but also because of their contempt. It is as if he said that Israel found that not only people were incensed against them, but also wild beasts. For it is degrading if God allows us to be torn apart by wild animals. It is as if he said that Israel was being treated so miserably that they were not only killed by the hands of their enemies but were also exposed to beasts of prey.

In order to underline this point Jeremiah adds (verse 16), **"Also, the men of Memphis and Tahpanhes have shaved the crown of your head."** The Egyptians, although they had a treaty with Israel, would be against them.

In short, Jeremiah teaches us that the cause of all evils lay in the people. It is as if he said, "You have concocted for yourself all this evil. Now you must swallow it and know that you cannot blame God for it. He would have been faithful to you, but your impiety prevented him."

Jeremiah further underlines their sin by saying, **"when he led you in the way."** To "lead in the way" is to govern people so as to make them happy. God says he had **"led"** them **"in the way,"** but they preferred to give their allegiance to idols.

18. "Now why go to Egypt to drink water from the Shihor? And why go to Assyria to drink water from the River?" The people could not blame other people for their own sin. "If you look into this matter carefully," says God, "and ask why you are so miserable, you will not be able to blame me, but only your own sins. So what should you have done? You should have asked for my pardon, and I would have healed you at once. If you had come to me, you would have come to the best doctor.

But in fact you turn to people who are unable to help you. You run off to Egypt, you run off to Assyria, but you will gain nothing from them." Now we understand what the prophet is saying. From this we learn that we are not to search for water from either the Nile or the Euphrates—that is, from the enticing things of the world. Instead, we are to drink from the hidden spring inside us.

19. "Your wickedness will punish you; your backsliding will rebuke you." It is as if he said, "You have now seen all this evidence proving that your own unfaithfulness has brought evil on your own head. God will pile evil on top of evil, so that you will at last realize, even against your will, that you will receive the just reward for all your evil."

"Consider then and realize how evil and bitter it is for you when you forsake the LORD your God and have no awe of me." This shows that the evils that the people suffered did not happen by chance but came as a result of their impiety.

"Have no awe of me." "You cannot," Jeremiah says, "object and say that you have been deceived. For it is clear that you have acted shamelessly in forsaking God, for there is no fear of God in you."

Declares the Lord, the LORD Almighty. Jeremiah adds this to lend authority to his pronouncement.

20. "Long ago you broke off your yoke and tore off your bonds." The prophet refers to many deliverances here. The people were delivered from Egypt, but when they were oppressed later on, God again rescued them. God had from ancient times, on numerous occasions, shaken off the yoke that lay on the people. This is clear from the book of Judges.

God complains that the people of Israel said, "I will not serve you!" This is like saying, "You were ungrateful—in the first place, when you did not take me as your Redeemer, and in the second place, in that you have not seen that I have been kind to you just so you can be mine."

"Indeed, on every high hill and under every spreading tree you lay down as a prostitute." We know that the Israelites, whenever they deserted God, went to some special places, on hills and under trees, as if such places possessed some special holiness. He says in effect, "That is what you have done with your freedom! You have used it to follow your own evil lusts."

21. "I had planted you like a choice vine of sound and reliable stock. How then did you turn against me into a corrupt, wild vine?" "When I redeemed you from your enemies, I did not give you permission to prostitute yourself without shame or restraint. I planted you like a choice vine. That vine should have been fruitful but has degenerated so much that it produces nothing except wild grapes."

22. "Although you wash yourself with soda and use an abundance of soap, the stain of your guilt is still before me," declares the Sovereign LORD. That is, Jeremiah says, "You fool no one when you try

to disguise your impiety. Even if you wash yourself, your sin remains in God's sight." The prophet speaks in the place of God, to add weight to his denunciations of the Israelites. **Soda** and **soap** were used to remove stains from cloth. But, says Jeremiah, "No matter how you attempt to deceive yourself and hide your sins from the world, you achieve nothing. For in my sight the stain of your guilt remains."

23. **"How can you say, 'I am not defiled; I have not run after the Baals'? See how you behaved in the valley; consider what you have done. You are a swift she-camel running here and there."** The prophet could not fully express the Jews' furious passions without comparing them to **a swift she-camel.** She is called **swift** not just because of her speed but because of her impetuous lust.

24. Jeremiah now compares the untamed madness of the people to **"a wild donkey accustomed to the desert, sniffing the wind in her craving—in her heat who can restrain her? Any males that pursue her need not tire themselves; at mating time they will find her."** Nothing can bridle their lusts.

25. **"Do not run until your feet are bare and your throat is dry. But you said, 'It's no use! I love foreign gods, and I must go after them.'"** Jeremiah's words are concise here and may appear obscure at first sight. He simply means: The people are so insane that they cannot be reformed, no matter how much God tries to check their excesses, through which they were led away into following idols and superstitions. Whenever there was any danger they ran until their feet were bare and their throats were parched, for they went off to Egypt and then to Assyria, as we have already seen.

"But you said, 'It's no use!'" This is like saying, "You prophets never stop bombarding our ears, but all your labor is in vain. We have once and for all made up our minds, and nothing will ever make us change."

"'I love foreign gods, and I must go after them.'" Jeremiah shows that the people shamelessly resolved to worship idols of their own imagination and to reject the only true God.

26. **"As a thief is disgraced when he is caught, so the house of Israel is disgraced—they, their kings and their officials, their priests and their prophets."** Jeremiah is not just speaking about ordinary people. He condemns **their kings and their officials, their priests and their prophets.** It is as if he said they were corrupt from top to bottom and now showed total contempt for God.

27-28. The prophet continues to emphasize the wickedness of the people: **"They say to wood, 'You are my father,' and to stone, 'You gave me birth.'"** By these words the prophet shows that idolatry was so rampant among the people that they openly ascribed to their wooden and stone statues the honor that is only due to the true God.

"**They have turned their backs to me and not their faces.**" God shows that the apostasy of the people could not be hidden.

"**When they are in trouble, they say, 'Come and save us!'**" God complains that the Jews have abused his kindness, for they came to him only whenever they were in deep trouble. "What have I to do with you?" he asks in effect; "you are totally devoted to your idols, you call them your father, you ascribe to them the glory of your salvation when things go well with you. But when your idols do not help you in your times of distress, you return to me and say, 'Come and save us!' But since idols are your fathers and you expect salvation from them, I will have nothing to do with you. Be content with your idols, and do not trouble me anymore, for I have been forsaken by you."

"**Where then are the gods . . . ?**" Here God laughs at the false confidence the Jews placed in these idols and how they deceived themselves. "**Where then are the gods you made for yourselves? Let them come if they can save you when you are in trouble!**" We now see what the prophet means. For he shows that the people behaved most strangely. They worshiped idols when they were safe and so denied the power of the true God. God shows them that they could expect no help from him, for they had robbed him of his own power when they devised idols for themselves.

God uses sarcasm as he derides them. "**Where then are the gods you made for yourselves? Let them come if they can save you when you are in trouble!**" That is, "Let them use all their power to help you." "**For you have as many gods as you have towns, O Judah.**" As the people were not satisfied with one God, every city chose a patron for itself. "Since, then, innumerable gods are invoked by you, why is it that they do not help you?"

29. "**Why do you bring charges against me? You have all rebelled against me,**" declares the LORD. Jeremiah says that the Jews would gain nothing by alleging they were innocent. God convicts them of impiety; so none of their excuses holds water.

30. "**In vain I punished your people; they did not respond to correction.**" God now adds that he had tried many ways to bring his people back to their senses, but it had all been in vain (see Isaiah 1:6).

"**Your sword has devoured your prophets like a ravening lion.**" When God healed the vices of the people, the true prophets, the ministers of salvation, were cruelly killed by the people. This is the best way to understand the expression, **devoured your prophets.** God says that they raged against the prophets as if those prophets had gone into a forest full of lions.

31. "**You of this generation, consider the word of the LORD.**" The prophet shows that however blind they were, they could see with their own eyes what the Lord says. It is as if he said, "The Lord through me

expostulates with you. Even though there are no witnesses present, nor any judge or arbiter, you yourselves can understand this matter."

"Have I been a desert to Israel or a land of great darkness?" He makes the Jews themselves the judges of this matter. Had they experienced God's bounty? Had God forsaken them?

"Why do my people say, 'We are free to roam; we will come to you no more'?" This is the language of vain boasting. See 1 Corinthians 4:8. It is like saying, "Your happiness has not come from me. Whatever you have been, and whatever has been given to you, should have been ascribed to me and to my bounty. Without me [God], you are kings, but by what right? What have you as your own?" They were so bloated with pride that they despised God's favor, as if they did not need anybody's help.

32. "Does a maiden forget her jewelry, a bride her wedding ornaments? Yet my people have forgotten me, days without number." "How is it, then," asks God, "that my people have forgotten me? Can anything be found among the most valuable jewels and the most precious stones that can be compared with me?"

33. "How skilled you are at pursuing love! Even the worst of women can learn from your ways." The prophet means that the Jews are like lascivious women, who not only despise their husbands at home but ramble here and there in all directions, put makeup on their faces, and seek for themselves all the charms of wantonness.

The prophets often compared the people to lovers, for the Jews, who should have been firmly attached to God (like a chaste woman, who does not turn her eyes here and there), sought safety from the Assyrians and from the Egyptians.

34. "On your clothes men find the lifeblood of the innocent poor, though you did not catch them breaking in. Yet in spite of all this . . ." The prophet repeats that the wickedness of his nation was incorrigible. The Jews were not only obstinate in their vices but also raged furiously against the prophets. The prophets were slaughtered, and the whole land was filled with and polluted by their blood. He seems to say that these slaughters were not hidden, for the blood splashed to the edges of their clothes. It is as if God said, "There is no reason for me to rebuke you severely in this matter, for your filthiness is apparent to all. You have not only rebelled against my teaching, but you have also cruelly murdered my prophets. You may ask, 'Where is the evidence for such killings?' But you only have to look on the edges of your clothes, and you will see that your sins are clearly evident."

35. "You say, 'I am innocent; he is not angry with me.' But I will pass judgment on you because you say, 'I have not sinned.'" Jeremiah says, "How dare you pretend to be innocent since you are proved to be guilty, not by allegations, but by glaring evidence!" In short, the prophet shows that the condition of these people was hopeless.

36. "Why do you go about so much, changing your ways? You will be disappointed by Egypt as you were by Assyria." Their love was never constant. They went here and there, depending on who allured them. Before Hezekiah's time the Jews had made a treaty with the Egyptians against the Syrians and the Israelites. Then, after they broke their treaty with the Egyptians, they fought against them and went to the Assyrians for help. Later on they made a peace treaty with Egypt, but this proved as useless as their first pact with Egypt. So the prophet says they would repeat the experience they had previously been through. God had indeed punished their ungodly defection when they went to Assyria. Now, he says, they will fare no better by looking for help from Egypt. We know that the Jews suffered more from the hands of their so-called allies than they did from their avowed enemies. This was the just reward for their impiety and defection. God declares that he would be the avenger of this second defection, just as he had been of the former one.

37. "You will also leave that place with your hands on your head." To place **your hands on your head** is a gesture of extreme despair. In effect he is saying, "The treaty that fills the Jews with so much confidence will be of no advantage to them. On the contrary, it will bring them utter ruin and disgrace." The reason for this is then given by the prophet: **"for the LORD has rejected those you trust; you will not be helped by them."** The prophet says why he had spoken so severely. It might have been thought he was using hyperbolic language when he compared them to an abandoned prostitute. But the reason given here should have been enough to dispel all notions like that. They had foolishly trusted in fallacious helps that they knew were condemned by God.

Jeremiah
Chapter 3

1. **"If a man divorces his wife and she leaves him and marries another man, should he return to her again? Would not the land be completely defiled? But you have lived as a prostitute with many lovers—would you now return to me?" declares the LORD.** The main point of this verse is that God shows that he wished to be reconciled to the Jews, provided they left their sinful ways. He had previously said that he held the place of a husband and that the people occupied the position of a wife. Then he complained about the unfaithfulness of the people, who had forsaken him, and said they had behaved like a wife who, despising her husband, committed adultery with everyone she met. But now God adds in effect, "If a man dismisses his wife, and she becomes the wife of another man, he will never receive her again." This was forbidden by law. "But I am ready," God says, "to receive you, although I had not given you the usual divorce, as husbands do who repudiate their wives when there is anything displeasing in them." It is not as simple a comparison as many think. God does not just compare himself to a husband who has repudiated his wife because of her adultery, for the Jews divorced their wives for the slightest of reasons or for no reason at all.

There is a twofold comparison here. "Even if a husband should fastidiously send away his wife, and she, through his fault, should marry another man, as if in contempt for her first husband, the first husband could hardly ever bear that indignity and be reconciled to her. But you have not been repudiated by me but are like a perfidious woman who shamelessly commits adultery with whomever she meets. And yet I am ready to receive you and to forget all your evil behavior."

"Would not the land be completely defiled?" Freedom was given to the women by divorce, although God did not allow divorce. But as the women were innocent, they were released, for God imputed no fault to the husbands. And when the repudiated wife married another man, this second marriage was considered legitimate. If, then, the first husband sought to recover the wife whom he had divorced, he violated the bond of the second marriage. For this reason and according to this sense, the prophet says that the land would by this become polluted. It is as if he said, "It is not lawful for husbands to take back their wives, however ready they may be to forgive them; but I require nothing but your return to me."

Then the prophet adds, **"But you have lived as a prostitute with many lovers."** The people had been guilty not only of one act of adultery but had become like common prostitutes who commit adultery with many. Those he calls **lovers** were rivals. He asks, **"Would you now return to me?"** By this he means, "Pardon is ready for you, provided that you repent."

2. **"Look up to the barren heights and see. Is there any place where you have not been ravished?"** The Lord says, "I bring forward witnesses who are well-known to you. There is no hill in the land where you have not been connected with idols. See if there is any hill free from your fornicating."

He adds, **"By the roadside you sat waiting for lovers, sat like a nomad in the desert. You have defiled the land with your prostitution and wickedness."** The Jews were not enticed by others to break the marriage vow they had made to God but were, on the contrary, moved by their own desires to gratify their lusts. Nomads sat in the deserts in order to rob travelers.

3. **"Therefore the showers have been withheld, and no spring rains have fallen. Yet you have the brazen look of a prostitute; you refuse to blush with shame."** This is like saying, "You Jews have not been subdued at all by punishment." The Jews had not only gone exactly where their lusts took them, but they had also been checked by evident judgments, since God had from heaven openly shown himself to be the vindicator of his own glory. There had been such a great drought that it seemed clear that the curse of the law had been fulfilled toward them: "I will break down your stubborn pride and make the sky above you like iron and the ground beneath you like bronze" (Leviticus 26:19).

4. **"Have you not just called to me: 'My Father, my friend from my youth . . . ?'"** God asks, "Will they not call on me again as their Father and the guide of their youth?" In short, he shows that he is ready to pardon them if they seek reconciliation.

5. **"'Will you always be angry? Will your wrath continue forever?' This is how you talk, but you do all the evil you can."** In effect the prophet was reasoning like this: "God is not inexorable, for he is as ready to forgive as he is long-suffering. So what stops you from living happily again under his rule? For he will spare you, provided that he finds in you genuine repentance."

God had previously put on, as it were, the character of someone in grief and sorrow, kindly exhorted his people to repent, said he would be prepared to pardon them, and at the same time showed in general that he would be propitious, for he is by nature inclined to mercy. Having set out these things, he now adds that he despaired of those people because they gloried in their own wickedness: **"This is how you talk, but you do all the evil you can."** In other words, the people were so impudent that they boasted about their rebellion against God and dared to call darkness light. The superstitious, as we know, glory against God without any shame.

6. The prophet begins a new discourse here. He cites what God has committed to him and mentions the time: **During the reign of King Josiah.** At this time the king worked hard to establish the pure worship of God, and no one dared to oppose him.

What is contained in this commission? **The LORD said to me, "Have you seen what faithless Israel has done?"** God compares the ten tribes with the tribe of Judah and the half tribe of Benjamin. He introduces the kingdom of Israel, as well as the kingdom of Judah, as women. God depicts himself as the husband of his people; he says he had two wives, Israel and Judah. God has indeed married all the descendants of Abraham in one contract. Although the Israelites had departed from God, he had not wholly rejected them. The kingdom of Israel had become adulterous, but God bore with that sin for a time, so that the covenant, in part, remained. For this reason he acknowledges as his wives both Israel and Judah.

"She has gone up on every high hill and under every spreading tree and has committed adultery there." In short, God complains that the ten tribes had violated the sacred bond of marriage when they prostituted themselves to idols on the high hills under the shady trees, as if these places were especially holy.

7. **"I thought that after she had done all this she would return to me."** God here records that he had called the ten tribes back to himself by his servants the prophets, although by their sins they had provoked his wrath.

"But she did not [return to me], and her unfaithful sister Judah saw it."

8. **"I gave faithless Israel her certificate of divorce and sent her away because of all her adulteries. Yet I saw that her unfaithful sister Judah had no fear; she also went out and committed adultery."** That is, "Judah saw that I gave the bill of divorce to her sister because she had been a prostitute, and yet she still had no fear." The people of Judah refused to learn from the lessons of others. They saw that the kingdom of Israel had been abolished, and yet all of them derived their origin from the same father—that is, Abraham. How could they despise God's judgments like this? It was because they **had no fear.**

9. **"Because Israel's immorality mattered so little to her, she defiled**

the land and committed adultery with stone and wood." Whenever the people departed from the pure worship of God, they were justly said to have committed adultery, for they had violated their pledged faith.

10. **"In spite of all this, her unfaithful sister Judah did not return to me with all her heart, but only in pretense," declares the LORD.** The prophet says, "Although they have shown some signs of repentance, they are only trying to fool God—there is no integrity in them."

11. **The LORD said to me, "Faithless Israel is more righteous than unfaithful Judah."** We now see why Jeremiah compared the ten tribes with the kingdom of Judah. It was done to show that the Jews, who wanted to be thought of as being more holy than other people, were more unfaithful to God and deserved greater punishment because they had acted so deceitfully with God. The obstinacy of the people of Judah was greater, and less excusable, than that of the people of Israel. For the people of Judah had seen God judge the ten tribes, but they looked down on this and derived no benefit from it.

12. **"Go, proclaim this message toward the north: 'Return, faithless Israel,' declares the LORD, 'I will frown on you no longer, for I am merciful,' declares the LORD, 'I will not be angry forever.'"** The prophet has shown that the tribe of Judah deserved heavier punishment than the ten tribes of Israel; now he turns his attention to the Israelites themselves, and he promises that God will be propitious to them. The kingdom of Israel had been overthrown, and the people had been banished into Assyria, Persia, and Media. They had been scattered, and the name of the kingdom had been obliterated. The prophet addresses his words to the north as God had a regard for the capital of the monarchy.

If God's people returned to him they would obtain pardon, because God of his own free will invited them and promised that the punishment he had inflicted on account of their sins would be only for a time.

13. **"'Only acknowledge your guilt—you have rebelled against the Lord your God, you have scattered your favors to foreign gods under every spreading tree, and have not obeyed me,'" declares the LORD.** In other words, "I do not now in vain remind you to admit your sins, for God himself condemns you. Do not think you can gain anything by your subterfuge." They went astray because they closed their ears to God's Word and so became wholly unteachable.

14. **"Return, faithless people," declares the LORD, "for I am your husband."** Jeremiah repeats the same words, but God by using so many words shows clearly how ready he would be to grant pardon, provided the Israelites really repented.

"I will choose one of you from every town and two from every clan." It would have been possible to argue like this: "What connection have I with God except that I am born into the race of Abraham? I do not see anyone turning to God, so I must perish with the rest of the people."

To prevent this kind of thinking among godly people, the Lord says, **"I will choose one of you from every town and two from every clan and bring you to Zion."** This means, "If only one person comes to me from a city, he will find an open door. If only two come to me from a tribe, I will receive them."

"And bring you to Zion." God intimates that the exile will be temporary, and the Israelites will again have a part in his inheritance, if they return to God in sincerity and truth.

15. **"Then I will give you shepherds after my own heart, who will lead you with knowledge and understanding."** God promises that he will provide for the salvation of his people after their return from exile, so that they will not perish again. We learn from this that the church cannot continue without having faithful pastors to show the way of salvation.

16. **"In those days, when your numbers have increased greatly in the land,"** declares the LORD, **"men will no longer say, 'The ark of the covenant of the LORD.' It will never enter their minds or be remembered; it will not be missed, nor will another one be made."** There was contention between the kingdom of Judah and the ten tribes. The Israelites were elated because of their numbers, their riches, and other temporal advantages; the people of Judah gloried in their temple and the ark of the covenant. And what does the prophet now say? He declares that there will be such agreement between the Israelites and the people of Judah that the people of Judah will no longer say **"the ark of the covenant of the LORD"** or "the temple of God," for God will be present with them all.

17-18. **"At that time they will call Jerusalem The Throne of the LORD, and all nations will gather in Jerusalem to honor the name of the LORD. No longer will they follow the stubbornness of their evil hearts. In those days the house of Judah will join the house of Israel, and together they will come from a northern land to the land I gave your forefathers as an inheritance."** The prophet promises here that there will be concord between the ten tribes of Israel and the kingdom of Judah, when both return from exile. In other words, their condition will be better than it has ever been.

19. **"I myself said, 'How gladly would I treat you like sons and give you a desirable land, the most beautiful inheritance of any nation.' I thought you would call me 'Father' and not turn away from following me."** God says that the Israelites were like dead people and that their salvation was hopeless without a resurrection. Yet he promises them salvation on this condition—that they call on him and do not turn away from following him. That is, if they will always be obedient to God, he will prove that he will not be called **Father** in vain.

20. **"But like a woman unfaithful to her husband, so you have been unfaithful to me, O house of Israel,"** declares the LORD. Even though

the Israelites were like an adulteress, God did not want to take all hope away from them.

21. A cry is heard on the barren heights, the weeping and pleading of the people of Israel, because they have perverted their ways and have forgotten the LORD their God. The prophet declares that the Israelites cried because they had departed from God. The Israelites did not yet show signs of true repentance. The prophet does not commend their piety but says the reason they were severely afflicted like this was because they had forsaken their God.

22-23. "Return, faithless people; I will cure you of backsliding." "Yes, we will come to you, for you are the LORD our God. Surely the idolatrous commotion on the hills and mountains is a deception; surely in the LORD our God is the salvation of Israel." God here exhorts the Israelites to repent, so he can use their example to move the people of Judah. The prophet cites the evidence of their repentance. This is like saying, "We have been deceived by the hills and the many mountains. We thought there would be more defense from a large number of gods than if we worshiped one God. This deception led to ruin. Let all these deceits now be discarded, for we will be content with the only true God."

24. "From our youth shameful gods have consumed the fruits of our fathers' labor—their flocks and herds, their sons and daughters." All the evils they had endured could only be accounted for by their own wickedness.

25. "Let us lie down in our shame, and let our disgrace cover us. We have sinned against the LORD our God, both we and our fathers; from our youth till this day we have not obeyed the LORD our God." The Israelites are explaining what they confessed. The labor of their fathers had been consumed by their shame—that is, by their wickedness. It was as if they said that the cause of all their evils was to be found in their sins, and nowhere else.

Jeremiah
Chapter 4

1. "If you will return, O Israel, return to me," declares the LORD. "If you put your detestable idols out of my sight and no longer go astray . . ." The prophet requires the people to **return** to God and sincerely confess their sins.

2. "And if in a truthful, just and righteous way you swear, 'As surely as the LORD lives,' then the nations will be blessed by him and in him they will glory." The Jews groundlessly blamed God for their being oppressed with so many evils. In fact, they had brought all these calamities on themselves and at the same time gave the godless an opportunity to profane God's name.

3. This is what the LORD says to the men of Judah and to Jerusalem: "Break up your unplowed ground and do not sow among thorns." The Scripture often compares us to a field when it represents us as God's heritage. God says they were like rough ground full of thorns and therefore needed a great deal of cultivation.

4. "Circumcise yourselves to the LORD, circumcise your hearts, you men of Judah and people of Jerusalem, or my wrath will break out and burn like fire because of the evil you have done—burn with no one to quench it." Circumcision was their great boast, but only before men, for nothing but ambition and vanity ruled in them, though they openly exulted and boasted that they were God's holy and special people. So the prophet says, "circumcise your hearts." Genesis 17:10-12 says: "This is my covenant with you and your descendants after you, the covenant you are to keep: Every male among you shall be circumcised. You are to undergo circumcision, and it will be the sign of the covenant between me and you. For the generations to come every male among you who is eight days old must be circumcised, including those born in your household or bought with money from a foreigner—those who are not your offspring." In effect the prophet is saying, "When God commanded the descendants of Abraham to be circumcised, it was not his aim to have a small part of

skin cut off. He had something higher in mind—that you should be circumcised in heart."

He then adds, **"Or my wrath will break out and burn like fire."** The prophet tells them to anticipate in due time God's judgment. For once his fury starts, it will **burn like fire** and consume them, and it will be impossible to put out.

5-6. "Announce in Judah and proclaim in Jerusalem and say: 'Sound the trumpet throughout the land!' Cry aloud and say: 'Gather together! Let us flee to the fortified cities!' Raise the signal to go to Zion! Flee for safety without delay! For I am bringing disaster from the north, even terrible destruction." Jeremiah here treats his own people of Judah more severely, for he sees that they are so obstinate in their vices that no wise counsel can restore them to the way of safety. It is as if he said, "When distress seizes you, you will then experience for yourselves that God is angry with you. Today you do not believe my warnings. To prevent God from punishing you and to bring you back to himself, you will sound the trumpet and proclaim, 'The enemies are coming. Let everyone flee to Jerusalem.'" But God, says Jeremiah, will bring **disaster from the north.** In other words, "Whatever you think is safe will prove useless to protect you."

7. A lion has come out of his lair; a destroyer of nations has set out. He has left his place to lay waste your land. Your towns will lie in ruins without inhabitant. Jeremiah now describes the evil that will come from the north. He compares the king of Babylon to a lion and calls him **a destroyer of nations.** Jeremiah uses past tenses; he has set out to show the certainty of the prediction, as if Nebuchadnezzar had already arrived with a powerful army.

8. So put on sackcloth, lament and wail, for the fierce anger of the LORD has not turned away from us. The prophet tells his own nation that a time of most serious mourning has almost arrived.

9. "In that day," declares the LORD, "the king and the officials will lose heart, the priests will be horrified, and the prophets will be appalled." The prophet wants to shake the false confidence that made the Jews drunk, for they thought they would be safe because of their king and rulers. He says the same thing about the priests and the prophets.

10. Then I said, "Ah, Sovereign LORD, how completely you have deceived this people and Jerusalem by saying, 'You will have peace,' when the sword is at our throats." The prophet tauntingly exposes how the prophets praised the poor Jews falsely and so caused their ruin: They had promised them God's forgiveness, and their predictions were always favorable (see Micah 2:11). This is like saying, "See, Lord, how these people deserve this turn of events. They have sought flattery and would not accept any kind of correction; so let them now begin to learn that they have been deceived by others rather than by you."

11-12. At that time this people and Jerusalem will be told, "A scorching wind from the barren heights in the desert blows toward my people, but not to winnow or cleanse; a wind too strong for that comes from me." Jeremiah continues with the same prediction. He says that a terrible wind is coming that will overthrow everything. He then says how great the calamity will be.

"Now I pronounce my judgments against them." Here God, as judge, declares that the wind has come that will disperse all of Judah. He shows that the Chaldeans will not come of their own accord but will be sent to execute orders. In other words, God will be the author of the calamities that are about to hit Judah.

13. Look! He advances like the clouds, his chariots come like a whirlwind, his horses are swifter than eagles. Woe to us! We are ruined! The prophet here concludes the prediction that referred to the dreadful vengeance that was coming. He mentions several metaphors that might rouse the Jews and make them fearful. He says that the chariots of God will advance **like the clouds,** and his horses will be **swifter than eagles.** By the **clouds, chariots** and **eagles** (the meaning of these metaphors is the same), the prophet depicts the speed of God's vengeance.

14. O Jerusalem, wash the evil from your heart and be saved. The prophet now exhorts the people to repent. By telling Jerusalem to **wash** the evil from her **heart** so that she might **be saved,** he shows that there is no remedy except for the Jews to be reconciled to God.

How long will you harbor wicked thoughts? That is, "Even if the whole world were to absolve you, how would that help you? For vain thoughts remain in the midst of you—that is, in the recesses of your heart. God knows them, for nothing is hidden from him. There is then no reason for you to think you will gain anything by your outward display or your excuses, for God searches your hearts. Do not let these thoughts continue with you."

15. A voice is announcing from Dan, proclaiming disaster. The prophet repeats that the Jews are given over to final ruin because of their perverseness. The whole passage is a graphic picture of the ruin that was at hand. **A voice,** he says, **is announcing from Dan.** Dan was on the extreme northern border. Jeremiah has already said that evil will come from the north. God had chosen the Chaldeans as the executors of his vengeance.

Disaster from the hills of Ephraim. Ephraim was close to the tribe of Judah and Jerusalem.

16. "Tell this to the nations, proclaim it to Jerusalem: 'A besieging army is coming from a distant land, raising a war cry against the cities of Judah.'" In other words, "I have long ago reminded this people that God had other teachers. Despite our efforts, the people degenerate more and more. Because of this, the Lord now says, 'Declare to the nations about Jerusalem.' Let the Jews hear nothing more about the ruin, but let God's vengeance on them be made known to the heathen."

17. "'They surround her like men guarding a field, because she has rebelled against me,'" declares the LORD. The prophet says there will be no escape for the Jews when God brings the Chaldeans.

18. "Your own conduct and actions have brought this upon you. This is your punishment. How bitter it is! How it pierces to the heart!" The Jews will not suffer ill fortune, as the saying goes, but will be summoned by God to judgment, so that, touched by the fear of God, they might repent, or at least, although destroyed in the body, yet be humbled and receive pardon and be saved by the Spirit.

19. "Oh, my anguish, my anguish! I writhe in pain. Oh, the agony of my heart! My heart pounds within me, I cannot keep silent. For I have heard the sound of the trumpet; I have heard the battle cry." The people were so insensitive that Jeremiah and other servants of God had to embellish what they said, so that they not only taught their hearers but forced them to wake up. Jeremiah spoke in earnest because he saw God's vengeance as if it had already happened.

20. "Disaster follows disaster; the whole land lies in ruins. In an instant my tents are destroyed, my shelter in a moment." The prophet continues the same theme but adds a new circumstance: God will heap evils upon evils.

21. "How long must I see the battle standard and hear the sound of the trumpet?" He concludes this part of his discourse, which he had embellished with figures of speech in order to wake them up. He repeats what he has already said: "You are greatly deceived if you think that your enemies, after marching through the land for a short time, will return home. The evil of war will afflict you for a long time, and God will protract your calamities. The sound of the trumpet will continue, and the standard will be raised often, even daily."

22. "My people are fools; they do not know me. They are senseless children; they have no understanding. They are skilled in doing evil; they know not how to do good." Notice two things here. First, a sort of madness is mentioned: the people did not know God. From this we learn that we are only wise when we fear God. Second, we must realize that those people were not allowed to excuse themselves by ignorance or mistakes, for God had made himself known to them.

23-26. I looked at the earth, and it was formless and empty; and at the heavens, and their light was gone. I looked at the mountains, and they were quaking; all the hills were swaying. I looked, and there were no people; every bird in the sky had flown away. I looked, and the fruitful land was a desert; all its towns lay in ruins before the LORD, before his fierce anger. In highly metaphorical language the prophet expands on the terror of God's vengeance, that he might arouse the

Jews, who were so stupid and careless. Four times he repeats the words **I looked**, as though he turned his eyes to four different quarters. And wherever he looked, he saw dreadful tokens of God's wrath that threatened the Jews with utter ruin.

27. This is what the LORD says: "The whole land will be ruined, though I will not destroy it completely." The prophet briefly explains here what he understood by the four things he has mentioned in the previous verses. He then declares, as though God were saying it, that there would be a dreadful desolation throughout Judea.

28. "Therefore the earth will mourn and the heavens above grow dark, because I have spoken and will not relent, I have decided and will not turn back." The mourning of the land stands for its desolation. God says he will not retract his sentence.

29. At the sound of horsemen and archers every town takes to flight. Some go into the thickets; some climb up among the rocks. The enemies will come so rapidly that the Jews will not dare to wait for them to arrive but will flee here and there before they are attacked.

All the towns are deserted; no one lives in them. We see that the prophet was forever trying to rouse the Jews, who had deaf ears and stony hearts and felt no concern for their own calamities. They even boldly despised God, as if they had made a covenant with death and so were safe (see Isaiah 28:15).

30. What are you doing, O devastated one? Why dress yourself in scarlet and put on jewels of gold? Why shade your eyes with paint? You adorn yourself in vain. Your lovers despise you; they seek your life. The prophet boldly ridicules the Jews in order to puncture their pride and haughtiness. The prophet says, "It will do you no good to adorn yourself. Although you put on scarlet, although you shine with gold from head to foot, this will all be superfluous and useless. Even if you paint your face, it will not help you at all."

Your lovers. The prophet is referring to the Egyptians and Assyrians here. The Jews, when oppressed by the Egyptians, sought help from the Assyrians. When they were attacked by the Assyrians, they ran to Egypt for help. So the prophet is saying: "Even if the Egyptians promise wonderful things to you, like a lover allured by your beauty and by your ornaments, they will still deceive you. And if the Assyrians say they will come to rescue you, they too will disappoint you. You will be like a destitute prostitute, reduced to extreme need."

31. I hear a cry as of a woman in labor, a groan as of one bearing her first child—the cry of the Daughter of Zion gasping for breath, stretching out her hands and saying, "Alas! I am fainting; my life is given over to murderers." Jeremiah uses different words to drive home his message to his own hard-hearted nation. He means that the final destruction of his people is near.

Jeremiah
Chapter 5

1. **"Go up and down the streets of Jerusalem, look around and consider, search through her squares. If you can find but one person who deals honestly and seeks the truth, I will forgive this city."** In this verse, and those that follow, God shows that he was not too severe in denouncing utter ruin on his people, because their wickedness was incurable. He says in effect, "If one honest man can be found in the city, I am ready to forgive." The whole priestly order was corrupt and in open war against God, and the people were no better. The prophet wanted to shut the mouths of the Jews and to expose their slanders, so they would not blame God for their impending calamities.

2. **"Although they say, 'As surely as the LORD lives,' still they are swearing falsely."** Jeremiah takes away from hypocrites their false confidence in thinking that God would be propitious to them provided they said his name even if they did not consider how precious that name is. The prophet derides their false pretense and says in effect, "Even when they swear most solemnly and show great concern for religion, they nevertheless swear falsely."

3. The prophet has just said that the Jews are destitute of all integrity, and now, by contrast, he says, **O LORD, do not your eyes look for truth?** Though the Jews make a show of religion through their ceremonies and outward displays, God searches the heart with his piercing eyes.

You struck them, but they felt no pain; you crushed them, but they refused correction. The prophet here reprimands the people for their hardness: they had been **struck** and **crushed**, yet **refused correction.**

They made their faces harder than stone and refused to repent. The prophet means that they were totally without shame. They had thrown away all reason and made no distinction between right and wrong, between honesty and falsehood.

4-5. **I thought, "These are only the poor; they are foolish, for they do not know the way of the LORD, the requirements of their God. So**

I will go to the leaders and speak to them; surely they know the way of the LORD, the requirements of their God." But with one accord they too had broken off the yoke and torn off the bonds. Jeremiah might have said, "Not only the lowest orders, the multitude, have become corrupt, but also the leaders, who should have been better than the rest." Jeremiah makes an even more striking comparison when he says in effect, "It may be that these miserable people have sinned like this because they did not understand the law of God, and that would be hardly surprising. But greater integrity will be found in the leaders." But it was not so.

6. Therefore a lion from the forest will attack them, a wolf from the desert will ravage them, a leopard will lie in wait near their towns to tear to pieces any who venture out, for their rebellion is great and their backslidings many. Jeremiah mentions three wild animals: a lion, a wolf, and a leopard. By these wild animals he doubtless understands the enemies who would soon attack them with the greatest cruelty.

7. "Why should I forgive you? Your children have forsaken me and sworn by gods that are not gods. I supplied all their needs." God seems here to seek the judgment of the adverse party. "If," he says, "I am the judge of the world, is it possible that people can escape unpunished when they openly provoke me? Would I not then expose my glory to ridicule? I would cease to be what I am if I did not punish such a wicked people."

"Yet they committed adultery and thronged to the houses of prostitutes." I think that adultery here is to be understood figuratively, as meaning that they had no spiritual chastity inasmuch as they did not give God glory.

8. "They are well-fed, lusty stallions, each neighing for another man's wife." Jeremiah mentions one kind of evil, but his purpose is to show that there is no chastity, no faithfulness, no honesty in that people.

9. "Should I not punish them for this?" declares the LORD. "Should I not avenge myself on such a nation as this?" God holds, as it were, a conference with them so that he might check all their complaints, in case they should complain that they were dealt with too severely.

10. "Go through her vineyards and ravage them, but do not destroy them completely. Strip off her branches, for these people do not belong to the LORD." Here God, through the mouth of his prophet, addresses the enemies of his people, whom he had appointed to be the ministers of his vengeance. This was normal with the prophets when they were trying to rouse people's hearts (see Isaiah 5:26; 7:18).

11. "The house of Israel and the house of Judah have been utterly unfaithful to me," declares the LORD. In other words, "There is no reason for you to argue with me, as though I had dealt with you severely." God himself declares that they are unfaithful.

12. They have lied about the LORD; they said, "He will do nothing! No harm will come to us; we will never see sword or famine." As we see

further in the next verse, the Holy Spirit has declared that all who trifle with the prophets say in their hearts that there is no God. They deprive him of his power and of his office and make him a product of their own imagination.

13. "The prophets are but wind and the word is not in them; so let what they say be done to them." Jeremiah exposes the contempt the people had for God. They said, "Oh, these are fine words the preachers speak from their pulpits. But everything they say comes to nothing. Whatever they denounce on us will fall on their own heads."

14. Therefore this is what the LORD God Almighty says: "Because the people have spoken these words, I will make my words in your mouth a fire and these people the wood it consumes." God shows here how intolerable it was for him that they should despise the prophets through whom he spoke his message. See Luke 10:16.

"I will make my words in your mouth a fire." God compares his own Word to fire. The prophetic word would consume the people like dry wood or straw.

15. "O house of Israel," declares the LORD, **"I am bringing a distant nation against you—an ancient and enduring nation, a people whose language you do not know, whose speech you do not understand."** God had said that the word in the prophet's mouth would be like fire among his people. He now transfers this to the Assyrians and Chaldeans.

16. "Their quivers are like an open grave; all of them are mighty warriors. The nations of the East used arrows a great deal. They were so skillful in using them that they destroyed everyone they fought against.

17. "They will devour your harvests and food, devour your sons and daughters; they will devour your flocks and herds, devour your vines and fig trees. With the sword they will destroy the fortified cities in which you trust." Jeremiah continues to speak about the cruelty of their enemies, as if victory was already at hand, for they were God's scourges.

18. "Yet even in those days," declares the LORD, **"I will not destroy you completely."** In other words, "Do not think that it will be all over when your enemies plunder you of your possessions and deprive you of your children. You will not be freed from all evils, for I will continue my vengeance on you further."

19. "And when the people ask, 'Why has the LORD our God done all this to us?' you will tell them, 'As you have forsaken me and served foreign gods in your own land, so now you will serve foreigners in a land not your own.'" In other words, "I will put a tyrannical yoke on you. Your conquerors will plunder you because you have been disobedient and unteachable."

20-21. "Announce this to the house of Jacob and proclaim it in Judah: Hear this, you foolish and senseless people, who have eyes but do not see, who have ears but do not hear." Wars were usually proclaimed by heralds. Enemies did not attack at once but proclaimed war so that the cause might seem to be just. Hence God declares that he had spoken in earnest through the mouth of Jeremiah, as though war had been duly proclaimed and armed enemies were now at hand.

22. "Should you not fear me?" declares the LORD. "Should you not tremble in my presence? I made the sand a boundary for the sea, an everlasting barrier it cannot cross. The waves may roll, but they cannot prevail; they may roar, but they cannot cross it." God shows here why he had said the people were foolish and had no understanding. It was indeed most foolish not to fear God's presence, since even inanimate elements obey his bidding.

23. "But these people have stubborn and rebellious hearts; they have turned aside and gone away." This verse completes what was said in the previous one. God had often tried, through his servants, to make his people return to him, but they only showed how perverse they were.

24. "They do not say to themselves, 'Let us fear the LORD our God, who gives fall and spring rains in season, who assures us of the regular weeks of harvest.'" The people were more senseless than lifeless elements. "For you have eyes," he says in summary, "and you have ears, and all human faculties. God gave you rain. Every year the earth has been fruitful. Are not your minds filled with God's bounty? Yet you do not think he should be worshiped."

25. "Your wrongdoings have kept these away; your sins have deprived you of good." Hypocrites often attacked God. Here the Lord through the prophet replies to what they may have alleged. He says his beneficence had been restrained by them, and that it was indeed their fault that it did not flow to them.

26. "Among my people are wicked men who lie in wait like men who snare birds and like those who set traps to catch men." In other words, "The wicked are not to be found only among the heathen; iniquity reigns among the chosen people so that there is nothing sound in them, nothing pure."

27-28. "Like cages full of birds, their houses are full of deceit; they have become rich and powerful and have grown fat and sleek. Their evil deeds have no limit; they do not plead the case of the fatherless to win it, they do not defend the rights of the poor." No further proof was needed that the Jews neglected the poor and helpless, for their houses were full of spoils that made their wickedness evident.

29. "Should I not punish them for this?" declares the LORD. "Should I not avenge myself on such a nation as this?" The prophet repeats this because of the indifference the Jews showed toward God.

30-31. "A horrible and shocking thing has happened in the land: The prophets prophesy lies, the priests rule by their own authority, and my people love it this way. But what will you do in the end?" The prophet speaking for the Lord says that what has happened is beyond human understanding. The two words he uses—**horrible** and **shocking**—indicate that the impiety of the people could not be expressed in words.

"And my people love it this way." The world is never deceived except when it consents to be deceived. See John 3:20. Here the same is said of the church.

"But what will you do in the end?" In other words, "You deceive yourselves if you think this city will last forever, for it is about to be destroyed. What will you do then? You will all be destroyed together with it."

Jeremiah
Chapter 6

1. "Flee for safety, people of Benjamin! Flee from Jerusalem! Sound the trumpet in Tekoa! Raise the signal over Beth Hakkerem! For disaster looms out of the north, even terrible destruction." The prophet often says that punishment is at hand or even, as here, is already before his hearers' eyes. He presents the event as being a present one in order to wake the people up. Jeremiah now addresses the tribe of Benjamin, for half of Jerusalem belonged to that tribe. As Jeremiah himself was from Anathoth, he could address his own people with greater freedom.

"For disaster looms out of the north." The prophet points out where destruction will come from. The Chaldeans had been appointed by God as his ministers and the executioners of his vengeance in destroying Jerusalem and the whole tribe of Judah.

2-3. "I will destroy the Daughter of Zion, so beautiful and delicate. Shepherds with their flocks will come against her; they will pitch their tents around her, each tending his own portion." The whole of Jerusalem would be so much in the power of the enemies that each one would freely choose his own part or his own portion of the city. When there is any fear, the shepherds gather their flocks, so they can help each other. But when everything is in their power, they move here and there as they please.

4-5. "Prepare for battle against her! Arise, let us attack at noon! But, alas, the daylight is fading, and the shadows of evening grow long. So arise, let us attack at night and destroy her fortresses!" Using a personification, Jeremiah pictures the Chaldeans encouraging one another to fight.

"So arise, let us attack at night and destroy her fortresses!" That is, "As we cannot capture the city in six hours, from noon until evening, let us attack at night." We see here how graphically Jeremiah describes the extreme zeal of their enemies.

6. This is what the LORD Almighty says: "Cut down the trees and

build siege ramps against Jerusalem. This city must be punished; it is filled with oppression." This is like saying, "The time of extreme vengeance has arrived. I have tried every way to see if there is any hope of repentance. But I now find that she is totally irreclaimable. Ruin cannot be delayed any longer."

7. **"As a well pours out its water, so she pours out her wickedness. Violence and destruction resound in her; her sickness and wounds are ever before me."** Jeremiah expands on what he said in the previous verse. He says that violence, oppression, devastation, and grief pour out like water from a spring. When people refuse to repent, they pile vice upon vice and appear to swell with wickedness and even burst with it. They are like a spring that bubbles up and cannot contain its water.

8. **"Take warning, O Jerusalem, or I will turn away from you and make your land desolate so no one can live in it."** In other words, "Even though I am now angry and have resolved to punish your faithlessness and rebellion severely, I will still be reconciled to you, provided that you return to me."

9. **This is what the LORD Almighty says: "Let them glean the remnant of Israel as thoroughly as a vine; pass your hand over the branches again, like one gathering grapes."** In other words, "What will become of you? What indeed! You have seen that your brethren have been plundered and that they and their children have been killed. After the name of Israel has been obliterated, God will punish the remnant. You will see that this punishment will soon overtake them. So what are you still looking for? Will your unfaithfulness never end? Why do you not seek to be reconciled to God when such an opportunity is offered to you?"

10. **To whom can I speak and give warning? Who will listen to me? Their ears are closed so they cannot hear. The word of the LORD is offensive to them; they find no pleasure in it.** Jeremiah teaches here that the Jews were so used to sinning that they were no longer free to do right. This remarkable verse shows the degraded and corrupt state of the nation.

11. **But I am full of the wrath of the LORD, and I cannot hold it in. "Pour it out on the children in the street and on the young men gathered together; both husband and wife will be caught in it, and the old, those weighed down with years."** Jeremiah is full of righteous indignation. He is in effect saying, "If I speak to you strongly, do not think that I have neglected to be moderate, for God's Spirit leads and impels me. Whatever indignation is found in my words, it is all from God's Spirit, and not from my own feelings as a man."

"Children . . . young men . . . the old." No one would be exempt from suffering God's vengeance, since impiety had pervaded all stations, ranks, and ages.

12. **"Their houses will be turned over to others, together with their**

fields and their wives, when I stretch out my hand against those who live in the land," declares the LORD. He mentions here only one kind of vengeance—the Jews would be deprived of their land, which they thought they would possess in peace forever.

13. "From the least to the greatest, all are greedy for gain; prophets and priests alike, all practice deceit." The prophet says that the whole community showed their contempt for God.

14. "They dress the wound of my people as though it were not serious. 'Peace, peace,' they say, when there is no peace." This verse applies to the priests and prophets. The prophet, speaking for God, takes the words, as it were, from their mouth: "You are very good doctors! For by your flattery you have soothed my people. There was need not only for serious medicine but for amputations, but you have only applied superficial remedies. This is your way of healing! This is how you have healed the wound of my people—with plasters and ointments to drive the disease inward."

15. "Are they ashamed of their loathsome conduct? No, they have no shame at all; they do not even know how to blush. So they will fall among the fallen; they will be brought down when I punish them," says the LORD. Jeremiah now addresses all the people. "Look," he says, "their wickedness is obvious, and yet they have no shame. Their disgrace is visible to heaven and earth; angels and mortals are witnesses of their corruption. But they are left untouched by any sense of shame."

16. This is what the LORD says: "Stand at the crossroads and look; ask for the ancient paths, ask where the good way is, and walk in it, and you will find rest for your souls. But you said, 'We will not walk in it.'" If the Jews had obeyed God's counsel, they would have been given divine rest. In short, they were miserable because of their own willfulness.

17. "I appointed watchmen over you and said, 'Listen to the sound of the trumpet!' But you said, 'We will not listen.'" Clearly, the sound of the trumpet should have penetrated their minds more than anything else, for it was louder than any human voice, and we usually only hear the trumpet when war is at hand.

18-19. "Therefore hear, O nations; observe, O witnesses, what will happen to them. Hear, O earth: I am bringing disaster on this people, the fruit of their schemes, because they have not listened to my words and have rejected my law." Jeremiah now turns to address the nations who had never before heard anything about true religion. His purpose was to make the Jews ashamed of their deafness to God's teachings.

We may learn from this passage that nothing is more abominable in God's sight than contempt for divine truth.

20. "What do I care about incense from Sheba or sweet calamus from a distant land? Your burnt offerings are not acceptable; your sacrifices do not please me." The prophet replies to those hypocrites

who thought they had made expiation when they offered incense and sacrifices, as if that were all that was necessary in serving God. See Jeremiah 7:21-22; Psalm 50:8-10; Micah 6:7.

21. Therefore this is what the LORD says: "I will put obstacles before this people. Fathers and sons alike will stumble over them; neighbors and friends will perish." Jeremiah means that no matter how they might conspire together, they would all be exposed to the same punishment.

22-23. This is what the LORD says: "Look, an army is coming from the land of the north; a great nation is being stirred up from the ends of the earth. They are armed with bow and spear; they are cruel and show no mercy. They sound like the roaring sea as they ride on their horses; they come like men in battle formation to attack you, O Daughter of Zion." It is not pointless repetition when the prophet says: This is what the LORD says. He could have just said, "Look, an army is coming from the land of the north." But he deliberately says that this message is from God. He introduces God as the speaker to add weight to the message.

"Look, an army is coming from the land of the north." For forty years Jeremiah proclaimed that war would be declared against the Jews, openly naming their enemies. Yet all this preaching bore no fruit. This was indeed dreadful. But we can see from this how great men's hardness is and how great God's fury is.

24. We have heard reports about them, and our hands hang limp. Anguish has gripped us, pain like that of a woman in labor. Jeremiah sets before them God's judgment and draws them, as it were, against their will into the middle of the scene.

25. Do not go out to the fields or walk on the roads, for the enemy has a sword, and there is terror on every side. The prophet speaks as if the war has already started, hoping that they will be changed by this fearful prospect.

26. O my people, put on sackcloth and roll in ashes; mourn with bitter wailing as for an only son, for suddenly the destroyer will come upon us. Nothing but extreme mourning remained for the Jews. So he says that the destroyer will come on them suddenly. For many years they had so misused the forbearance of God that they thought they could sin with impunity.

27. "I have made you a tester of metals and my people the ore, that you may observe and test their ways." Jeremiah introduces God as the speaker in order to gain more authority for his prophecy. The Lord tells Jeremiah to watch how the Jews behave.

28. "They are all hardened rebels, going about to slander. They are bronze and iron; they all act corruptly." Like bronze and iron they are inflexible.

29. "The bellows blow fiercely to burn away the lead with fire,

but the refining goes on in vain; the wicked are not purged out." In Scripture God is said to melt, purge, and refine people when he punishes them. But the prophet says there is only dross in the people. From this we learn how stubborn they were. Although they were tried by fire, they did not melt but continued to be perverse.

30. "They are called rejected silver, because the LORD has rejected them." Jeremiah concludes by saying that if the Jews had been cast in the furnace a hundred times, they would not have improved; their hopeless obstinacy meant they would never become soft.

Jeremiah
Chapter 7

1-4. This is the word that came to Jeremiah from the LORD: "Stand at the gate of the LORD's house and there proclaim this message: 'Hear the word of the LORD, all you people of Judah who come through these gates to worship the LORD. This is what the LORD Almighty, the God of Israel, says: Reform your ways and your actions, and I will let you live in this place. Do not trust in deceptive words and say, "This is the temple of the LORD, the temple of the LORD, the temple of the LORD!"'" Here the prophet gives a summary of the sermon in which he severely reproved the people because his work had been in vain even though he had reproved them sharply.

The prophet repeated the words **the temple of the LORD** because the Jews boasted, as it were, "We are invincible. How can enemies come to us? How can any calamity reach us? God lives in the middle of us. He has his court, his temple, and his Most Holy Place with us."

5-7. "'If you really change your ways and your actions and deal with each other justly, if you do not oppress the alien, the fatherless or the widow and do not shed innocent blood in this place, and if you do not follow other gods to your own harm, then I will let you live in this place, in the land I gave your forefathers for ever and ever.'"

This is what the prophet means: "Although God seems to treat you with great severity, he still promises to be kind to you, if you order your lives according to his law. Is this unjust? Can the condition that is proposed by God be liable to any calumnies, as if God treated you cruelly?"

8. "'But look, you are trusting in deceptive words that are worthless.'" Jeremiah says that deceptive words are those that hypocrites use as they indulge in a pretense of glorifying God. The prophet's reply amounts to, "As you seek to trifle with God, he will frustrate your purpose."

9-11. "'Will you steal and murder, commit adultery and perjury, burn incense to Baal and follow other gods you have not known, and then come and stand before me in this house, which bears my Name, and say, "We are safe"—safe to do all these detestable things? Has this house, which bears my Name, become a den of robbers to you? But I have been watching! declares the LORD.'" The prophet shows how foolish the Jews were in trying to make an agreement with God, so they could provoke him by their many vices and still go unpunished. When they went into the temple, they thought God was under some obligation to receive them, as though that was a true reconciliation. But the prophet exposes this folly. What can be more absurd than that God should allow people to commit murder, theft, and adultery with impunity?

12-14. "'Go now to the place in Shiloh where I first made a dwelling for my Name, and see what I did to it because of the wickedness of my people Israel. While you were doing all these things, declares the LORD, I spoke to you again and again, but you did not listen; I called you, but you did not answer. Therefore, what I did to Shiloh I will now do to the house that bears my Name, the temple you trust in, the place I gave to you and your fathers.'" The prophet confirms by an example what he had said in the previous verses—that the Jews deceived themselves when they thought they were covered by the shadow of the temple, while they engaged in open rebellion against God. He says what had happened before. The temple did not excel in dignity on its own account, but on account of the ark of the covenant and the altar. It was indeed adorned in a splendid way, but the holiness of the temple was derived from the ark of the covenant and the sacrifices. This ark had been at Shiloh for a long time. Hence Jeremiah shows how foolish the Jews were in being proud just because they had the ark of the covenant and the altar among them: Shiloh, where sacrifices had been offered to God, was not preserved in safety.

15. "'I will thrust you from my presence, just as I did all your brothers, the people of Ephraim.'" Here the prophet concludes what he has said in the previous verses. He now calls the Israelites "your brothers." He calls them "the people of Ephraim" because of their first king, and also because that tribe was more illustrious than the other nine tribes. And in many passages the prophets say "Ephraim" when they mean Israel— that is, the second kingdom, which flourished in wealth and power.

16. "So do not pray for this people nor offer any plea or petition for them; do not plead with me, for I will not listen to you." God, in order to exonerate his servant from charges of ill will toward the people, forbids him from praying for them.

17-19. "Do you not see what they are doing in the towns of Judah and in the streets of Jerusalem? The children gather wood, the fathers light the fire, and the women knead the dough and make cakes of bread for the Queen of Heaven. They pour out drink offerings to other gods to provoke me to anger. But am I the one they are provoking? declares the LORD. Are they not rather harming themselves, to their own shame?" Here God shows why he was so implacable toward the people.

"**They pour out drink offerings to other gods to provoke me to anger.**" When God complains about being provoked, it is like saying the Jews were engaging in open war with him: "They sin, but not through ignorance. It is, as it were, their aim to provoke me by their acts of impiety."

20. "'**Therefore this is what the Sovereign LORD says: My anger and my wrath will be poured out on this place, on man and beast, on the trees of the field and on the fruit of the ground, and it will burn and not be quenched.'**" Jeremiah continues the same theme, explaining it in more detail.

"'**On man and beast, on the trees of the field and on the fruit of the ground.'**" Strictly speaking, God does not punish animals and trees; this happens because of mankind, so that this spectacle may fill men with fear.

21-24. "'**This is what the LORD Almighty, the God of Israel, says: Go ahead, add your burnt offerings to your other sacrifices and eat the meat yourselves! For when I brought your forefathers out of Egypt and spoke to them, I did not just give them commands about burnt offerings and sacrifices, but I gave them this command: Obey me, and I will be your God and you will be my people. Walk in all the ways I command you, that it may go well with you. But they did not listen or pay attention; instead, they followed the stubborn inclinations of their evil hearts. They went backward and not forward.'**" The Lord here taunts the Jews for being so tireless in their attention to sacrifices while not caring about piety. So he ridicules them by saying, "Offer your sacrifices, accumulate burnt offerings and victims, eat the meat. You are really making sacrifices to yourselves, not to me."

At first sight it may appear that the Lord through Jeremiah condemns sacrifices too much: "'**I did not just give them commands about burnt offerings and sacrifices.'**" But he is only repudiating these sacrifices because these false worshipers adulterated them. To them, they were only an external rite, for they had overlooked their purpose, and even despised them.

Note how detestable a sacrilege it is to follow the wickedness of our hearts rather than to obey God when he points out to us the way of salvation. We must also observe that nothing will do us any good, although we may appear to be wise in our own eyes, if God declares that we have **evil hearts,** which is what we have every time we turn away from his pure Word.

25-26. "'**From the time your forefathers left Egypt until now, day after day, again and again I sent you my servants the prophets. But they did not listen to me or pay attention. They were stiff-necked and did more evil than their forefathers.'**" God complains about the perverse wickedness of the people. All his efforts to lead them to repentance proved in vain, not only in one age, but in succeeding generations. This passage deserves special note, for God not only condemned those who were living and whom Jeremiah addressed, but also linked with them the dead, to demonstrate their greater obstinacy, as impiety had been, as it were, handed down from one age to another.

27. "When you tell them all this, they will not listen to you; when you call to them, they will not answer." This shows still more fully the people's perverseness. Not only were they deaf to God's voice, neglecting plain teaching—they also disregarded the most vehement exhortations.

28. "Therefore say to them, 'This is the nation that has not obeyed the LORD its God or responded to correction. Truth has perished; it has vanished from their lips.'" In short, Jeremiah is saying there is no hope of their repenting. Had they promised God a hundred times that they would be teachable and obedient and showed evidence of this before the world, they would have been only deceiving everyone.

29. "'Cut off your hair and throw it away; take up a lament on the barren heights, for the LORD has rejected and abandoned this generation that is under his wrath.'" Jeremiah, speaking for God, tells his people to lament. First, he tells them to **cut off** their **hair**. The word for **hair**, *nesar*, is derived from the Nazirites, who allowed their hair to grow. Here there may be here a striking allusion to the Nazirites, who were sacred to God. It is as if God said, "My people are profane and therefore ought to have nothing in common with the Nazirites." So these people, rejected by God, are told to cut off their hair and **throw it away.**

30. "'The people of Judah have done evil in my eyes, declares the LORD. They have set up their detestable idols in the house that bears my Name and have defiled it.'" Though the Jews always flattered themselves, the prophet here reminds them of God's judgment. "It is enough," he says, "that the Judge condemns you. Even if you do not see your wickedness or acknowledge your sin, that will not help you. For God declares that you are guilty in his sight."

31. "'They have built the high places of Topheth in the Valley of Ben Hinnom to burn their sons and daughters in the fire—something I did not command, nor did it enter my mind.'" Jeremiah condemns the superstitions by which the Jews had corrupted the true and pure worship of God.

He mentions one particular place, **Topheth in the Valley of Ben Hinnom.** The prophets, in order to render the place detestable, no doubt designated the infernal regions by **Topheth** and *gai enom*. When Isaiah speaks about the eternal punishment of the wicked (Isaiah 30:33), he mentions "Topheth"—the same word as we have here. As the Valley of Ben Hinnom, it is called in Greek *Gehenna* and is taken to designate eternal death or the torments that await all the wicked. They chose this filthy place to worship God according to their own will, or rather according to their own wantonness. In such a place, Jeremiah says, they "'have built . . . high places.'"

He adds, "'to burn their sons and daughters in the fire.'" It was a horrible and prodigious madness for parents not to spare their own children but rather to throw them into the fire. They must have been devoid of all human feeling and filled with diabolic fury. And yet they dredged up a reason for this: To show their zeal for God, they preferred him to even their children.

As the words *Topheth* and *Gehenna* were so stigmatized by the prophets, we may learn from this how much God is displeased with all idolatry and profanation of his true and pure worship.

32. "'So beware, the days are coming, declares the LORD, when people will no longer call it Topheth or the Valley of Ben Hinnom, but the Valley of Slaughter, for they will bury the dead in Topheth until there is no more room.'" The prophet predicts a punishment, although the Jews thought they deserved a reward.

The Valley of Slaughter. He says the slaughter will be so great that Jerusalem will not be able to contain the dead. So, he says, graves will be made in **Topheth**, where many will also be killed.

33. "'Then the carcasses of this people will become food for the birds of the air and the beasts of the earth, and there will be no one to frighten them away.'" The prophet says there will be no one to perform the humane office of driving the beasts away from dead bodies.

34. "'I will bring an end to the sounds of joy and gladness and to the voices of bride and bridegroom in the towns of Judah and the streets of Jerusalem, for the land will become desolate.'" The prophet continues with the same subject. Speaking for God, he says that the Jews deserved the punishment they would receive. By referring to marriage, **the voices of bride and bridegroom,** the prophet, representing a part for the whole, means whatever was necessary for the preservation of society. In other words, "There will now be no marrying." For without marriage the human race cannot continue.

Jeremiah
Chapter 8

1-2. "'At that time, declares the LORD, the bones of the kings and officials of Judah, the bones of the priests and prophets, and the bones of the people of Jerusalem will be removed from their graves. They will be exposed to the sun and the moon and all the stars of the heavens, which they have loved and served and which they have followed and consulted and worshiped. They will not be gathered up or buried, but will be like refuse lying on the ground.'" Jeremiah repeats in the first verse what he has just said—the Jews will be deprived of their graves so there will be a mark of God's vengeance on the dead. In other words, after they were destroyed by the hand of enemies, they would receive more punishment by having their dead bodies exposed to wild animals and birds.

"'They will not be gathered up or buried, but will be like refuse lying on the ground.'" They had despised God and had prostrated themselves before their idols; so after death they would be made detestable, so people would be revolted by such a terrible sight.

3. "'Wherever I banish them, all the survivors of this evil nation will prefer death to life, declares the LORD Almighty.'" He says in this verse that all survivors will be doubly miserable, and that it would have been better for them to die at once than to pine away in unceasing evils.

4-5. "Say to them, 'This is what the LORD says: When men fall down, do they not get up? When a man turns away, does he not return? Why then have these people turned away? Why does Jerusalem always turn away? They cling to deceit; they refuse to return.'" God, partly to aggravate the sin of the godly and partly to provide for his faithful people, exhorts the people to repent even though they are totally intractable.

"'When men fall down, do they not get up?'" In other words, "When anyone falls, he immediately thinks about how to get up. When anyone deviates from the right course and is warned that he is going astray, he immediately looks for the right road. This is what is usually done. So what does this great stupidity mean, that the people of Jerusalem do not repent when they should long ago have acknowledged their fall and their wandering?"

6. "'I have listened attentively, but they do not say what is right. No one repents of his wickedness, saying, "What have I done?" Each pursues his own course like a horse charging into battle.'" Jeremiah says that he was not being inconsiderate in reproving the people, but that he found such perversity in them that no one said, "What is right?" No one repented because they did not examine their own lives but slept securely in their sins.

7. "'Even the stork in the sky knows her appointed seasons, and the dove, the swift and the thrush observe the time of their migration. But my people do not know the requirements of the LORD.'" Jeremiah continues to condemn the people's shameful lack of awareness. He says they had less wisdom than birds that are not even endued with reason and understanding. He says the Jews were more foolish than "'the stork . . . and the dove, the swift and the thrush.'" He no doubt deeply wounded the feelings of the people with such a severe reproof, but it was necessary to use a sharp rebuke because the people had become so hardened in their vices.

8. "'How can you say, "We are wise, for we have the law of the LORD," when actually the lying pen of the scribes has handled it falsely?'" Jeremiah describes the kind of wisdom they claimed to possess: "we have the law of the LORD." There is no doubt that to attend to God's law is the way to become really wise. Had they just boasted that they had the law, the prophet would not have charged them with being doubly foolish. But as they made a false claim to wisdom, he asks them, "How can you say . . . ?" He is really asking, "Why are you so foolish to think you are wise, as if God's law was with you? If that were the case, the law would have been written in vain, for your life demonstrates that you do not know anything about God's law."

9. "'The wise will be put to shame; they will be dismayed and trapped. Since they have rejected the word of the LORD, what kind of wisdom do they have?'" He says, "the wise will be put to shame . . . dismayed and trapped." He means that the Jews gained nothing from their craftiness as they arrogated to themselves wisdom and under this pretense rejected all warnings and sought to be spared.

10. "'Therefore I will give their wives to other men and their fields to new owners. From the least to the greatest, all are greedy for gain; prophets and priests alike, all practice deceit.'" Having seen that his exhortations were ignored, the Lord through Jeremiah now becomes more severe and says, "I will give their wives to other men." Jeremiah shows that the most atrocious thing that happens to conquered nations was about to happen to the Jews—men would be deprived of their wives.

He then says the same thing would happen to **their fields**, meaning they would permanently lose them.

11. **"'They dress the wound of my people as though it were not serious. "Peace, peace," they say, when there is no peace.'"** By repeating the word **peace**, the prophet shows more clearly how unsure their security was. They did not just deceive the people once but proceeded obstinately in the work of deceiving the wretched people by their false promises.

12. **"'Are they ashamed of their loathsome conduct? No, they have no shame at all; they do not even know how to blush. So they will fall among the fallen; they will be brought down when they are punished, says the LORD.'"** The prophet shows even more clearly that the people were wholly irreclaimable, for they had divested themselves of all shame. It is a sure proof of wickedness beyond remedy when there is no shame.

13. **"'I will take away their harvest, declares the LORD. There will be no grapes on the vine. There will be no figs on the tree, and their leaves will wither. What I have given them will be taken from them.'"** The prophet means that by various ways the Jews would be reduced to penury. Either their enemies would rob them of grapes and figs, or God himself would send sterility; or, when they thought their provisions were safe, they would not be allowed to enjoy them.

14. **"Why are we sitting here? Gather together! Let us flee to the fortified cities and perish there! For the LORD our God has doomed us to perish and given us poisoned water to drink, because we have sinned against him."** Jeremiah is carrying out the duty of his prophetic office. The people never willingly acknowledged that they were suffering just punishment for their sins. But the prophet here reproves them for hoping to be safe by fleeing to **fortified cities**, as though God could not follow them there. He then says that God's vengeance would be in close pursuit and that wherever they fled, they would still be exposed to evils, for they carried their impieties with them, and these would bring God's wrath upon them.

15. **"We hoped for peace but no good has come, for a time of healing but there was only terror."** The Jews flattered themselves by entertaining false hopes.

16. **"The snorting of the enemy's horses is heard from Dan; at the neighing of their stallions the whole land trembles. They have come to devour the land and everything in it, the city and all who live there."** Jeremiah tells them that God will send hostile armies who will devour their cities and the inhabitants.

17. **"See, I will send venomous snakes among you, vipers that cannot be charmed, and they will bite you, declares the LORD."** The prophet now says that the Jews will have to wage war on **venomous snakes**, showing that they will have no way of escape.

18. **O my Comforter in sorrow, my heart is faint within me.**

Jeremiah says that their hearts will become weak, and the debility will overwhelm them.

19. Listen to the cry of my people from a land far away: "Is the Lord not in Zion? Is her King no longer there?" "Why have they provoked me to anger with their images, with their worthless foreign idols?" In this verse the prophet assumes different characters. He first implied ruin that, although near, was not yet dreaded by the people. He then represents the people and relates what they would say. In the third place he adds an answer, in God's name, to check the clamors of the people.

20. "The harvest is past, the summer has ended, and we are not saved." In other words, "We thought the people we had made alliances with would come to our help, but we have been deceived in this."

21. Since my people are crushed, I am crushed; I mourn, and horror grips me. The astonishment that overcomes Jeremiah contrasts with the people's insensibility, for they had no fear of God.

22. Is there no balm in Gilead? Is there no physician there? Why then is there no healing for the wound of my people? Jeremiah says that the people had an incurable disease and that their destruction could not be avoided.

Jeremiah
Chapter 9

1. **Oh, that my head were a spring of water and my eyes a fountain of tears! I would weep day and night for the slain of my people.** Jeremiah continues the same theme. During times of tranquillity, when nothing but joyful voices were heard among the Jews, he bewails, as one in the greatest grief, the miseries of the people. Their ruin would be so dreadful that the usual lamentation would not suffice.

2. **Oh, that I had in the desert a lodging place for travelers, so that I might leave my people and go away from them; for they are all adulterers, a crowd of unfaithful people.** Jeremiah shows that the Jews had become so detestable that all of God's true servants wanted to go far away from them.

3. **"They make ready their tongue like a bow, to shoot lies; it is not by truth that they triumph in the land. They go from one sin to another; they do not acknowledge me," declares the LORD.** The Jews ridiculed all warnings, thinking they were far from danger.

4-6. **"Beware of your friends; do not trust your brothers. For every brother is a deceiver, and every friend a slanderer. Friend deceives friend, and no one speaks the truth. They have taught their tongues to lie; they weary themselves with sinning. You live in the midst of deception; in their deceit they refuse to acknowledge me," declares the LORD.** The prophet describes the extreme wickedness of the people. During times of calamity, some regard for close relatives remains. At such times, even among the most wicked people, there remains some natural affection, called *storge* by philosophers. So it is monstrous when all such affections are destroyed. When people depart wholly from nature and become wild animals, natural affections no longer exist.

7-9. **Therefore this is what the LORD Almighty says: "See, I will refine and test them, for what else can I do because of the sin of my people? Their tongue is a deadly arrow; it speaks with deceit. With his mouth each speaks cordially to his neighbor, but in his heart** he sets a trap for him. Should I not punish them for this?" declares the LORD. "Should I not avenge myself on such a nation as this?" Jeremiah, speaking in God's name, concludes that the punishment he had spoken about was necessary. He exposes their sins so they would realize they could not escape the hand of God, who is a just avenger of wickedness.

10. **I will weep and wail for the mountains and take up a lament concerning the desert pastures. They are desolate and untraveled, and the lowing of cattle is not heard. The birds of the air have fled and the animals are gone.** The prophet had exhorted others to lament, but nobody listened to him. So he himself prepares to lament and mourn, thus indirectly condemning the people's lack of awareness.

The desert pastures. The richest pastures were on the mountains, but the Jews often called them deserts. Jeremiah is condemning the foolish confidence of the people, who thought they lived in safety.

11. **"I will make Jerusalem a heap of ruins, a haunt of jackals; and I will lay waste the towns of Judah so no one can live there."** The prophet turns to Jerusalem and the neighboring cities, having said that ruin would extend to the mountains. But it seemed incredible that a well-fortified city, full of people to defend it, having a treaty with Egypt, could ever be destroyed.

12. **What man is wise enough to understand this? Who has been instructed by the LORD and can explain it? Why has the land been ruined and laid waste like a desert that no one can cross?** If the people had a particle of understanding, they would have known that a dreadful calamity was about to overtake them.

13-15. **The LORD said, "It is because they have forsaken my law, which I set before them; they have not obeyed me or followed my law. Instead, they have followed the stubbornness of their hearts; they have followed the Baals, as their fathers taught them." Therefore, this is what the LORD Almighty, the God of Israel, says: "See, I will make this people eat bitter food and drink poisoned water."** Jeremiah now confirms that although no teacher was given a hearing, yet there was enough power in God's Word alone to carry out God's will. God's judgment did not depend on the will or perceptions of men.

"See, I will make this people eat bitter food and drink poisoned water." Jeremiah refers to God's dreadful vengeance: God would not only deprive the Jews of his benefits but would also turn their bread into bitterness and their water into poison.

16. **"I will scatter them among nations that neither they nor their fathers have known, and I will pursue them with the sword until I have destroyed them."** Jeremiah declares that since they have abused God's forbearance, he will punish them until they are completely destroyed.

17-18. This is what the LORD Almighty says: "Consider now! Call for the wailing women to come; send for the most skillful of them. Let them come quickly and wail over us till our eyes overflow with tears and water streams from our eyelids." In this passage, as in many others, the prophet presents a striking picture in order to touch the hearts of the people.

19. "The sound of wailing is heard from Zion: 'How ruined we are! How great is our shame! We must leave our land because our houses are in ruins.'" The people enjoyed tolerably good conditions at that time, but Jeremiah is warning them that in the future they will be exiled.

20-21. Now, O women, hear the word of the LORD; open your ears to the words of his mouth. Teach your daughters how to wail; teach one another a lament. Death has climbed in through our windows and has entered our fortresses; it has cut off the children from the streets and the young men from the public squares. Jeremiah now says, in effect, that hiring women to mourn for them will not be enough, for the calamities will reach all hearts, and mercenary wailing will not be real.

22. Say, "This is what the LORD declares: 'The dead bodies of men will lie like refuse on the open field, like cut grain behind the reaper, with no one to gather them.'" Jeremiah means that no one will be left of the people, for all, from the least to the greatest, will be given up to destruction.

23-24. This is what the LORD says: "Let not the wise man boast of his wisdom or the strong man boast of his strength or the rich man boast of his riches, but let him who boasts boast about this: that he understands and knows me, that I am the LORD, who exercises kindness, justice and righteousness on earth, for in these I delight," declares the LORD. Jeremiah forbids anyone to glory except in God alone. All are greatly deceived who think themselves blessed when they are alienated from God.

25-26. "The days are coming," declares the LORD, "when I will punish all who are circumcised only in the flesh—Egypt, Judah, Edom, Ammon, Moab and all who live in the desert in distant places. For all these nations are really uncircumcised, and even the whole house of Israel is uncircumcised in heart." The prophet pronounces ruin not only on the Jews but also on the Egyptians and other surrounding nations. However, he only speaks to his own people.

Moses and the prophets often called an unrenewed heart "uncircumcised." Circumcision, while evidence of free salvation in Christ, at the same time initiated the Jews into the worship and service of God and proved the necessity of a new life. In short, it was a sign of both repentance and of faith. When, therefore, the Jews presented only the sign, Moses and the prophets quite rightly derided them. They seemed to be trying to pacify God by a thing of no substance, without taking into account its purpose.

We may say the same of baptism. Baptism itself avails hypocrites nothing, for they only receive the mere sign. Therefore we must come to the *spirit* of baptism, to the thing itself. For the interior power is renovation, when our old self is crucified in us, and when we rise again with Christ to newness of life.

Jeremiah
Chapter 10

1-2. Hear what the LORD says to you, O house of Israel. This is what the LORD says: "Do not learn the ways of the nations or be terrified by signs in the sky, though the nations are terrified by them." Jeremiah begins a new topic here. He starts to attack those superstitions to which the Jews were extremely addicted. He tells them, "Do not suppose that prosperity or adversity depends on the position or aspect of the stars." He tells them not to **"be terrified by signs in the sky."** The Chaldeans, no doubt, prophesied that they would have a new empire, and so they frightened the miserable Jews: "It is all over with us, for the astrologers among the Chaldeans have said so. The Egyptians also say they have seen this foreshadowed by the position of the stars." In this way the Jews became, as it were, wholly lifeless.

3-5. "For the customs of the peoples are worthless; they cut a tree out of the forest, and a craftsman shapes it with his chisel. They adorn it with silver and gold; they fasten it with hammer and nails so it will not totter. Like a scarecrow in a melon patch, their idols cannot speak; they must be carried because they cannot walk. Do not fear them; they can do no harm nor can they do any good." In other words, "When the Chaldeans and Egyptians astonish you through the influence of a false opinion derived from nothing, saying they are alone wise, do you not see that you are doubly mad? Where is their wisdom when they make gods from tree trunks?"

"Do not fear them; they can do no harm nor can they do any good." The prophet says that the idols of the Gentiles, their fictitious gods, **"can do no harm"**; that is, they have no power to inflict punishment on people.

6. "No one is like you, O LORD; you are great, and your name is mighty in power." Anyone who does not understand that there is a God and does not know who or what he is can never really be influenced by the truth that the gods of the heathens are demons, and all their superstitions sacrilegious.

7-8. "Who should not revere you, O King of the nations? This is your due. Among all the wise men of the nations and in all their kingdoms, there is no one like you. They are all senseless and foolish; they are taught by worthless wooden idols." In other words, "Lord, why are you not feared throughout the world? Surely where people have any spark of right knowledge they will acknowledge you as the only true God and, having learned this truth, will submit to your power. When, therefore, people invent for themselves various gods, and when everyone is led here and there without understanding, it is monstrous. And how is it that those who say that God ought to be worshiped fall away and adopt many gods and can never say who is the true God or how he is to be worshiped?"

9-10. "Hammered silver is brought from Tarshish and gold from Uphaz. What the craftsman and goldsmith have made is then dressed in blue and purple—all made by skilled workers. But the LORD is the true God; he is the living God, the eternal King. When he is angry, the earth trembles; the nations cannot endure his wrath." The prophet, anticipating what might be said, refers to the splendor and pomp of idols and declares that it is all frivolous and extremely childish. Why did the world show so much honor to idols unless they were dazzled by their pomp? In this way the devil has always deluded the unbelieving. For he has exhibited in idols something that involved people's minds in darkness.

"When he is angry, the earth trembles; the nations cannot endure his wrath." Jeremiah is saying, "Even though unbelievers now boldly despise God, when he appears as the Judge of the world, the whole earth will tremble and will not be able to stand in his presence, although they now proudly reproach true religion."

11. "Tell them this: 'These gods, who did not make the heavens and the earth, will perish from the earth and from under the heavens.'" In other words, "Even though now you are in the most miserable bondage, and although the Chaldeans disdainfully oppress you, you must still proclaim the glory of God and make an open confession of your religion."

We see that there is no true religion in people's hearts unless they witness to it, for the tongue should say what the heart feels.

12-13. But God made the earth by his power; he founded the world by his wisdom and stretched out the heavens by his understanding. When he thunders, the waters in the heavens roar; he makes clouds rise from the ends of the earth. He sends lightning with the rain and brings out the wind from his storehouses. In other words, "There is one who has created the earth; there is one who has set in order the world and extended the heavens. Since these things cannot be ascribed to many, it follows that it is absurd to imagine that there are various gods."

14-16. Everyone is senseless and without knowledge; every gold-smith is shamed by his idols. His images are a fraud; they have no breath in them. They are worthless, the objects of mockery; when their judgment comes, they will perish. He who is the Portion of Jacob is not like these, for he is the Maker of all things, including Israel, the tribe of his inheritance—the LORD Almighty is his name. Whenever the prophets spoke about idols, they also spoke about the true God. That is why the prophet repeats that God, who is **the Portion of Jacob,** is not like idols. He calls God **the Portion of Jacob** in order to preserve the people in the pure truth of the law that they had learned and with which they had been favored. In this way he draws the attention of the Israelites away from the inventions of the heathen.

17-18. Gather up your belongings to leave the land, you who live under siege. For this is what the LORD says: "At this time I will hurl out those who live in this land; I will bring distress on them so that they may be captured." This means that the whole country was going to be exposed to the will of their enemies so they could plunder it.

19. Woe to me because of my injury! My wound is incurable! Yet I said to myself, "This is my sickness, and I must endure it." Jeremiah is not grieving on his own account, but he represents the grief that all the people should have felt but did not feel at all. Note how the confession of sin and patience or endurance are linked here, for those who experience the severity of God quietly submit to him as long as he exercises his office of judge toward them.

20. My tent is destroyed; all its ropes are snapped. The prophets often compare the church to a tent.

My sons are gone from me and are no more; no one is left now to pitch my tent or to set up my shelter. Jeremiah says the people will be so bereaved that no one will help them.

21. The shepherds are senseless and do not inquire of the LORD; so they do not prosper and all their flock is scattered. Jeremiah says that this dreadful visitation has been brought about by **senseless shepherds** (including the priests and the prophets).

22. Listen! The report is coming—a great commotion from the land of the north! It will make the towns of Judah desolate, a haunt of jackals. In effect, God is saying to the people through his prophet, "You would not listen to me or any other of God's servants; so the Chaldeans will be your teachers. I will send you to their school since I have spent so many years laboring over you in vain."

23. I know, O LORD, that a man's life is not his own; it is not for man to direct his steps. This verse teaches the general truth that people are deceived if they think fortune or the outcome of events lies in their own hands. No matter how much they may consult other people, what they do will be unsuccessful if God does not bless their counsels.

24. Correct me, LORD, but only with justice—not in your anger, lest you reduce me to nothing. The prophet personifies the whole people and undertakes a public lamentation, even though the people still refuse to change their sinful ways.

25. Pour out your wrath on the nations that do not acknowledge you, on the peoples who do not call on your name. For they have devoured Jacob; they have devoured him completely and destroyed his homeland. As his reason for his prayer in the last verse, the prophet says that God had sufficient grounds to execute his vengeance on the wicked and ungodly nations.

Jeremiah does not say that the Israelites had been badly treated but that the nations had **devoured** them. He repeats this: **they have devoured Jacob;** then adds that their **homeland** is **completely . . . destroyed.** We see how God's children have been afflicted and so are not surprised if today's church is exposed to terrible calamities.

Jeremiah
Chapter 11

1-5. This is the word that came to Jeremiah from the LORD: "Listen to the terms of this covenant and tell them to the people of Judah and to those who live in Jerusalem. Tell them that this is what the LORD, the God of Israel, says: 'Cursed is the man who does not obey the terms of this covenant—the terms I commanded your forefathers when I brought them out of Egypt, out of the iron-smelting furnace.' I said, 'Obey me and do everything I command you, and you will be my people, and I will be your God. Then I will fulfill the oath I swore to your forefathers, to give them a land flowing with milk and honey'—the land you possess today." I answered, "Amen, LORD."

The prophet teaches us that the Jews, though they continued to profess God's holy name, had departed from following God's law. The theme of this passage is that the Jews gloried in the name of God while they violated his covenant. It is as if he said, "You have no case for saying that God defrauded you if he throws you out of the land, for it is not God who is disinheriting you—it is your own wickedness."

6-8. The LORD said to me, "Proclaim all these words in the towns of Judah and in the streets of Jerusalem: 'Listen to the terms of this covenant and follow them. From the time I brought your forefathers up from Egypt until today, I warned them again and again, saying, "Obey me." But they did not listen or pay attention; instead, they followed the stubbornness of their evil hearts. So I brought on them all the curses of the covenant I had commanded them to follow but that they did not keep.'" The prophet explains in more detail why he had been commanded to promulgate the words of the covenant. Most of the people were all too ready to say, "What do you mean? Are we not Moses' disciples? We are not barbarians. We have been taught God's law since we were children. We know all about the teaching that you say we are ignorant of. Go off to the Chaldeans or Assyrians or Egyptians. As for us, we know all about the law." Jeremiah doubtless had to face such insolence. He says that he is right to set before them God's law, for they did not really know it.

9-10. Then the LORD said to me, "There is a conspiracy among the people of Judah and those who live in Jerusalem. They have returned to the sins of their forefathers, who refused to listen to my words. They have followed other gods to serve them. Both the house of Israel and the house of Judah have broken the covenant I made with their forefathers." Jeremiah says that these people are worse than their forefathers and that their **conspiracy** against God had been discovered. "They were previously two peoples, but they are now one, for their conspiracy against God unites them to each other."

11-13. "Therefore this is what the LORD says: 'I will bring on them a disaster they cannot escape. Although they cry out to me, I will not listen to them. The towns of Judah and the people of Jerusalem will go and cry out to the gods to whom they burn incense, but they will not help them at all when disaster strikes. You have as many gods as you have towns, O Judah; and the altars you have set up to burn incense to that shameful god Baal are as many as the streets of Jerusalem.'" They had been so given over to destruction that it was hopeless for them to expect God to be merciful to them. Jeremiah points out that they were not genuinely repentant, for they could cry out indiscriminately to God and to idols.

14. "Do not pray for this people nor offer any plea or petition for them, because I will not listen when they call to me in the time of their distress." So that the Jews might understand that their sin was serious and God could not be appeased, the prophet is told not to pray for them.

15. "What is my beloved doing in my temple as she works out her evil schemes with many? Can consecrated meat avert your punishment? When you engage in your wickedness, then you rejoice." When the Lord says **"my beloved,"** he is speaking ironically. It is as if he were saying, "I truly do not owe you anything. You do indeed come to my courts, but for what reason? You only wear out the pavement of my temple. Stay at home, and do not think that I owe you anything just because you come to my temple."

16-17. The LORD called you a thriving olive tree with fruit beautiful in form. But with the roar of a mighty storm he will set it on fire, and its branches will be broken. The LORD Almighty, who planted you, has decreed disaster for you, because the house of Israel and the house of Judah have done evil and provoked me to anger by burning incense to Baal. The prophet says that the Jews had indeed been for a time like a fruitful and fair olive tree. Then he adds that this beauty would not prevent God from breaking its branches and entirely eradicating it.

18-20. Because the LORD revealed their plot to me, I knew it, for at that time he showed me what they were doing. I had been like a

gentle lamb led to the slaughter; I did not realize that they had plotted against me, saying, "Let us destroy the tree and its fruit; let us cut him off from the land of the living, that his name be remembered no more." But, O LORD Almighty, you who judge righteously and test the heart and mind, let me see your vengeance upon them, for to you I have committed my cause. This passage teaches us that even if the whole world unites to suppress the light of truth, prophets and teachers should not be despondent but rather persevere in their work. We also see that there is no point in the ungodly trying to elude the authority of the prophets, for they eventually have to come before God's tribunal.

21-23. "Therefore this is what the LORD says about the men of Anathoth who are seeking your life and saying, 'Do not prophesy in the name of the LORD or you will die by our hands'—therefore this is what the LORD Almighty says: 'I will punish them. Their young men will die by the sword, their sons and daughters by famine. Not even a remnant will be left to them, because I will bring disaster on the men of Anathoth in the year of their punishment.'" The citizens of Anathoth, Jeremiah's hometown, had sinned very badly; so Jeremiah pronounces that they will be severely punished.

Jeremiah
Chapter 12

1. You are always righteous, O LORD, when I bring a case before you. Yet I would speak with you about your justice: Why does the way of the wicked prosper? Why do all the faithless live at ease? The Israelites scorned and laughed at all of Jeremiah's warnings; so now he addresses God himself. It appears as if he is saying he would have nothing more to do with them, for he had labored wholly in vain. The prophet did this to arouse them and so they would realize that they were summoned, so to speak, by this outburst before the celestial tribunal.

2. You have planted them, and they have taken root; they grow and bear fruit. You are always on their lips but far from their hearts. When the happiness of the wicked disturbs us, two false thoughts come to mind. First, that this world is ruled by chance and not governed by God's providence; or, second, that God is not a just Judge when he allows light to be mixed with darkness. The prophet takes it for granted that this world is governed by God's providence. He does not agree with Ovid's words, "I am disposed to think that there are no gods." So the prophet now asks, How could God be so patient?

3. Yet you know me, O LORD; you see me and test my thoughts about you. Drag them off like sheep to be butchered! Set them apart for the day of slaughter! The prophet clearly intended not just to touch the Jews with these words, but to deeply wound them, to make them understand that the only reason they were not destroyed was because God had spared them.

4. How long will the land lie parched and the grass in every field be withered? Because those who live in it are wicked, the animals and birds have perished. Moreover, the people are saying, "He will not see what happens to us." In other words, "Wild animals and birds appear to be under God's judgment, but what have they done to deserve this? They are cursed by God because of you evil people. Will God spare you when he has already begun to punish innocent animals? How can he bear with you to the end who are full of such atrocious sins?"

5. **"If you have raced with men on foot and they have worn you out, how can you compete with horses? If you stumble in safe country, how will you manage in the thickets by the Jordan?"** In this and the following verses, God is speaking. He starts by speaking to the people and reproving them for their presumption. The opposition they have experienced so far is nothing in comparison with the **horses** that will carry the Chaldeans and Assyrians as they conquer them.

6. **"Your brothers, your own family—even they have betrayed you; they have raised a loud cry against you. Do not trust them, though they speak well of you."** God addresses the prophet as if to say, "You have faithfully pleaded my cause, and your own people are unfaithful. Your own brothers have conspired against you, but there is no reason for you to doubt that I will defend you."

7. **"I will forsake my house, abandon my inheritance; I will give the one I love into the hands of her enemies."** It is as if God said to them, "You are the house of God, you are his heritage, you are his beloved, you are his portion—his richest portion; but all this will not stop me from being your Judge."

8. **"My inheritance has become to me like a lion in the forest. She roars at me; therefore I hate her."** These people had acted so insolently toward God that they even dared to attack him **like a lion** that roars against people **in the forest.** God accuses the Jews of being filled with the fury of a wild animal and of violently attacking him.

9. **"Has not my inheritance become to me like a speckled bird of prey that other birds of prey surround and attack? Go and gather all the wild beasts; bring them to devour."** The people are now compared with **a speckled bird of prey.** It is as if God said, "I had chosen this people for myself, that they might be my friends. They were like birds that are gathered together into a cage, or sheep into their own folds. When I gathered this people, I thought they would be like domesticated sheep, but they have turned out to be like speckled birds of prey." Their bright coloring was bound to catch people's attention.

"Go and gather all the wild beasts; bring them to devour." In other words, "Since you have dared to become like wild birds that cannot be tamed, I will send for all the birds of the air and the wild animals of the forest, that they may all attack you."

10. **"Many shepherds will ruin my vineyard and trample down my field; they will turn my pleasant field into a desolate wasteland."** The people who are here called **shepherds** are the leaders or chiefs from Assyria and Chaldea. There is an implied antithesis here, as if God were saying, "I have until now been your shepherd, but as you no longer want me, other shepherds will come who will treat you according to their own will and disposition."

11. **"It will be made a wasteland, parched and desolate before me; the**

whole land will be laid waste because there is no one who cares." God declares that their enemies will become their masters who will destroy them and commit dreadful atrocities.

12. "Over all the barren heights in the desert destroyers will swarm, for the sword of the LORD will devour from one end of the land to the other; no one will be safe." No corner of the land will be exempt from the attacks of the enemy. The Chaldeans would do God's work. He wanted the Jews to realize that **the sword of the Lord will devour** them, not blind chance.

13. "They will sow wheat but reap thorns; they will wear themselves out but gain nothing. So bear the shame of your harvest because of the LORD's fierce anger." The prophet sets out God's curse that the people would soon experience.

14. This is what the LORD says: "As for all my wicked neighbors who seize the inheritance I gave my people Israel, I will uproot them from their lands and I will uproot the house of Judah from among them." The prophet now begins to moderate what might have exasperated people's minds beyond measure. He does this not so much for the sake of the people in general as for the sake of the elect, a few of whom still remained. It would be a sign of God's paternal favor that he would treat his elect in this way.

"I will uproot the house of Judah from among them." This second uprooting is to be taken in a good sense, as it refers to the return of God's elect from Moab and other heathen nations.

15. "But after I uproot them, I will again have compassion and will bring each of them back to his own inheritance and his own country." Here God promises mercy not only to the Jews, but also to heathen nations, of whom he said he would be Judge, to punish them for the sake of his people.

16. "And if they learn well the ways of my people and swear by my name, saying, 'As surely as the LORD lives'—even as they once taught my people to swear by Baal—then they will be established among my people." God declares that he will be merciful and propitious to those miserable nations that have no grounds for hoping for salvation. The condition God lays down is that the Gentiles must "swear by my name"— that is, worship and serve God.

17. "But if any nation does not listen, I will completely uproot and destroy it," declares the LORD. God threatens extreme vengeance on the Gentiles if they do not submit to his yoke and obey him. So we see that God, on the one hand, is allured to the Jews who must willingly obey his law, but on the other hand he issues warnings to them. Since God could not bear with the perverseness of the Gentiles, much less could the Jews hope to escape punishment. That is this meaning of this passage.

Jeremiah
Chapter 13

1-9. This is what the LORD said to me: "Go and buy a linen belt and put it around your waist, but do not let it touch water." So I bought a belt, as the LORD directed, and put it around my waist. Then the word of the LORD came to me a second time: "Take the belt you bought and are wearing around your waist, and go now to Perath and hide it there in a crevice in the rocks." So I went and hid it at Perath, as the LORD told me. Many days later the LORD said to me, "Go now to Perath and get the belt I told you to hide there." So I went to Perath and dug up the belt and took it from the place where I had hidden it, but now it was ruined and completely useless. Then the word of the LORD came to me: "This is what the LORD says: 'In the same way I will ruin the pride of Judah and the great pride of Jerusalem.'"

This is the start of a new prophecy. The application is given: God declares that he will deal with the Jews in the same way as Jeremiah had with the belt. Although God had them as his belt, he would throw them away. They would then be hidden and become rotten in a cave of the Euphrates, that is, in Assyria and Chaldea.

Doubtless a vision is being narrated here, and not a real transaction, as some people think.

10. "'These wicked people, who refuse to listen to my words, who follow the stubbornness of their hearts and go after other gods to serve and worship them, will be like this belt—completely useless!'" It is ridiculous in the extreme to devise two sets of worship—one peculiar to God, and another for people and dead idols. The Lord through the prophet draws the conclusion that the Jews would become like a useless, good-for-nothing belt.

11. "'For as a belt is bound around a man's waist, so I bound the whole house of Israel and the whole house of Judah to me,' declares the LORD, 'to be my people for my renown and praise and honor. But they have not listened.'" The Jews could not complain that God had been too severe

with them. They had provoked his wrath, rejected his yoke, and refused his offers.

12-13. "Say to them: 'This is what the LORD, the God of Israel, says: Every wineskin should be filled with wine.' And if they say to you, 'Don't we know that every wineskin should be filled with wine?' then tell them, 'This is what the LORD says: I am going to fill with drunkenness all who live in this land, including the kings who sit on David's throne, the priests, the prophets and all those living in Jerusalem.'" Here the prophet pronounces God's vengeance, using another metaphor: He says that all will be filled with **drunkenness.** The general statement might have appeared to carry no weight, for what do we learn from **"Every wineskin should be filled with wine"**? Every child knows that. Indeed, they did object to the prophet's address and contemptuously asked, **"Don't we know that every wineskin should be filled with wine?"** But it was God's particular object to wake the people up in this way, for they were asleep in their delusions; he wanted them to pay attention to spiritual instruction. There would have been less force in his words if God through Jeremiah had said, "As a bottle is filled with wine, so will the Lord fill you with drunkenness." But because he said, **"Every wineskin should be filled with wine,"** they answered with disdain, "Everyone knows that, even children."

So Jeremiah drives his point home and says they were like bottles.

14. "'I will smash them one against the other, fathers and sons alike, declares the LORD. I will allow no pity or mercy or compassion to keep me from destroying them.'" This is not inconsistent with the promise of mercy given elsewhere, when God declares that he is patient and full of mercy (see Numbers 14:18; Psalm 103:8). Although God then destroyed his people in a dreadful way, he did not divest himself of his own nature or throw away his mercy. He executed his judgments on the reprobate in such a way that he lost nothing of his eternal mercy and still remained faithful concerning his election.

15-16. Hear and pay attention, do not be arrogant, for the LORD has spoken. Give glory to the LORD your God before he brings the darkness, before your feet stumble on the darkening hills. You hope for light, but he will turn it to thick darkness and change it to deep gloom. The reason for their stubborn resistance was pride, for they dared to quarrel with God. So also the main principle of obedience is humility, when people acknowledge that they are nothing and ascribe to God what is due to him.

Darkness means adversities, and **light** peace and prosperity. The prophet says that the Jews deceive themselves if they think their present happiness will be perpetual though they despise God and his prophets. In short, he shows that dreadful vengeance is at hand unless the Jews submit themselves to God.

17. But if you do not listen, I will weep in secret because of your pride;

my eyes will weep bitterly, overflowing with tears, because the LORD's flock will be taken captive. In other words, "Until now I have never stopped exhorting you, for God has commanded me to do so. But there will be no remedy if you as usual harden yourselves against what I teach. There remains then nothing for me except to hide myself in some secret place and there to mourn. For my prophetic office among you is at an end, as you are unworthy of such a favor from God."

18. Say to the king and to the queen mother, "Come down from your thrones, for your glorious crowns will fall from your heads." The prophet is now told to address his discourse directly to King Jehoiakim and his mother. By showing that he would not spare even the king and queen mother, God hoped to arouse the community in general.

19. The cities in the Negev will be shut up, and there will be no one to open them. All Judah will be carried into exile, carried completely away. Since the Jews thought Egypt would be an asylum for them, the prophet declares that all these cities will be shut against them, and no one will open them. This is like saying, "The Lord will drive you out and will prevent you from taking refuge there."

20. Lift up your eyes and see those who are coming from the north. Where is the flock that was entrusted to you, the sheep of which you boasted? We see here that Egypt and Chaldea are set in opposition to each other. It is as if the prophet were saying, "Whenever anything is said to you about the Chaldeans, you turn your eyes to Egypt, as though that would be a quiet place to live. But God will prevent you from having any escape there. Lift up your eyes—your enemies are coming from a different place, from Chaldea." Since they were so content with their present ease, he tells them to lift up their eyes, that they might see further than they were used to seeing.

21. What will you say when the LORD sets over you those you cultivated as your special allies? Will not pain grip you like that of a woman in labor? The prophet says to them, "Surely, sorrows will take hold of you, although you are not looking for them. You will gain nothing by endlessly promising yourselves peace and quietness. The Chaldeans have become your leaders, but they will cause you trouble."

22. And if you ask yourself, "Why has this happened to me?"—it is because of your many sins that your skirts have been torn off and your body mistreated. The prophet again declares that God's judgment will be just.

Your skirts. Clothes in those days were made to keep a person warm and to cover what should not be decently shown or left bare without shame. The prophets use this expression about skirts being torn off when they want to say that someone is exposed to public reproach.

23. Can the Ethiopian change his skin or the leopard its spots? Neither can you do good who are accustomed to doing evil. In this verse God declares that the people are so hardened in their wickedness that there

is no hope of their repentance. If an Ethiopian washed a hundred times a day, he would still remain black. Jeremiah condemns the Jews for their habitual practice of doing evil. They were unable to repent, for their wickedness had become inherent or firmly fixed in their hearts, like the blackness that is inherent in the skin of the Ethiopians or the spots belonging to the leopard.

24. **"I will scatter you like chaff driven by the desert wind."** As long as there is any hope of repentance, there is also room for mercy. God often declares that he is patient. But it was fair for God to bring extreme calamity on the Jews because they had obstinately hardened themselves in their vices and wickedness.

25. **"This is your lot, the portion I have decreed for you,"** declares the LORD, **"because you have forgotten me and trusted in false gods."** A contrast should be seen in this verse. God was the lot or portion of the people, and they were also the lot of God, the heritage of God, and they boasted that God was their heritage. The land was a symbol and a pledge of this heritage. The Lord through the prophet now says, "This lot will be for you the portion I have decreed for you." He is referring to the ancient custom when they divided up fields by lines and, later, by poles.

The Jews boasted that God was their heritage. But God now says that a different **lot** is prepared for them, greatly different from their heritage. God will banish them from the Promised Land, which they have polluted by their vices.

26-27. **"I will pull up your skirts over your face that your shame may be seen—your adulteries and lustful neighings, your shameless prostitution! I have seen your detestable acts on the hills and in the fields. Woe to you, O Jerusalem! How long will you be unclean?"** To **pull up your skirts over your face** means to uncover the private parts. It is as if a vile woman was condemned to bear the disgrace of being stripped of her clothes and exposed in public, that all might abhor a disgraceful spectacle.

God assumed the character of a husband to his people. As he had been so shamefully despised, he now says he was ready to punish them by throwing the skirts of his people over their faces, that their reproach or baseness might appear by exposing their private parts.

The people were justly punished by God because they had continually sinned. The Lord through the prophet does not mention all their sins here. They were not only given over to superstition but also to prostitution, drunkenness, and other outrages. Here God only speaks of their superstitions. They have rejected him and followed their own idols. By **adulteries** he no doubt means idolatries. He condemns them for falling away into ungodly and false forms of worship.

Lustful neighings. This metaphor is used elsewhere to reproach the Jews for following their own ideas.

Jeremiah
Chapter 14

1. **This is the word of the LORD to Jeremiah concerning the drought.**
As there was a **drought** at hand, which would cause great scarcity,
Jeremiah's purpose was to forewarn the Jews about it, so they would
know that it did not happen by chance but was evidence of God's
vengeance.

2-3. **"Judah mourns, her cities languish; they wail for the land, and
a cry goes up from Jerusalem. The nobles send their servants for water;
they go to the cisterns but find no water. They return with their jars
unfilled; dismayed and despairing, they cover their heads."** In these
words the Lord through the prophet is saying that such an unusual event
could not be ascribed to natural causes but could only be attributed to the
extraordinary judgment of God. That is why he uses so many figurative
expressions. He could have just said, in one sentence, that there would be
a terrible famine in the land. But hardly one person in a hundred would
have been moved if it had been stated like that. Therefore, in order to
rouse them from their stupor, the prophet uses more striking expressions.

4. **"The ground is cracked because there is no rain in the land; the
farmers are dismayed and cover their heads."** When the heavens supply
moisture, the earth retains its solid character; but in constant heat it dis-
solves into dust, as if it were pounded in a mortar. This all happened to
teach the Jews that they were not deprived of water by chance but because
God had cursed their land.

5-6. **"Even the doe in the field deserts her newborn fawn because
there is no grass. Wild donkeys stand on the barren heights and pant
like jackals; their eyesight fails for lack of pasture."** Jeremiah now comes
to the animals. He says that the **doe** and **wild donkeys** would experience
the same scarcity as the farmers.

Now we understand the object of this prediction. It was God's purpose
not only to tell the Jews in advance what would soon happen, but also to

point out his vengeance, that they might not attribute all to secondary causes but might know that they would suffer punishment for their sins.

7. Although our sins testify against us, O LORD, do something for the sake of your name. For our backsliding is great; we have sinned against you. The prophet urges the Jews to seek pardon and does so by his own example. Like Daniel, he does not just confess the sins of the people but confesses his own sins (see Daniel 9:4-5).

It is as if he said, "In ourselves we find nothing but reasons for being condemned. Seek then in yourself a reason for forgiving us. For as long as you look at us, you of necessity will hate us and thus be a rigid Judge. So stop looking for anything in us or calling us to account, and seek from yourself a reason for sparing us."

Do something for the sake of your name. The prophet mentions to God his own name. He does this because God had chosen that people and promised that they would be his special people. It is then on the basis of that covenant that the prophet now prays to God that he will glorify his name. So we see why the prophet dares to introduce God's name, saying in effect, "Deal with us for your name's sake."

8-9. O Hope of Israel, its Savior in times of distress, why are you like a stranger in the land, like a traveler who stays only a night? Why are you like a man taken by surprise, like a warrior powerless to save? The Israelites had not relied on God as they should have, for the ten tribes had long ago rebelled against him, and Judah was so corrupted that less than one in a thousand could be said to be faithful to God. Hope then among the people had become extinct. But the prophet here recalls the permanent nature of the covenant, as if he said, "Even though we are unworthy to be protected by you, yet as you have promised to be always ready to bring us help, you are our hope." In short, the word **hope** or "expectation" refers to God's promise and to his constant faithfulness, and not to human faithfulness, which did not exist or at least was found in very few people.

You are among us, O LORD, and we bear your name; do not forsake us! Let us learn from this that whenever we pray to God, we should not concentrate on our own desires, which are filthy and abominable in God's sight, but should simply call on his name and recall his promise, especially the covenant he has made with us in his only Son, confirmed by his blood.

10. This is what the LORD says about this people: "They greatly love to wander; they do not restrain their feet. So the LORD does not accept them; he will now remember their wickedness and punish them for their sins." The prophet continues the same theme but rebukes the Jews more severely, exposing their sins.

"They greatly love to wander." At first sight this might appear to be a small offense. But if we consider its source, that they distrusted God and his power and trusted the Egyptians or the Chaldeans for their safety, it will be apparent that they were committing a shameful and intolerable sacrilege. Unbelief, then, is condemned here. The Jews looked around for help from foreigners and took no account of God.

11-12. Then the LORD said to me, "Do not pray for the well-being of this people. Although they fast, I will not listen to their cry; though they offer burnt offerings and grain offerings, I will not accept them. Instead, I will destroy them with the sword, famine and plague." The prophet is told by God, **"Do not pray for the well-being of this people,"** as in 7:16 and 11:14. We must remember that this prohibition refers to the Exile. Since God had already decreed that the people should be banished from the Promised Land, the prophet was forbidden to pray, for that decree was immutable. This was not, therefore, a general prohibition, as if the prophet was not allowed to ask God's forgiveness on behalf of the whole people.

"Although they fast." We pray to God daily, it may be said, and yet we do not fast daily. When fasting is joined to prayer, prayer becomes more earnest, which usually happens when there is danger or when God's wrath is evident. It is therefore as if God said, "Even if they pray daily and earnestly, and even if they add fasting to their praying, I will not hear their cries because their heart is false." We gather from this passage that fasting is not in itself a religious duty or exercise, but that it is used so there may be a greater alacrity in prayer.

13. But I said, "Ah, Sovereign LORD, the prophets keep telling them, 'You will not see the sword or suffer famine. Indeed, I will give you lasting peace in this place.'" Jeremiah now makes public the prayers he had offered by himself in order to help restore the Jews from their impiety. Jeremiah made known his secret prayers to help the Jews.

"'You will not see the sword or suffer famine.'" We see that Jeremiah had a running battle with other prophets as soon as the people were warned about exile or famine or God's judgment. "You are secure," they reassured the people, "for God has chosen this place where he is to be worshiped. He will not banish his church from its quiet rest. There is no reason then to fear that he will ever allow this kingdom to perish or his temple to be destroyed." Hence the complaint of the prophet. Not that he himself was affected by such false thoughts, but he had the good of the people in his mind and wanted to win back those who had been deceived.

14. Then the LORD said to me, "The prophets are prophesying lies in my name. I have not sent them or appointed them or spoken to them. They are prophesying to you false visions, divinations, idolatries and the delusions of their own minds." God says that the prophets prophesy **"in my name,"** as though he said, "My name is often profaned by men. Many people pass themselves off as my servants and prophets, but they are so depraved that they are not ashamed to abuse my name. So you must exercise wisdom in this matter."

Note the three things God says about these false prophets. He had **"not sent them or appointed them or spoken to them."** So we see that as soon as people depart in even the smallest degree from God's Word, they cannot preach anything but falsehoods, vanities, errors, and deceits.

15-16. **"Therefore, this is what the LORD says about the prophets who are prophesying in my name: I did not send them, yet they are saying, 'No sword or famine will touch this land.' Those same prophets will perish by sword and famine. And the people they are prophesying to will be thrown out into the streets of Jerusalem because of the famine and sword. There will be no one to bury them or their wives, their sons or their daughters. I will pour out on them the calamity they deserve."** When people are led astray by impostures, the people can only blame themselves, for they are so ready to embrace vanity rather than submit to God and his Word. (See Romans 1:28.) God says that he tests the hearts of people whenever false prophets spread their message. Everyone who really fears God will not be led astray by the deceits of Satan and of impostors.

17. **"Speak this word to them: 'Let my eyes overflow with tears night and day without ceasing; for my virgin daughter—my people—has suffered a grievous wound, a crushing blow.'"** The prophet shows how obtuse the people were, for no amount of warning could induce them to return to their senses.

God calls them **"my virgin daughter"** here not to honor them but because until then he had spared the Jews. *Virgin* is sometimes taken in a good sense. God, when speaking about holy marriage, by which he had bound the Jews to himself, compares his people to a virgin. But the daughter of Babylon is also often called a virgin, because the Chaldeans, as a result of an extended peace, had become used to enjoying delicacies. So in this place Jeremiah, by way of concession, says that the people of his own nation were soft and tender because they had been borne with through God's indulgence. But just as in war virgins are exposed to violation, and the lust of men rages without shame, knowing no bounds, God intended here to show the fierceness of his vengeance. It is as if he said, "Now indeed you are tender and delicate young women, but in a short time your condition will be changed. Do not be deceived by the constant happiness you have enjoyed so far."

18. **"'If I go into the country, I see those slain by the sword; if I go into the city, I see the ravages of famine. Both prophet and priest have gone to a land they know not.'"** Jeremiah says the city will offer the people no shield against the impending punishment and that if they go into the fields the whole land will be covered with enemies who will destroy them.

19. **Have you rejected Judah completely? Do you despise Zion? Why have you afflicted us so that we cannot be healed? We hoped for**

peace but no good has come, for a time of healing but there is only terror. The prophet now turns to prayer and to complaints, so that by his example he might at last arouse the people to lamentation, so that they might humbly implore God's forgiveness, sincerely confess their sins, and be displeased with themselves. At the same time he indirectly reproves the hardness about which we have spoken before. As he has achieved nothing by teaching, Jeremiah stops speaking to them and instead addresses God.

20. O LORD, we acknowledge our wickedness and the guilt of our fathers; we have indeed sinned against you. The prophet prescribes to the Jews the way to appease God. He uses a simple form of prayer when he says, **O LORD, we acknowledge our wickedness.** He dictates for posterity a right form of prayer, so that in their exile they might know that only this one thing remains for them—to confess their sins. Otherwise they cannot be forgiven.

21. For the sake of your name do not despise us; do not dishonor your glorious throne. Remember your covenant with us and do not break it. Jeremiah continues with his prayer. He made it out of love, and in order to encourage the faithful who remained among the people to seek forgiveness.

Your glorious throne. He calls Jerusalem God's **glorious throne** because God chose to be worshiped in that city. He was not confined to the temple, but his name was remembered there (see Exodus 20:24). The ark was not a vain symbol of God's covenant, for God really dwelt there; the presence of his power and grace were seen by the clearest proofs. As this way of speaking is often found in the prophets, it was enough for Jeremiah just to mention it. God indeed, as is well known, fills heaven and earth, but he gives symbols of his presence wherever he pleases. As it was his will to be worshiped in the temple, it is called his **throne**; elsewhere it is called his footstool. The Scripture describes the same thing in various ways. So we see what Scripture means whenever it calls Jerusalem or the temple the throne or the house of God.

22. Do any of the worthless idols of the nations bring rain? Do the skies themselves send down showers? No, it is you, O LORD our God. Therefore our hope is in you, for you are the one who does all this. Jeremiah teaches that in desperate situations the people must turn to God and ask him to be merciful. It is as if he said, "What will become of us unless you show yourself to be propitious? The Gentiles have their gods from whom they seek safety. But with us it is a fixed principle to hope for and to seek salvation from you alone."

Do the skies themselves send down showers? Here Jeremiah argues from the lesser to the greater. It is as if he said, "Not even the heavens give rain. How then can worthless idols? For even if man could invent for himself a thousand gods, he cannot make one drop of rain fall from heaven. Since, then, the heavens do not of themselves give rain, but only at God's command, how can the idols of the heathen and their vain inventions send rain for us from heaven?" The prophet's purpose is now clear: He wants to show that if God rejects the people and resolves to punish their sins with the utmost rigor and in an implacable manner, they will have no hope of salvation.

From this we learn that there is no reason why punishments, which are signs of God's wrath, should discourage us from venturing to seek God's pardon. On the contrary, a model prayer for this is given to us here. If we are convinced that we have been punished by God's hand, we are on this very account encouraged to hope for salvation. For the one who wounds also heals, and the one who kills also brings back to life.

Jeremiah
Chapter 15

1-2. Then the LORD said to me: "Even if Moses and Samuel were to stand before me, my heart would not go out to this people. Send them away from my presence! Let them go! And if they ask you, 'Where shall we go?' tell them, 'This is what the Lord says: Those destined for death, to death; those for the sword, to the sword; those for starvation, to starvation; those for captivity, to captivity.'" God repeats that as the sins of the people reached their highest pitch, there was no more room for pardon or for mercy. However, Jeremiah's prayer at the end of chapter 14 was not in vain. In detail it was not heard, for he wanted everyone to be saved. But God had resolved to destroy the ungodly, people who were beyond hope because of their constant obstinacy, and so Jeremiah obtained only part of what he prayed for—that God would preserve his church, which at that time was hidden.

"Even if Moses and Samuel were to stand before me, my heart would not go out to this people." This means that even if all godly intercessors came forward on their behalf, they could do nothing, for God had rejected the people.

"And if they ask you, 'Where shall we go?' tell them, 'This is what the LORD says: Those destined for death, to death; those for the sword, to the sword; those for starvation, to starvation; those for captivity, to captivity." In other words, "It is no good complaining about their own miseries." No doubt God had in mind the hypocrites who always complained about the way God treated them. "Alas, how far will God go?" they asked. "Will our punishment never end? What does all this mean? Why are we afflicted so severely? Why does not God give us a little respite from our miseries?" God anticipates such questions and says, "If they say to you, 'Where will we flee?' say to them, 'Either to death or to famine or to the sword or to exile.' It is all the same with me, for there is no longer any hope for you since I have rejected you. Know, then, that it is all over with you and that I will never deliver you."

3. **"I will send four kinds of destroyers against them,"** declares the
LORD, **"the sword to kill and the dogs to drag away and the birds of
the air and the beasts of the earth to devour and destroy."** Jeremiah
continues with the same theme. He says that God will prepare for them
ravenous birds as well as wild animals, the sword, and dogs; it is as if he
were saying that all animals would be hostile to them and would be the
executors of God's vengeance.

4. **"I will make them abhorrent to all the kingdoms of the earth
because of what Manasseh son of Hezekiah king of Judah did in
Jerusalem."** Jeremiah now speaks about exile. He seems to have taken
these words from Moses (see Deuteronomy 28).

God through Jeremiah says that the Exile will take place because of
Manasseh. But he was already dead. So why did God transfer the vengeance that king deserved to posterity? The prophet commends God's
great patience because the destruction of his people had been suspended
until that time.

5-6. **"Who will have pity on you, O Jerusalem? Who will mourn
for you? Who will stop to ask how you are? You have rejected me,"**
declares the LORD. **"You keep on backsliding. So I will lay hands on
you and destroy you; I can no longer show compassion."** In case the
Jews should complain, the prophet says that all the evils that are about
to fall on them are fully deserved, and so they will find no pity, not even
among men. We know that even with the worst of people, when the Lord
punishes them, they have someone who sympathizes with them. But the
prophet shows that the Jews were not only inexcusable before God, but
they did not deserve any sympathy from men.

7. **"I will winnow them with a winnowing fork at the city gates of
the land. I will bring bereavement and destruction on my people, for
they have not changed their ways."** God rebukes their extreme hardness. For although he brought **bereavement** to his people (the ten tribes)
and destroyed them, and although the kingdom of Judah had been greatly
oppressed, they still did not turn from their evil ways.

8. **"I will make their widows more numerous than the sand of the
sea. At midday I will bring a destroyer against the mothers of their
young men; suddenly I will bring down on them anguish and terror."**
He talks first about **"widows"** because nearly all the men had been killed
in battle. The prophet wanted to show just how obstinate the Jews were
as they struggled against all of God's judgments. It is evidence of people's
great impiety when they pay no attention to any of God's punishments.

"At midday." The fact that the enemies of the Jews dared to attack
them in the middle of the day, during the clearest light, was a greater
proof of God's vengeance. God's hand, not man's cunning, came from
heaven in this open and visible way.

9. **"The mother of seven will grow faint and breathe her last. Her**

sun will set while it is still day; she will be disgraced and humiliated. I will put the survivors to the sword before their enemies," declares the LORD. Jeremiah says that fruitful women had been weakened not as a result of frequent childbearing but because the strength the mothers normally derived from their numerous children had been taken from them. They were bereaved of their children as if they were barren.

"I will put the survivors to the sword." In other words, "They have not yet suffered all the punishment allotted to them, for they are not subdued even though I have punished them severely. As they are incurable, the sword will kill the rest of them. For my vengeance will not end until I have destroyed them all."

10. Alas, my mother, that you gave me birth, a man with whom the whole land strives and contends! I have neither lent nor borrowed, yet everyone curses me. Jeremiah addresses his mother as if he counted his life a curse. What does this mean? "Why," he asks, "have you given birth to me, my mother? Woe is me, that I have been born a man of strife and contention!" We learn from these words that the prophet was not composed and calm in his mind but felt angry when he saw he had achieved less than he had hoped for. It is clear from the context that all this was said for the benefit of the public, that the Jews might know that their hardness of heart would not benefit them.

11. The LORD said, "Surely I will deliver you for a good purpose; surely I will make your enemies plead with you in times of disaster and times of distress." God says at the beginning of this verse that he will grant Jeremiah what he asked for. So we conclude that the prophet's prayer was heard. So it becomes clear that the prophet was not just overcome with grief, but that he mainly spoke like this for the benefit of the people.

God tells Jeremiah that the latter part of his life will be happy and that although he will suffer just like everyone else, yet the enemy will be kind to him, so that he will be better treated than other people.

12. "Can a man break iron—iron from the north—or bronze?" This verse shows that the purpose of the holy man was to divest the Jews of the false confidence in which they boasted. They were so sure that they were secure that they were unmoved by any predictions. So Jeremiah attempted to break through this wall of indifference by saying they would suffer greater hardships under the Chaldeans, who would be like iron, and even like bronze.

13. "Your wealth and your treasures I will give as plunder, without charge, because of all your sins throughout your country." I think this is a metaphorical way of speaking about counsels, as if God said, "On account of your wicked deeds and on account of all your plans, that is, of all your counsels, I will give away your wealth and your treasures as

plunder." Or, "Your enemies will freely plunder all that you have without your permission."

14. "I will enslave you to your enemies in a land you do not know, for my anger will kindle a fire that will burn against you." God would be implacable until they were consumed, for his wrath had been kindled by their perverse wickedness.

15. You understand, O LORD; remember me and care for me. Avenge me on my persecutors. You are long-suffering—do not take me away; think of how I suffer reproach for your sake. The prophet turns again to God. Jeremiah abruptly turned from the people to God and from God to the people because the people would not pay any attention to his teaching. The prophet bore this great wickedness and could not but speak in a hasty way.

The prophet asks for a favor for himself—that God would make a distinction between him and the reprobate people.

16. When your words came, I ate them; they were my joy and my heart's delight, for I bear your name, O LORD God Almighty. This verse sheds light on the previous one where he said he was burdened with reproaches on account of God's name. The prophet now indicates that he knew there was nothing better than to receive whatever God sent, and he testifies that he found sweetness in God's Word.

17. I never sat in the company of revelers, never made merry with them; I sat alone because your hand was on me and you had filled me with indignation. The prophet gives more detail about how he was hated by all of the people because he pleased God. Jeremiah confesses that he had separated himself from the people. But he did this because there was no other way in which he could obey God.

You had filled me with indignation. Jeremiah confirms what he said in the previous verse—that he had eaten the Word of God, that he had not been moved superficially but had been inflamed with zeal for God. We cannot carry out a commission unless zeal for God burns inside us, for the prophetic office requires such fervor.

18. Why is my pain unending and my wound grievous and incurable? Will you be to me like a deceptive brook, like a spring that fails? Jeremiah had previously shown that he courageously despised all the splendor of the world and had no regard for proud men who boasted they were rulers of the church. But he now confesses his frailty. When we think of the apostles and the prophets we must always distinguish between the pure truth they spoke and their own personal anxieties and fears. Jeremiah's worries stemmed from this human weakness. That is the meaning of this verse.

Will you be to me like a deceptive brook, like a spring that fails? The prophet was often accused of being a deceiver and was frequently harassed by the ungodly. So he complains that God was not to him like perennial springs, because everyone rejected his message. But we also have to remember that the prophet did not just speak here for his own sake but rather to reprove the impiety of the people.

19. Therefore this is what the LORD says: "If you repent, I will restore you that you may serve me; if you utter worthy, not worthless, words, you will be my spokesman. Let this people turn to you, but you must not turn to them." From God's answer we can see more clearly the prophet's purpose, which was to expose the people's guilt.

The Lord tells his prophet to separate himself from the people and not to link himself with those who might easily disturb him, for they refused to follow God's Word.

20. "I will make you a wall to this people, a fortified wall of bronze; they will fight against you but will not overcome you, for I am with you to rescue and save you," declares the LORD. Because the prophet is almost alone, and God has told him to contend with many powerful enemies, God promises to stand at his side, as if he were saying, "Although you are defenseless and unarmed, and they are equipped with great wealth and power, you will still be like a fortified city. You will be impregnable despite all their assaults."

"I am with you to rescue and save you." In other words, "You will not stand alone, nor will you carry on the war single-handed. But you must learn to flee to me."

21. "I will save you from the hands of the wicked and redeem you from the grasp of the cruel." God had promised Jeremiah his help. He now says that he will be strong enough to deliver the prophet from the hands of his enemies.

Jeremiah
Chapter 16

1-4. Then the word of the LORD came to me: "You must not marry and have sons or daughters in this place." For this is what the LORD says about the sons and daughters born in this land and about the women who are their mothers and the men who are their fathers: "They will die of deadly diseases. They will not be mourned or buried but will be like refuse lying on the ground. They will perish by sword and famine, and their dead bodies will become food for the birds of the air and the beasts of the earth." This is a new discourse, not unlike many others, except that the prophet is commanded not to marry or have any children in that land. The instruction against marriage was full of meaning. It was to show that the people were wholly given up to destruction. We know that the law of man's creation was to increase and multiply (see Genesis 1:22; 8:17; 9:1, 7). Humankind is perpetuated through marriage. But here God shows that the land is not worthy of the general blessing that is enjoyed by the whole human race. It is the same as if he said, "They are indeed at the moment alive, but a quick end awaits them, for I will deprive them of the universal favor that I have until now shown to all mankind."

5-7. For this is what the LORD says: "Do not enter a house where there is a funeral meal; do not go to mourn or show sympathy, because I have withdrawn my blessing, my love and my pity from this people," declares the LORD. "Both high and low will die in this land. They will not be buried or mourned, and no one will cut himself or shave his head for them. No one will offer food to comfort those who mourn for the dead—not even for a father or a mother—nor will anyone give them a drink to console them." At the beginning of the chapter Jeremiah was told not to marry, for a dreadful devastation was about to overtake the land. Now God confirms what he had said previously: The slaughter will be so great that nobody will be found to carry out the common task of lamenting for the dead. He also says something even more dreadful:

Those who perish will be unworthy of any kind of burial. Their deaths will be so ignominious that they will be deprived of the honor of a grave.

8. "And do not enter a house where there is feasting and sit down to eat and drink." In other words, "Have nothing more to do with this people. If they lament their dead, leave them, for they are not worthy of any act of kindness. And if they indulge in joyful feasts, keep clear of them, for all links you have with them will be blighted."

9. "For this is what the LORD Almighty, the God of Israel, says: Before your eyes and in your days I will bring an end to the sounds of joy and gladness and to the voices of bride and bridegroom in this place." This verse explains the previous verse: Every connection with that people would be accursed. The Lord states one thing in particular: The time will come when they will be deprived of all joy.

"I will bring an end to . . . the voices of bride and bridegroom in this place." By this God through Jeremiah intimates that they will become like the dead rather than the living. The continuance of the human race is preserved by marriage. Since there was no more time left for marriages, it was a token of final destruction.

10-13. "When you tell these people all this and they ask you, 'Why has the LORD decreed such a great disaster against us? What wrong have we done? What sin have we committed against the LORD our God?' then say to them, 'It is because your fathers forsook me,' declares the LORD, 'and followed other gods and served and worshiped them. They forsook me and did not keep my law. But you have behaved more wickedly than your fathers. See how each of you is following the stubbornness of his evil heart instead of obeying me. So I will throw you out of this land into a land neither you nor your fathers have known, and there you will serve other gods day and night, for I will show you no favor.'" God shows here that the people indulged themselves so much in their vices that nothing could make them repent. It was great blindness, even madness, not to examine themselves when they were struck by God's hand. This is what God now confirms to his own prophet, as if he said, "There is no reason for their perverseness to discourage you. They will oppose you at once and will treat you as if you had greatly harmed them. They will claim they are not guilty of any sins. So if they petulantly ignore all your warnings, you have no reason to be disheartened, for you will have an answer ready for them."

"Then say to them . . ." The prophet says that the Jews who refuse to worship God in their own land will be led away to Chaldea, where they will be constrained, willingly or unwillingly, to worship strange gods.

14-15. "However, the days are coming," declares the LORD, "when men will no longer say, 'As surely as the LORD lives, who brought the Israelites up out of Egypt,' but they will say, 'As surely as the LORD lives, who brought the Israelites up out of the land of the north and

out of all the countries where he had banished them.' For I will restore them to the land I gave their forefathers." I think Jeremiah is amplifying what he has just said. God had said, "I will expel you from this land and will send you to a land that neither your fathers nor you know." Now follow some circumstances that increased the horror of the exile. The people knew how cruel slavery was because of that from which God had rescued their fathers. When they were forced into slavery, their condition was worse than a hundred deaths. All justice was denied them, and their babies were killed at birth. Because they knew how cruelly the Egyptians had treated their fathers, the prophet states in his comparison what dreadful punishment awaited them, and thus their redemption would be much more incredible.

It is as if the prophet said, "You know what your fathers came through, from the depths of death as it were; so that redemption should be remembered throughout the world. But God will now throw you into an abyss deeper than that of Egypt from which your fathers were delivered. When he redeems you from there, it will be a miracle far more wonderful for your posterity, so that it will almost eclipse or at least obscure the memory of the first redemption. 'However, the days are coming,' declares the LORD, 'when men will no longer say, "As surely as the LORD lives, who brought the Israelites up out of Egypt."' That Egyptian captivity was more bearable than this latter one will be. When God rescues from this, it will be a more wonderful work."

16. "But now I will send for many fishermen," declares the LORD, "and they will catch them. After that I will send for many hunters, and they will hunt them down on every mountain and hill and from the crevices of the rocks." Jeremiah shows that the Chaldeans will easily defeat the Jews, for they will take them like fish drawn into nets. This is one thing. In the second place, he says that if they hide themselves in caves or in the crevices of the rocks, their enemies will be like hunters who track down wild beasts in forests. No recesses in the mountains will be hidden from the Chaldeans.

17. "My eyes are on all their ways; they are not hidden from me, nor is their sin concealed from my eyes." In other words, "This one thing is enough: God knows their sins, and he is a fit Judge. So it is pointless for them to try to excuse themselves."

18. "I will repay them double for their wickedness and their sin, because they have defiled my land with the lifeless forms of their vile images and have filled my inheritance with their detestable idols." Jeremiah introduces nothing new here but continues with the theme of the previous verse.

Double for their wickedness. The prophet does not mean God will be excessively severe. Double indicates a just and complete measure. Isaiah says this as well: "She has received from the Lord's hand double for all her sins" (Isaiah 40:2). In Isaiah God assumes the character of a father and, according to his great kindness, says that the Jews had been punished more than enough. So here in Jeremiah, in speaking about punishment, he calls it **double** not because it will exceed the limits of justice, but because God will show himself differently to them from what he had done before, when he patiently bore with them. It is as if he were saying, "I will punish them to the limit, for there will be no remission, no leniency, no mercy." We see from this that what is meant here is only extreme rigor, which was just and right.

19. **O LORD, my strength and my fortress, my refuge in time of distress, to you the nations will come from the ends of the earth and say, "Our fathers possessed nothing but false gods, worthless idols that did them no good."** Jeremiah contrasts the conversion of the Gentiles with the destruction he has just announced. The truth of God and his mercy were so linked with the salvation of the chosen people that their destruction seemed to obliterate them. Therefore the prophet contrasts with this the conversion of the Gentiles, as if he were saying, "Although the tribe of Abraham perishes, God's covenant will not fail, nor will there be any diminution of his grace, for he will convert Gentiles to himself."

20. **"Do men make their own gods? Yes, but they are not gods!"** The prophet reasons as follows: "Can he who is not God make a god?" That is, "Can he who is created be the Creator?" No one can give, as the proverb has it, what he has not got. And there is in man no divine power. We indeed see that this is our condition. There is nothing more frail and perishable. As man, then, is all vanity and has in him nothing of substance, can he create a god for himself? This is the prophet's argument. It is drawn from what is absurd, in order that men might at last acknowledge not only their presumption but their monstrous madness.

21. **"Therefore I will teach them—this time I will teach them my power and might. Then they will know that my name is the LORD."** God cannot be rightly worshiped unless people are humbled. Humility is the best preparation for faith, so that there may be submission to the Word of God. Idolaters do indeed pretend to have some kind of humility, but then they involve themselves in such stupidity that they are unwilling to make any distinction between light and darkness.

Jeremiah
Chapter 17

1. "Judah's sin is engraved with an iron tool, inscribed with a flint point, on the tablets of their hearts and on the horns of their altars." The sin of the Jews had increased so much that it was apparent to all, and in vain did they try to hide it.

Engraved. It is as if he said, "They are not only slightly imbued with iniquity, for then there might be some healing. But iniquity is engraved on their inner feelings, as if someone had engraved it with an iron pen."

Then he adds, **"the horns of their altars."** He had spoken about their **hearts.** But if he had spoken only of their **hearts,** the Jews might have objected and said, "Jeremiah, how can you penetrate into our hearts? Are you God? Can you examine our inner emotions?" So the prophet adds that their iniquity was well known from their own **altars.** At the same time he intimates that there was no point on their calling on the name of religion, for under that pretense they had especially sinned against God. They had compromised pure worship of him.

2. "Even their children remember their altars and Asherah poles beside the spreading trees and on the high hills." The prophet here amplifies their wickedness. Their posterity remembered the superstitions they had received from their fathers.

3. "My mountain in the land and your wealth and all your treasures I will give away as plunder, together with your high places, because of sin throughout your country." The prophet again repeats that punishment was close at hand for the Jews, and there was no point in their trying to hide, for God would draw them out from the mountains and expose them like a prey to their enemies.

4. "Through your own fault you will lose the inheritance I gave you. I will enslave you to your enemies in a land you do not know, for you have kindled my anger, and it will burn forever." The prophet, speaking for the Lord, says this so they will not complain that their own inheritance has been taken away from them. "How has the land,"

God asks, "become your inheritance? You have received it through my bounty. And now, since you are so ungrateful, why should I be blamed for taking away what I had given you? What wrong is done to you? It has always been my inheritance, even though for a time I gave it to you. Had you been grateful to me it would have been yours permanently. But now that I deprive you of it, you must realize that you are to blame for this."

5. This is what the LORD says: "Cursed is the one who trusts in man, who depends on flesh for his strength and whose heart turns away from the LORD." Anyone who places the smallest hope in men departs from God to some extent. In short, the Holy Spirit declares briefly but very solemnly that anyone who fixes his hope on man is an apostate and has deserted God. So the inference the prophet teaches here is that we should remain dependent only on God.

6. "He will be like a bush in the wastelands; he will not see prosperity when it comes. He will dwell in the parched places of the desert, in a salt land where no one lives." The prophet does not compare the unbeliever to dry branches but to a bush that has roots and gives the appearance of being alive. Unbelievers are like that while fortune, as they say, smiles on them. They think they are happy but reject every divine instruction, as if they were free from the authority of God, and they do not listen to God's prophets. So the prophet, conceding something to them, says they are like bushes that have roots and leaves but no fruit and that dry up when heat comes. The heat of the sun consumes whatever moisture, beauty, and life may appear in shrubs, and God will scorch and dry up the hopes of unbelievers, although they may think they have roots to preserve them and their life. (See Psalm 129:6.)

7-8. "But blessed is the man who trusts in the LORD, whose confidence is in him. He will be like a tree planted by the water that sends out its roots by the stream. It does not fear when heat comes; its leaves are always green. It has no worries in a year of drought and never fails to bear fruit." The prophet points out the difference between God's true servants, who trust in him, and those who are inflated with their own false imaginations, so that they seek refuge either in themselves or in others. The faithful are like trees planted by water, sending their roots out to the river. God's servants are planted, as it were, in a moist soil, irrigated continually by streams of water. Hence the prophet adds that this tree does not fear when heat comes.

9-10. The heart is deceitful above all things and beyond cure. Who can understand it? "I the LORD search the heart and examine the mind, to reward a man according to his conduct, according to what his deeds deserve." What is taught here depends on what has gone before; so the two should be read together. If we want to derive benefit from reading the prophets, we must consider why a thing is said and then elicit a general doctrine. Thus we will be able to rightly apply this passage in a general way if we first understand why the prophet said, **The heart is deceitful.** He wanted to instruct the Jews. They were unmoved by the declaration that people who trust in men are cursed by God, so he adds, **The heart is deceitful above all things and beyond cure.** "Do you think you are so cunning that you can deceive God and his ministers with impunity?"

"I," says Jehovah, "**search the heart.** I have a right to examine the hearts of men." We see from this that it is an implied reproof when the prophet says **the heart is deceitful above all things and beyond cure.** It is as if he said, "You think you are wise in this instance? Is not God also wise?" Isaiah says the same thing in an ironic way: "Woe to those who go down to Egypt for help, who rely on horses, who trust in the multitude of their chariots and in the great strength of their horsemen, but do not look to the Holy One of Israel, or seek help from the Lord" (Isaiah 31:1). God says, "You may be very cunning, but it is my work to search the hearts of men."

11. **Like a partridge that hatches eggs it did not lay is the man who gains riches by unjust means. When his life is half gone, they will desert him, and in the end he will prove to be a fool.** The prophet shows that those who make themselves rich by unlawful means or so acquire great wealth are subject to God's curse, so that whatever they may have accumulated through much labor will vanish from them. God will take from them all they possess. The prophet is saying, "Those who accumulate riches in an unjust way are compelled to leave riches unlawfully acquired in the middle of their lives."

12. **A glorious throne, exalted from the beginning, is the place of our sanctuary.** The prophet refers to the singular favor that God granted the Jews when he chose to live among them. There is a twofold object here as the Scripture sets before us God's blessings. First, we may be fully persuaded that he will always be a Father to us, for he who starts his work in us will complete it in us (see Psalm 138:8). Also, the Scripture sometimes encourages us to give thanks to God when it shows how bountifully he has dwelt with us.

13. **O LORD, the hope of Israel, all who forsake you will be put to shame. Those who turn away from you will be written in the dust because they have forsaken the LORD, the spring of living water.** Because the Jews had been raised high, so that their elevation appeared eminent throughout the world, their unfaithfulness to God became the more detestable as they followed vain hopes, idols, and their own false counsels. It is the same as if the prophet said, "How does it benefit you that God dwells among you and that the temple is as it were his earthly habitation, where he speaks with you? For no one accepts this favor. We have willfully cast away from us this kindness that is freely offered to us."

14. **Heal me, O LORD, and I will be healed; save me and I will be saved, for you are the one I praise.** Here the prophet, as if terrified, hides

himself under God's wings. He sees that apostasy of every kind prevails throughout the land. When he sees that the land is thus infected, in order that fainting might not overcome him, he presents himself to God, as if he said, "What will become of me, Lord? I am surrounded by wickedness. Wherever I turn I find nothing but what allures me away from true religion. What will happen to me if you forsake me? I will be taken at once, and it will be all over for me, for there is no safety in the land, and no healing. It is as if disease prevailed everywhere so that nobody is prepared to travel in case they become infected." Thus the prophet in this verse, seeing the whole land so polluted with sin that there is not a corner free from it, flees to God for help and says, "O Lord, I cannot be kept safe unless you keep me. I cannot be pure unless my purity comes from you." We now understand the prophet's purpose and how this is linked with the preceding verses.

15. They keep saying to me, "Where is the word of the LORD? Let it now be fulfilled!" Here Jeremiah complains of the people's obstinate contempt. He found them not only discourteous but even petulant toward God. They did not hesitate to discredit all prophecies, to despise the promises, and boldly to reject all warnings. Now they publicly provoked God and said, "**Where is the word of the LORD?** Many years have passed, Jeremiah, and you have continually spoken of war, famine, and pestilence. But we still remain quiet, and God spares us. Where is the word of the Lord that you have announced?"

16. I have not run away from being your shepherd; you know I have not desired the day of despair. What passes my lips is open before you. The prophet here implores God as his defender, for the people are being so unfaithful to God. He refers the matter to God, as if saying, "Contend with God, for what have I to do with you or you with me? I do not plead my own cause, nor do I promote my own case. But as God has committed it to me to carry out this office, I had to obey him. As I am only God's instrument, what will you gain in the end after you have quarreled so much? No doubt God will show you that he is your adversary. Are you able to conquer him?"

17-18. Do not be a terror to me; you are my refuge in the day of disaster. Let my persecutors be put to shame, but keep me from shame; let them be terrified, but keep me from terror. Bring on them the day of disaster; destroy them with double destruction. Now the prophet, having appealed to God as a witness to his integrity, asks him to show himself as his defender.

You are my refuge in the day of disaster. That is, "I have chosen you as my protector, as if you were my shield. As I have promised myself the favor of having you as my help, see that I am not left destitute, since I have to fight for you under your banner."

The prophet doubtless knew that everyone on whom he announced

God's vengeance was reprobate, but as it is not up to us to distinguish between the elect and the reprobate, let us learn to suspend and check our zeal, so it may not be too fervent, for we may often make mistakes if we follow generally what the prophet says here: **Bring on them the day of disaster; destroy them with double destruction.** If we spoke in this indiscriminate way about everyone, our zeal would often hit the children of God. We must therefore bear in mind that before the prophet uttered this imprecation, he was taught by the Spirit of God that he had to deal with the reprobate and irreclaimable.

19-21. This is what the LORD said to me: "Go and stand at the gate of the people, through which the kings of Judah go in and out; stand also at all the other gates of Jerusalem. Say to them, 'Hear the word of the LORD, O kings of Judah and all people of Judah and everyone living in Jerusalem who come through these gates. This is what the LORD says: Be careful not to carry a load on the Sabbath day or bring it through the gates of Jerusalem.'" This discourse should be separated from the preceding one. Whoever divided the chapters was in my judgment deficient here, as well as in many other places. These verses mean that contempt for the law was so great that they neglected even to observe the Sabbath. And yet we know that hypocrites are very careful in this respect (see Isaiah 1:13). But the Jews were so audacious in the time of Jeremiah that they openly violated the Sabbath. Men had become so lost, as we often say, that they did not even pretend to be religious. As this was the case in Jerusalem, what do we think happened in obscure villages where religion hardly existed?

We now see that the prophet was sent by God to charge the people with this dreadful contempt of the law. It is as if he said, "How can you pretend that you retain the least vestiges of religion? For even in this matter of the observance of the Sabbath you are deficient. You **carry a load on the Sabbath day**; that is, you carry on business on the Sabbath as on other days. As, then, there is not even external sanctity for the Sabbath among you, why do you go on with your evasions? Your impiety is sufficiently proved."

22. "Do not bring a load out of your houses or do any work on the Sabbath, but keep the Sabbath day holy, as I commanded your forefathers." God was not just concerned about the external rite of keeping the Sabbath, but rather its end or purpose, about which he speaks in Exodus 31:13 and Ezekiel 20:12. In both passages he reminds us of the reason why he commanded the Jews to keep holy the seventh day—that it might be to them a symbol of sanctification. "I have given my Sabbaths to you," he says, "so that you might know that I am your God who sanctifies you." If we consider the purpose of the Sabbath, we cannot say that it is an unimportant rite.

As, then, the Jews had become apostates, Jeremiah is right to condemn them severely. And so he says that their extreme impiety was sufficiently proved because they disregarded the seventh day.

23. "'Yet they did not listen or pay attention; they were stiff-necked and would not listen or respond to discipline.'" The Jews were not only unteachable when the will of God was plainly known to them, but they were also perverse in their spirit. When exhortations were added to teaching, in order to stimulate them to be faithful, it was impossible to subdue their wantonness.

24-25. "'But if you are careful to obey me, declares the LORD, and bring no load through the gates of this city on the Sabbath, but keep the Sabbath day holy by not doing any work on it, then kings who sit on David's throne will come through the gates of this city with their officials. They and their officials will come riding in chariots and on horses, accompanied by the men of Judah and those living in Jerusalem, and this city will be inhabited forever.'" Jeremiah introduces a condemnation of their fathers, so he can make the Jews of his age ashamed of themselves, lest they should imitate the example of those who they saw had been so disobedient to God. Yet the prophet still says God desired to be reconciled to them, provided that they repented from the heart. It is as if he said, "Your fathers indeed provoked, for many years and even for ages, the vengeance of God. But as he is always inclined to be merciful, he is ready to forgive you, if only you stop following your fathers and return to him." In short, he promises them pardon for their past sins if they turn to God.

"'And this city will be inhabited forever.'" He adds this because Jerusalem was in great danger then. Each day there were new calamities, and the whole country was in danger. So Jeremiah's promise about Jerusalem seemed incredible—that is, that the city would be made safe if they truly and faithfully worshiped God and testified to that by observing the Sabbath. The meaning is that it would be their own fault if they did not find God's help enough for them. Even if they were besieged by enemies, God would protect them, provided they became his true and faithful servants.

26. "'People will come from the towns of Judah and the villages around Jerusalem, from the territory of Benjamin and the western foothills, from the hill country and the Negev, bringing burnt offerings and sacrifices, grain offerings, incense and thank offerings to the house of the LORD.'" Jeremiah mentions how God will greatly bless them. Everyone would be kept safe and retain their kingdom and priesthood, as God's favor appeared in both. The king and the priest were both types of Christ. By the priesthood they knew that God was propitious to them, as they were being reconciled to him by sacrifices. And by the kingdom they knew that God was the protector and guardian of their safety. These two things constituted a real and complete happiness.

"'People will come from the towns of Judah and the villages around Jerusalem, from the territory of Benjamin'" and from other places to offer sacrifices in the temple. Sacrifices could not of themselves save the people. But Jeremiah assumed the principle that the people were promised reconciliation through the sacrifices. Sins were really atoned for, and God as it were came forth to gather a people for himself. It was as though God said that he would by all means be gracious to them, if only they observed the Sabbath—that is, if they devoted themselves with a pure heart to his service.

27. "'But if you do not obey me to keep the Sabbath day holy by not carrying any load as you come through the gates of Jerusalem on the Sabbath day, then I will kindle an unquenchable fire in the gates of Jerusalem that will consume her fortresses.'" Now the prophet, speaking for God, warns the people what will happen if they do not listen to God's promises. God first kindly woos us, but when he sees that we are stubbornly resistant, he deals with us according to the hardness of our hearts. He therefore now adds warnings to promises.

Jeremiah
Chapter 18

1-6. This is the word that came to Jeremiah from the LORD: "Go down to the potter's house, and there I will give you my message." So I went down to the potter's house, and I saw him working at the wheel. But the pot he was shaping from the clay was marred in his hands; so the potter formed it into another pot, shaping it as seemed best to him. Then the word of the LORD came to me: "O house of Israel, can I not do with you as this potter does?" declares the LORD. "Like clay in the hand of the potter, so are you in my hand, O house of Israel."

The sum of what is taught here is that as Jews gloried in God's singular favor, which had been conferred on them for a different purpose than they supposed—that they might be his sacred heritage—it was necessary to take from them their wrong confidence. For at the same time they heedlessly despised God and the whole of his law. We know that in God's covenant there was a mutual stipulation—those in the race of Abraham were to serve God faithfully, and God was prepared to perform whatever he had promised. The perpetual law of the covenant, "walk before me and be blameless" (Genesis 17:1), once and for all imposed on Abraham, extended to all his posterity. The Jews thought that God was bound to them by an inviolable contract; yet they proudly rejected all his prophets and polluted and even (as far as they could) abolished his true worship. So it was necessary to deprive them of that foolish boasting by which they deluded themselves. Hence the prophet was ordered to go down to the potter's house, that he might tell the people what he saw there—namely, that the potter, according to his own will and pleasure, made and remade vessels.

7-10. "If at any time I announce that a nation or kingdom is to be uprooted, torn down and destroyed, and if that nation I warned repents of its evil, then I will relent and not inflict on it the disaster I had planned. And if at another time I announce that a nation or kingdom is to be built up and planted, and if it does evil in my sight and does not obey me, then I will reconsider the good I had intended to do for it." This is a fuller application of the prophet's teaching. Before, he had said generally that the people were in God's hand as the clay is in the hand of the potter; but here he adds something more comprehensive—that all people are in God's hand, so that he now favors one nation with his blessing and then deprives them of it, and that he raises up those whom he had previously brought low.

11-12. "Now therefore say to the people of Judah and those living in Jerusalem, 'This is what the LORD says: Look! I am preparing a disaster for you and devising a plan against you. So turn from your evil ways, each one of you, and reform your ways and your actions.' But they will reply, 'It's no use. We will continue with our own plans; each of us will follow the stubbornness of his evil heart.'" The prophet is now told to address the Jews, applying the doctrine of repentance. God shows in these verses that he was ready to receive the Jews if they repented. But if they continued to be perverse, as they so often did, he would not allow them to go unpunished. As he was the potter, he could do this; they were in his hand and power.

13. Therefore this is what the LORD says: "Inquire among the nations: Who has ever heard anything like this? A most horrible thing has been done by Virgin Israel." God shows that the Jews had arrived at the height of impiety by daring to reject the salvation he offered them. Because they were so deaf and stupid, God turns to the Gentiles.

"Inquire among the nations: Who has ever heard anything like this?" In essence, God was saying, "I will no more contend with brute beasts who are devoid of reason. But the Gentiles, who are destitute of the light of knowledge, can be made witnesses of such gross impiety." He had said the same thing before: "Cross over to the coasts of Kittim and look, send to Kedar and observe closely; see if there has ever been anything like this: Has a nation ever changed its gods? (Yet they are not gods at all)" (Jeremiah 2:10-11). It is as if he said, "Religion is prevalent among wretched idolaters, and they continue steadfast in their superstitions. They think it would be the greatest piety if they were to forsake the God whom they once welcomed; yet these new ones are not gods. My people have forsaken me, the source of living water."

14-15. "Does the snow of Lebanon ever vanish from its rocky slopes? Do its cool waters from distant sources ever cease to flow? Yet my people have forgotten me; they burn incense to worthless idols, which made them stumble in their ways and in the ancient paths. They made them walk in bypaths and on roads not built up." God highlights the sin of the people with the following comparison: When one can draw water in one's own field, how foolish it would be to travel a long way looking for water. And if water does not spring up nearby but flows from a distant pure and cold stream, who will not be satisfied with such water?

God was like a living spring, and at Jerusalem the Jews could drink as much as they liked from that spring. God's blessing also flowed to them through various channels, so that they lacked nothing. We see that a double madness in the people is condemned here: They despised God's kindness that was close at hand, as though someone close to the mountains of Lebanon refused their cold waters, or as though someone would not draw water from a river but only from its source. God offered himself to them in every way and presented his bounty to them; so it was inexcusable madness to reject both the flowing waters and the source itself.

16. **"Their land will be laid waste, an object of lasting scorn; all who pass by will be appalled and will shake their heads."** The prophet again announces the punishment that they deserved—the land would be desolated.

17. **"Like a wind from the east, I will scatter them before their enemies; I will show them my back and not my face in the day of their disaster."** He means that enemies would come to exterminate the Jews from the land. And he adds something else: These enemies would be full of terror, for God would give them the force of a whirlwind or a storm in order to disperse and scatter the Jews. They would not dare withstand God, for they were terrified of him.

18. **They said, "Come, let's make plans against Jeremiah; for the teaching of the law by the priest will not be lost, nor will counsel from the wise, nor the word from the prophets. So come, let's attack him with our tongues and pay no attention to anything he says."** Jeremiah relates how furious the people were on whom he had pronounced God's vengeance. It was doubtless a dreadful thing to hear that when they despaired, no help could be expected from God. For this is the meaning of, **"I will show them my back and not my face in the day of their disaster"** (verse 17).

The prophet shows that their attacks on him revealed their diabolical actions. They did not hesitate to reject what came from God. They refused to pay any attention to his commands.

19. **Listen to me, O LORD; hear what my accusers are saying!** As the prophet saw that his work was useless, he turned to God, as he had often done before. This way of speaking, no doubt, had more force than if he had continued to address the people. He might indeed have said, "Miserable people! Where are you rushing headlong to? What is the meaning of this madness? Where do you think this will lead you since you are resisting God? You cannot extinguish the light by your insolence!" The prophet might have reproved them in this way. But it was more effective for him to leave those people and to speak to God himself. It is as if Jeremiah says, "As they do not listen to me, you, Lord, listen to me." He saw that he was despised by God's enemies, and by this prayer he intimates that his teaching came from God and so could not fail.

20. Should good be repaid with evil? Yet they have dug a pit for me. Remember that I stood before you and spoke in their behalf to turn your wrath away from them. In other words, "Even if malice prevents people from saying what I am and how I have behaved toward them, God will be to me a sufficient witness, and I will be satisfied with his judgment."

21. So give their children over to famine; hand them over to the power of the sword. Let their wives be made childless and widows; let their men be put to death, their young men slain by the sword in battle. The prophet seems here to have been driven through indignation to utter imprecations that are inconsistent with a right feeling. For even if Christ had not said with his own lips that we are to pray for those who curse us, God's law, which was always known by the holy fathers, was sufficient. Jeremiah then should not have uttered these curses, although they were fully deserved. But it must be observed that he was moved by the Holy Spirit to become so indignant against his enemies. He could not have been excused on the grounds that indignation often goes beyond the bounds of patience, for the children of God should bear all injuries. But the prophet does not say anything rashly here but obediently proclaims what the Holy Spirit dictated, as his faithful instrument.

22. Let a cry be heard from their houses when you suddenly bring invaders against them, for they have dug a pit to capture me and have hidden snares for my feet. Jeremiah continues with his imprecation. He wants a cry to be heard from their houses, as if he said, "Let there be no refuge for them when their calamity arrives." One's own house is for everyone a place of safety in a time of trouble.

23. But you know, O LORD, all their plots to kill me. Do not forgive their crimes or blot out their sins from your sight. Let them be overthrown before you; deal with them in the time of your anger. Whenever the Scripture speaks of the time of God's wrath, we must realize that beneath this way of speaking there lies an exhortation to be patient. Excessive zeal must not lead us beyond the limits of moderation, but we ought to wait with resigned minds until the due time of judgment comes. But the prophet also expresses something else—he wants the reprobate he is talking about to remain under endless judgment. (Compare Psalm 106:40.)

Jeremiah
Chapter 19

1-3. This is what the LORD says: "Go and buy a clay jar from a potter. Take along some of the elders of the people and of the priests and go out to the Valley of Ben Hinnom, near the entrance of the Potsherd Gate. There proclaim the words I tell you, and say, 'Hear the word of the LORD, O kings of Judah and people of Jerusalem. This is what the LORD Almighty, the God of Israel, says: Listen! I am going to bring a disaster on this place that will make the ears of everyone who hears of it tingle.'" We see that the prophet was sent by God to show the people that the boasts of the hypocrites were empty. God, who had favored the people of Israel with special benefits, did not care less for them than did the potter for the jar he made. The prophet had previously shown the Jews that the potter formed his vessels as he pleased, and also that when the vessel did not please him, he made another. Now the prophet is told to **"buy a clay jar from a potter."** Then, where the people met, **near the entrance of the Potsherd Gate**, to break it (verse 10), so that everyone might understand that they were like pottery. They were thus reminded of their own fragility, so that they might no longer be proud.

The Lord says through the prophet that a calamity is about to take place that will make **the ears of everyone who hears of it tingle.** When there is a very loud noise, our ears are stunned, and then they ring or **tingle.** When one person is killed, or when a dozen people are killed, there is a dreadful cry. But in a great tumult caused by many people being killed, the noise is so great, like that which comes from waterfalls, that it seems to stun our ears. They say that the great noise of the Nile causes a degree of deafness. So God through the prophet says, **"I am going to bring a disaster on this place,"** which will not only terrify those who hear it but will totally astonish them, so that their **ears** will **tingle.**

4-5. **"For they have forsaken me and made this a place of foreign gods; they have burned sacrifices in it to gods that neither they nor their fathers nor the kings of Judah ever knew, and they have filled** this place with the blood of the innocent. They have built the high places of Baal to burn their sons in the fire as offerings to Baal—something I did not command or mention, nor did it enter my mind.'" God complains that he has been forsaken by them, because they have changed the worship prescribed by his law.

He adds that "they have filled this place with the blood of the innocent," for there they killed their children. By mentioning this, Jeremiah highlights the wickedness of the people. They had not only despised God and his law but also cruelly destroyed their innocent children.

6. "'So beware, the days are coming, declares the LORD, when people will no longer call this place Topheth or the Valley of Ben Hinnom, but the Valley of Slaughter.'" This seemed incredible to the Jews, for they had chosen that place themselves to perform their superstitious rites. They thought their safety depended on their false worship.

7. "'In this place I will ruin the plans of Judah and Jerusalem. I will make them fall by the sword before their enemies, at the hands of those who seek their lives, and I will give their carcasses as food to the birds of the air and the beasts of the earth.'" The prophet says their enemies will be so cruel that they will seek the life of all the people and will delight in slaughter. It was as if he said they would be deadly enemies and altogether implacable. God then adds, "I will give their carcasses as food to the birds of the air and the beasts of the earth." It was deemed to be a punishment inflicted by heaven when the carcasses of the dead remain unburied.

8. "'I will devastate this city and make it an object of scorn; all who pass by will be appalled and will scoff because of all its wounds.'" Jeremiah proceeds with his denunciation. All who pass by will be appalled because what befalls the people will not be a common calamity, but one in which can be seen God's dreadful judgment.

9. "'I will make them eat the flesh of their sons and daughters, and they will eat one another's flesh during the stress of the siege imposed on them by the enemies who seek their lives.'" Here the prophet goes further: The calamity will be so atrocious that mothers and fathers will even eat their children. We know from the writings of Josephus that during the last siege of Jerusalem, mothers killed their children in a brutal way. They also lay in wait for one another as they snatched at anything to eat. This was evidence of God's dreadful vengeance.

10-11. "Then break the jar while those who go with you are watching, and say to them, 'This is what the LORD Almighty says: I will smash this nation and this city just as this potter's jar is smashed and cannot be repaired. They will bury the dead in Topheth until there is no more room.'" Jeremiah did this in front of witnesses. It was not only an important sign, that they might learn from it about the doom of the city and of the whole land, but was also a solemn sealing of the prophecy.

He was commanded to **"break the jar"** so that he might show, through this visible act, the approaching vengeance of God, about which the Jews had no understanding.

"'They will bury the dead in Topheth until there is no more room.'" They had chosen that place when they thought they had some evidence of God's favor, and because they were joyful. But God declares that the place will be filled with dead bodies, for they will flee in great numbers into the city, which would later become so full of dead bodies that there would be no room to bury them except **in Topheth.**

12. "'This is what I will do to this place and to those who live here, declares the LORD. I will make this city like Topheth.'" He had previously said that the valley would be the place of slaughter (verse 6) and so get its name; now he declares that it will be the same for the city. That is, "As Topheth will be the valley of slaughter, so will Jerusalem be."

13. "'The houses in Jerusalem and those of the kings of Judah will be defiled like this place, Topheth—all the houses where they burned incense on the roofs to all the starry hosts and poured out drink offerings to other gods.'" Jerusalem was a broad city and splendidly built, with many large and elegant houses there, as well as the royal palaces. Yet all these things would not prevent God from demolishing the whole city.

They burned incense on the roofs to all the starry hosts and poured out drink offerings to other gods. Many kinds of superstitions existed among the people. Jeremiah spoke about Baal, in the singular, as well as Baals, and here he adds, **all the starry hosts**—that is, the sun, the moon, and all the stars.

14-15. Jeremiah then returned from Topheth, where the LORD had sent him to prophesy, and stood in the court of the LORD's temple and said to all the people, "This is what the LORD Almighty, the God of Israel, says: 'Listen! I am going to bring on this city and the villages around it every disaster I pronounced against them, because they were stiff-necked and would not listen to my words.'" Jeremiah had been led to the very place mentioned when he foretold the punishment that was at hand on account of the superstitions of Topheth or the valley of Hinnom.

"'They were stiff-necked and would not listen to my words.'" Although all people are hard-hearted, yet when the teaching of salvation is made known and not received, a greater impiety and pride is exposed, for in that case people hear God speaking and yet rob him of his authority.

Jeremiah
Chapter 20

1-2. When the priest Pashhur son of Immer, the chief officer in the temple of the LORD, heard Jeremiah prophesying these things, he had Jeremiah the prophet beaten and put in the stocks at the Upper Gate of Benjamin at the LORD's temple. Jeremiah now relates the kind of reward he received for his prophecy: He was attacked and thrown in prison, not by the king or his courtiers, but by a priest who looked after the temple. It was a bitter trial when God's servant was cruelly treated by one who belonged to the sacred order, who was of the same tribe and a colleague. The priests who were then in office had been appointed by God. Since their authority was based on the law and on God's inviolable decree, Jeremiah might well have been very frightened. He may have thought, "What is God's purpose in this? He has set priests from the tribe of Levi over his temple and over his whole people. Why, then, does he not rule over them by his Spirit? Why does he not make them fit for their office? Why does he allow his temple and his sacred office that he so highly commends to us in the law to be profaned in this way? Or why, at least, does he not stretch out his hand to defend me, since I also am a priest and sincerely engaged in my calling?"

Jeremiah was **beaten and put in the stocks.** But we must notice that Pashhur had heard Jeremiah prophesying before he became angry with him. He ought to have been moved by such a prophecy, but instead he became so enraged and audacious that he attacked God's prophet.

3. The next day, when Pashhur released him from the stocks, Jeremiah said to him, "The LORD's name for you is not Pashhur, but Magor-Missabib." Doubtless Pashhur called other priests to examine the case, but it was a specious pretense, for he made it appear that he did not want to condemn the holy prophet quickly or without hearing his defense. But Jeremiah only says briefly that he was brought out of prison. At the same time we gather that he was not acquitted, for he was summoned before Pashhur to give the reason for his prophecy.

Magor-Missabib means "terror on every side." That is, terror would so surround everyone that no escape would be possible.

4-5. "For this is what the LORD says: 'I will make you a terror to yourself and to all your friends; with your own eyes you will see them fall by the sword of their enemies. I will hand all Judah over to the king of Babylon, who will carry them away to Babylon or put them to the sword. I will hand over to their enemies all the wealth of this city— all its products, all its valuables and all the treasures of the kings of Judah. They will take it away as plunder and carry it off to Babylon.'" Jeremiah explains why he said that Pashhur would experience terror on every side—he and his friends would be afraid. He would find himself overwhelmed by God's vengeance and would become a spectacle to everyone else. In short, Jeremiah meant that God's vengeance would fill Pashhur and everyone else with fear. Pashhur would be made to acknowledge God's hand without being able to escape.

6. "'And you, Pashhur, and all who live in your house will go into exile to Babylon. There you will die and be buried, you and all your friends to whom you have prophesied lies.'" Now Jeremiah declares that Pashhur himself will be the evidence that he has truly foretold the destruction of the city and the desolation of the whole land. He has indeed already exposed his vanity, but now he brings the man himself before the public. For it was necessary to give a remarkable example, so that everyone might know that God's judgment should have been dreaded.

7. O LORD, you deceived me, and I was deceived; you overpowered me and prevailed. I am ridiculed all day long; everyone mocks me. Jeremiah is speaking ironically here, assuming the character of his enemies, who boasted that his prophecy of the city's ruin was presumptuous because no such thing would happen. The prophet declares here that God was the author of his teaching and that nothing could be alleged against him that would not be against God himself. It is as if he said that the Jews' argument was in vain, for they thought they were arguing against a mortal man. In fact, they were waging open war against God and were furiously assailing heaven itself. Jeremiah not only had the Spirit of God as a witness to his calling, but he also had a firm conviction in his heart that he had delivered the truth. He says all this to those who opposed his teaching, denied that he was God's servant, and gave him no credit, as if he were only an impostor.

This way of speaking was much more striking than if he had said in a commonplace way, "Lord, I am not deceived, for I have only obeyed your command and have received from you whatever I have made public. I have not put myself forward presumptuously or adulterated the truth of which you have made me a herald. I have, then, faithfully discharged my office."

8-9. Whenever I speak, I cry out proclaiming violence and destruc-

tion. So the word of the LORD has brought me insult and reproach all day long. But if I say, "I will not mention him or speak any more in his name," his word is in my heart like a fire, a fire shut up in my bones. I am weary of holding it in; indeed, I cannot. The prophet says here that he found no fruit from his labors; on the contrary, he saw that all his efforts and endeavors had the opposite effect. They exasperated all the Jews, inflamed their rage, and drove them to greater licentiousness in sinning. So he says that he intended to give up the office he had been given. But a secret impulse constrained him to persevere, and so he was not at liberty to desist from the course he had begun.

We are told how God helped his servant. The Word of God, says Jeremiah, became like a fire, a fire shut up in my bones. It was in his bones, so that he was led by an ardent zeal and could not be himself without continuing in his office. He concludes by saying that he was weary. In other words, it was not in his power either to abstain from teaching or to do what God commanded. But burning zeal forced him to go on. It is the same, then, as if he had said that he had learned what it was to have the whole world against him, but God prevailed. This was said because profane people take the opportunity to be secure and indifferent when they imagine that prophets and teachers are people with no feelings. "What do we care for fanatics, who do not possess common feelings? And it is no wonder, since they are stupid and unfeeling, that they are angry and violent, disregard others, and feel nothing that is human." Since they imagine that men are sticks when they speak of God's servants as being without discretion, the prophet seems to say, "Surely you are deceived, for I am not like iron, but I am influenced by many strong feelings. I know my weaknesses, and I do not hide the fact that I am a person subject to fear, sorrow, and other passions. But God has prevailed. There is no reason for you to think that I speak boldly because I have no human feelings. When I submitted myself to God and wanted to give up my calling, I was constrained, and God dealt powerfully with me, for his Word was like a burning fire in my heart, so that at length, through the strong influence of the Spirit, I was constrained to proceed and carry out my office."

10. I hear many whispering, "Terror on every side! Report him! Let's report him!" All my friends are waiting for me to slip, saying, "Perhaps he will be deceived; then we will prevail over him and take our revenge on him." Jeremiah continues with the same subject and accuses God before his enemies—they argued with him disgracefully, although he deserved no such treatment, for he had endeavored to secure their safety insofar as he was able.

All my friends are waiting for me to slip. We may deduce from these words that this holy servant of God was not only harassed openly by professed foes but was also secretly watched by people who pretended to be his friends but were all the time his worst enemies.

11. But the LORD is with me like a mighty warrior; so my persecutors will stumble and not prevail. They will fail and be thoroughly disgraced; their dishonor will never be forgotten. Whenever we fight against the world and the devil and his servants, we should remember that God stands on our side to defend our cause and to protect us.

12. O LORD Almighty, you who examine the righteous and probe the heart and mind, let me see your vengeance upon them, for to you I have committed my cause. We should never pray for vengeance on our enemies unless we are sure that our zeal is guided by a godly spirit of uprightness and wisdom.

13. Sing to the LORD! Give praise to the LORD! He rescues the life of the needy from the hands of the wicked. Here the prophet breaks into an open expression of joy and not only gives thanks to God himself for freeing him from the intrigues of the wicked but also summons others to sing God's praises.

14-16. Cursed be the day I was born! May the day my mother bore me not be blessed! Cursed be the man who brought my father the news, who made him very glad, saying, "A child is born to you—a son!" May that man be like the towns the LORD overthrew without pity. May he hear wailing in the morning, a battle cry at noon. It appears that the prophet is being inconsistent, seeming to move from joy and thanksgiving to curses and execrations. But it seems to me a levity unworthy of the holy man to pass suddenly from thanksgiving to God into imprecations, as though he had forgotten himself. Therefore, I am sure the prophet here is relating how grievously he had been harassed by his own thoughts. The whole of this passage, then, is connected with thanksgiving, for he amplifies the deliverance that he has just mentioned. Later he recalls what had previously happened to him, as if saying, "When I now declare that I have been rescued by God from the hand of the wicked, I cannot sufficiently express the greatness of that favor until I make it more clearly known to all the godly what great and dreadful agonies I suffered, so that I cursed the day I was born and abhorred everything that ought to have stimulated me to praise God."

In short, the prophet teaches us here that he was not only opposed by enemies but was also distressed inwardly in his mind, so that he was even led to utter vile blasphemies. What is said here cannot be excused. The prophet sinned when he deprecated God in this way, for a man must be in a wrong state of despair when he curses the day on which he was born. It used to be customary to celebrate one's birthday by acknowledging on that day that God had been responsible for one's birth. Birthdays used to be a reason for thanksgiving, and it is clear that when we curse what ought to make us praise God, we are no longer in our right mind.

17-18. For he did not kill me in the womb, with my mother as my grave, her womb enlarged forever. Why did I ever come out of the

womb to see trouble and sorrow and to end my days in shame? We must remember what aim the prophet had in recounting this. He mentioned what had passed through his mind in order to focus on God's grace in delivering him, as it were, from hell itself, into which he had plunged. The drift of what he said seems to be: "I was lost, and my mind could conceive of nothing but what was bitter, and with a full mouth I vomited out poison and blasphemies against God." The prophet's aim was to make more conspicuous God's kindness in bringing him into light from so deep an abyss.

Jeremiah
Chapter 21

1-4. The word came to Jeremiah from the LORD when King Zedekiah sent to him Pashhur son of Malkijah and the priest Zephaniah son of Maaseiah. They said: "Inquire now of the LORD for us because Nebuchadnezzar king of Babylon is attacking us. Perhaps the LORD will perform wonders for us as in times past so that he will withdraw from us." But Jeremiah answered them, "Tell Zedekiah, 'This is what the LORD, the God of Israel, says: I am about to turn against you the weapons of war that are in your hands, which you are using to fight the king of Babylon and the Babylonians who are outside the wall besieging you. And I will gather them inside this city.'"
Jeremiah relates how he received the king's messengers, who wanted him to give them a message of comfort in their hopeless situation. He says that two people were sent to him. One was Pashhur (not the priest mentioned in the last chapter, for he was the son of Immer), **Pashhur son of Malkijah.** The other person sent was the priest **Zephaniah son of Maaseiah.** Jeremiah indicates that they were disappointed with the answer he gave them, for they were expecting a favorable answer, hoping God would deliver Jerusalem. But the prophet answered as he was commanded by God, namely, that it was all over for the city, the kingdom, and the whole nation.

5. "'I myself will fight against you with an outstretched hand and a mighty arm in anger and fury and great wrath.'" Jeremiah states that God was the leader of the war, and that the Chaldeans were, as it were, his hired soldiers, whom he had guided with his own hand, and to whom he would give the signal to fight.

6-7. "'I will strike down those who live in this city—both men and animals—and they will die of a terrible plague. After that, declares the LORD, I will hand over Zedekiah king of Judah, his officials and the people in this city who survive the plague, sword and famine, to Nebuchadnezzar king of Babylon and to their enemies who seek their lives. He will put them to the sword; he will show them no mercy or pity or compassion.'" Jeremiah carries on with what he was saying: God had resolved to destroy Jerusalem and the people, at least for the time. But he points out here what God intends to do: He will consume them with pestilence and famine as long as they stay in the city. It is as if he said, "Although these Chaldeans may not at once take the city through a siege, its destruction will be worse, for famine will rage inside and kill people."

8-9. **"Furthermore, tell the people, 'This is what the LORD says: See, I am setting before you the way of life and the way of death. Whoever stays in this city will die by the sword, famine or plague. But whoever goes out and surrenders to the Babylonians who are besieging you will live; he will escape with his life.'"** The prophet means that there is no hope of safety unless the Jews surrender to their enemies. If they persist in defending themselves, God will be their enemy, for he has led the Chaldeans to attack them and has directed their counsels and their troops. Jeremiah confirmed that the Jews could not escape the correction they deserved.

10. **"'I have determined to do this city harm and not good, declares the LORD. It will be given into the hands of the king of Babylon, and he will destroy it with fire.'"** Jeremiah confirms that it will be **the way of death** for them if they remain in Jerusalem.

11-12. **"Moreover, say to the royal house of Judah, 'Hear the word of the LORD; O house of David, this is what the LORD says: Administer justice every morning; rescue from the hand of his oppressor the one who has been robbed, or my wrath will break out and burn like fire because of the evil you have done—burn with no one to quench it.'"** The prophet says that God's wrath might be alleviated, although not wholly pacified, if the king and his counselors begin to behave justly. He mentions the **house of David** by way of reproach, because David had ruled justly and was an upright king.

13-14. **"'I am against you, Jerusalem, you who live above this valley on the rocky plateau, declares the LORD—you who say, "Who can come against us? Who can enter our refuge?" I will punish you as your deeds deserve, declares the LORD. I will kindle a fire in your forests that will consume everything around you.'"** Although the whole nation was corrupt in the time of the prophet, Jerusalem was the center of all evils. Its inhabitants thought the prophets had no business rebuking them. The situation of the city also gave them courage, for they thought they were beyond all danger because of the height of their walls, towers, and fortresses. It is this security that the prophet condemns, and so he calls Jerusalem **"you who live above this valley on the rocky plateau."**

Jeremiah
Chapter 22

1-3. This is what the LORD says: "Go down to the palace of the king of Judah and proclaim this message there: 'Hear the word of the LORD, O king of Judah, you who sit on David's throne—you, your officials and your people who come through these gates. This is what the LORD says: Do what is just and right. Rescue from the hand of his oppressor the one who has been robbed. Do no wrong or violence to the alien, the fatherless or the widow, and do not shed innocent blood in this place.'" The prophet is again told to rebuke the king and his counselors. Later on he is told to include all the people. God will not spare even the king. This thought should have struck fear into the hearts of the whole nation.

4-5. "'For if you are careful to carry out these commands, then kings who sit on David's throne will come through the gates of this palace, riding in chariots and on horses, accompanied by their officials and their people. But if you do not obey these commands, declares the LORD, I swear by myself that this palace will become a ruin.'" The prophet declares that the kingdom will be restored by the Lord, if the king and his servants and all the people repent. If, however, they refuse to do this, they will be destroyed.

6-7. For this is what the LORD says about the palace of the king of Judah: "Though you are like Gilead to me, like the summit of Lebanon, I will surely make you like a desert, like towns not inhabited. I will send destroyers against you, each man with his weapons, and they will cut up your fine cedar beams and throw them into the fire." God means, "Who do you think you are? Why do you place such confidence in yourself? I did not spare Mount Gilead and that extensive country that was so superior to you. So why do you presume that you are out of danger? You will be like Gilead was to me. What happened to them will happen to you."

"I will send destroyers against you." The prophet distinctly says that the Chaldeans will be God's ministers and that they will come not of their own accord but through God's secret working.

8-9. "People from many nations will pass by this city and will ask one another, 'Why has the LORD done such a thing to this great city?' And the answer will be: 'Because they have forsaken the covenant of the LORD their God and have worshiped and served other gods.'" There are two contrasts in these verses. Jeremiah compares mortals with God, and the many nations with him alone. The Jews could not bear having God as their judge. But the prophet says that godless people would come and judge them.

10. Do not weep for the dead king or mourn his loss; rather, weep bitterly for him who is exiled, because he will never return nor see his native land again. The prophet wanted to show the miserable condition in which the people would be left. It is as if he said, "You lament the destruction of the city, but you should mourn more for those who remain alive than for those who die, for death will be as it were a rest, but life will be a continual succession of miseries."

11-12. For this is what the LORD says about Shallum son of Josiah, who succeeded his father as king of Judah but has gone from this place: "He will never return. He will die in the place where they have led him captive; he will not see this land again." What had been said previously in general Jeremiah now applies specifically to the king, so the people would know they could not escape that punishment from which even the king was not exempt.

13. "Woe to him who builds his palace by unrighteousness, his upper rooms by injustice, making his countrymen work for nothing, not paying them for their labor." The prophet shows here that the king's **palace** will be destroyed along with Jerusalem, for wickedness has reached its highest pitch there.

14. "He says, 'I will build myself a great palace with spacious upper rooms.' So he makes large windows in it, panels it with cedar and decorates it in red." The prophet reproves the ambition and pride of King Jehoiakim. He was not content with the moderation of his fathers but indulged in extravagant display and built for himself a palace in the clouds, so to speak, as if he did not want to live on the earth. Splendid houses are not in themselves condemned, but since they nearly always proceed from insatiable ambition, the prophets condemn sumptuous houses. They pronounced a curse on such displays because they knew the motivation that lay behind them. Such was the purpose of the prophet in this passage.

15. "Does it make you a king to have more and more cedar? Did not your father have food and drink? He did what was right and just, so all went well with him." The prophet here derides the foolish confidence of King Jehoiakim, because he has set up empty things against his enemies instead of strong defenses. Jeremiah's purpose was to show that the only true glory and the chief honor of kings, when they carry out their duties, only comes about when God's image shines in them, and not when they are blind slaves to pride.

16. "He [Shallum's father, Josiah; see verse 15] defended the cause of the poor and needy, and so all went well. Is that not what it means to know me?" declares the LORD. We have here a part stated that stands for the whole: The prophet mentions one thing that includes all the duties of a ruler. He says that King Josiah was upright, just, and equitable, that he not only abstained from wrongs but also helped the innocent whom he saw oppressed. This one example stands for everything that belongs to the office of an upright ruler.

17. "But your eyes and your heart are set only on dishonest gain, on shedding innocent blood and on oppression and extortion." Here the prophet shows more clearly how much Jehoiakim differed from Josiah his father. He indeed shows that he was completely unlike him, because Josiah had fought for justice, while Jehoiakim set his thoughts on fraud, plunder, and cruelty. The **eyes** and **heart** stand for all the faculties of the soul and body.

18-19. Therefore this is what the LORD says about Jehoiakim son of Josiah king of Judah: "They will not mourn for him: 'Alas, my brother! Alas, my sister!' They will not mourn for him: 'Alas, my master! Alas, his splendor!' He will have the burial of a donkey—dragged away and thrown outside the gates of Jerusalem." The prophet, having inveighed against Jehoiakim, now shows what kind of punishment he will receive from God. Otherwise he would have despised the prophet's reproof. We learn from these verses how great Jehoiakim's perverseness was in despising God's warnings. If there had been any teachable spirit in the king and the people, the prophet would have been content with the statement, "Jehoiakim will not be buried." That would have meant that God would punish him, even when he was dead. God's curse would not only be on him while living, but he would also take vengeance on him after death. But Jeremiah was not content with that kind of statement. Rather he says, **"He will have the burial of a donkey—dragged away and thrown outside the gates of Jerusalem."** Such was the eternal mark of infamy and disgrace.

20. "Go up to Lebanon and cry out, let your voice be heard in Bashan, cry out from Abarim, for all your allies are crushed." Jeremiah triumphs over the Jews and derides their presumption in thinking they would be safe, though God was against them. He then shows that they were deceived in promising themselves impunity. He tells them to **"Go up to Lebanon and cry out, let your voice be heard in Bashan,"** that they might know there would be no help for them when God's judgment came. They would cry and howl in vain. The prophet had to be ironical and deride the madness of their promising themselves safety as they continued to bring God's vengeance upon themselves.

21. **"I warned you when you felt secure, but you said, 'I will not listen!' This has been your way from your youth; you have not obeyed me."** God shows here that the people were so wicked that they had rebelled against him from their youth. It is as if he said, "You cannot make the excuse that you have been without a teacher for a long time, that you have been without any wisdom and understanding, and that on this account you have become hardened in evil ways. I have found you completely unteachable from your childhood."

22. **"The wind will drive all your shepherds away, and your allies will go into exile. Then you will be ashamed and disgraced because of all your wickedness."** The prophet says that their **shepherds** (that is, pastors) will be driven away by **the wind**; that is, they will vanish like a puff of smoke. In this way God shows that their presumption and fraud were nothing but smoke and emptiness.

23. **"You who live in 'Lebanon,' who are nestled in cedar buildings, how you will groan when pangs come upon you, pain like that of a woman in labor!"** God through the prophet repeats the same thing, using different words. He does not allow that the Jews will gain anything by thinking they will have a quiet time in Lebanon, by having nests in the cedars, for God will bring on them sudden pains like those women who, while laughing and full of mirth, are suddenly seized with the pangs of childbearing.

24. **"As surely as I live," declares the LORD, "even if you, Jehoiachin son of Jehoiakim king of Judah, were a signet ring on my right hand, I would still pull you off."** God here makes an oath that he has resolved to punish Jehoiachin, who was also called Jeconiah. He says that although he sat on David's throne, he would be a miserable exile. The king himself never thought he could be driven into exile, because he was David's successor and ordained by God. This is why God now declares, **"even if you, Jehoiachin son of Jehoiakim king of Judah, were a signet ring on my right hand, I would still pull you off."** However exalted Jeconiah was, God shows that the king would only last for a time and would soon fade away.

25. **"I will hand you over to those who seek your life, those you fear—to Nebuchadnezzar king of Babylon and to the Babylonians."** This verse is connected to the previous one and explains it more fully. The wrenching off of the signet ring from God's finger took place when Jeconiah was deprived of his glory and his kingdom and was made subject to the king of Babylon. Although that king spared his life at first, as sacred history testifies (2 Kings 25:7; 2 Chronicles 36:6; Jeremiah 52:11), when he surrendered to them, he trembled as if he saw the sword ready to cut off his head.

26. "I will hurl you and the mother who gave you birth into another country, where neither of you was born, and there you both will die." In order to emphasize what kind of indignity was taking place, it is added that the king's mother would be taken captive with him. Females were often spared being taken into exile for the sake of their gender and because, as in this case, they were elderly. But God executed his judgment on King Jehoiachin's mother because she was his associate in impiety.

27. "You will never come back to the land you long to return to." The prophet had said before that both the king and his mother would die in a foreign land, and now he confirms that fact. The foolish idea that the king of Babylon would eventually be merciful to them could not be easily erased from their minds. "When Nebuchadnezzar sees us coming to him to ask for mercy, will he not grant what we ask for? How much more does he want? He does not want to build a royal palace here in our land. It will be enough if the people are given to him as a tribute. And when he finds that I am a man with no courage, he will prefer to have me as king than to appoint a new one." This vain conviction was demolished by the prophet.

28. Is this man Jehoiachin a despised, broken pot, an object no one wants? Why will he and his children be hurled out, cast into a land they do not know? The prophet here speaks about what seemed incredible. He assumes the character of someone who was greatly wondering, so that others might cease to wonder. He then asks whether it was possible that Jeconiah should be driven into exile and there perish miserably. We now see the purpose of the prophet: The Jews thought the kingdom would last forever, and it was necessary to shake off such an idea, so that they might know that God had not warned them in vain about these things. There is in these questions a kind of irony, for the prophet could have made a positive assertion in plain words. But for the sake of others, he hesitates and seems to doubt it all, as if it were a monstrous idea.

29-30. O land, land, land, hear the word of the LORD! This is what the LORD says: "Record this man as if childless, a man who will not prosper in his lifetime, for none of his offspring will prosper, none will sit on the throne of David or rule anymore in Judah." The prophet repeats the word **land** three times. As the hardness of iron is overcome by repeated hammer blows, so the prophet tries to subdue the perverseness of the Jews, who had so hardened themselves that no warnings from God ever moved them.

"Record this man as if childless." It is no wonder that the prophet declares here that Jeconiah will be childless, for such a sad calamity as the throne of David being trodden underfoot with scorn and contempt for many ages might have overwhelmed the faithful with despair. This, then, was the reason why he said that king would be **childless** and his whole posterity under a curse. But we must bear in mind the exception, expressed by another prophet: "until he comes to whom it rightfully belongs" (Ezekiel 21:27). The throne was reserved for the head of Christ, although for a long time it had been exposed to dishonor and to the reproaches of the nations.

Jeremiah
Chapter 23

1-3. "Woe to the shepherds who are destroying and scattering the sheep of my pasture!" declares the LORD. Therefore this is what the LORD, the God of Israel, says to the shepherds who tend my people: "Because you have scattered my flock and driven them away and have not bestowed care on them, I will bestow punishment on you for the evil you have done," declares the LORD. "I myself will gather the remnant of my flock out of all the countries where I have driven them and will bring them back to their pasture, where they will be fruitful and increase in number." Here God through the prophet promises the restoration of the church. But he reminds hypocrites that there is no reason for them on that account to flatter themselves, especially the king, his advisers, and the priests. This prophecy is a mixture of promises and warnings. God promises that he will be propitious to the miserable Jews after having punished them, so that the descendants of Abraham will not be entirely cut off. But he also deprives hypocrites of vain confidence, so that they do not falsely apply to themselves the hope of salvation, from which they had excluded themselves by their impiety.

4. "I will place shepherds over them who will tend them, and they will no longer be afraid or terrified, nor will any be missing," declares the LORD. He confirms the promise that he will give them faithful and true pastors who will perform their office as they should. It will not be enough for the sheep to be restored to their folds; they must be fed. We know that a sheep is a silly animal and therefore needs a shepherd to rule and guide it.

5-6. "The days are coming," declares the LORD, "when I will raise up to David a righteous Branch, a King who will reign wisely and do what is just and right in the land. In his days Judah will be saved and Israel will live in safety. This is the name by which he will be called: The LORD Our Righteousness." Here God promises that he will be faithful to the covenant he made with David, because David himself was also faithful and embraced with true faith the promise made to him. God then, as if he would have nothing to do with that perverse and irreclaimable people, but only with his servant David, says, "I will raise up to David a righteous Branch." It is as if he said, "Although you were even a hundred times unworthy of having a Deliverer, yet the memory of David will stay with me forever, for he was perfect and faithful in keeping my covenant." It cannot be doubted that the prophet is speaking about Christ here.

He adds, "**This is the name by which he will be called: The LORD Our Righteousness.**" The prophet shows here that he is not speaking generally about David's posterity, however excellent they may have been, but of the Mediator who had been promised and on whom depended the salvation of the people. And he says his name will be "**The LORD Our Righteousness.**" By saying that God is **Our Righteousness,** the prophet shows that we have a righteousness in common with him, for Christ possesses a righteousness that he communicates to us. Here we do not see Christ coming to show divine justice but to bring righteousness, which would effect salvation. If, then, we want to have God as our righteousness, we must seek Christ, for it cannot be found except in him. Christ is made our righteousness (see 1 Corinthians 1:30), and we are counted the righteousness of God in him. He is not only righteous for himself, but he is our righteousness.

7-8. "**So then, the days are coming,**" declares the LORD, "**when people will no longer say, 'As surely as the LORD lives, who brought the Israelites up out of Egypt,' but they will say, 'As surely as the LORD lives, who brought the descendants of Israel up out of the land of the north and out of all the countries where he had banished them.' Then they will live in their own land.**" The prophet, after speaking about the Redeemer who is to be sent, now sets forth the great favor of God and says it will be so remarkable and glorious that the former redemption will be nothing compared to its greatness and excellency. When the children of Israel were brought out of Egypt, God showed his power by many miracles, so that his favor toward his people might be seen more brightly. But our prophet enhances the second redemption by this comparison: In the future, the kindness with which God favored his people when he delivered them from the slavery of Egypt will not be remembered. Something even more remarkable will be done, and everyone will talk about it and proclaim the immense benefit that God will confer on them in delivering them from their exile in Babylon.

9. **Concerning the prophets: My heart is broken within me; all my bones tremble. I am like a drunken man, like a man overcome by wine, because of the LORD and his holy words.** The prophet here inveighs against the wickedness of the people. The prophets had flattered the king and his princes, as well as the people, and led them astray. Now Jeremiah addresses them, saying that his heart is troubled because of the prophets.

Because of them, he says, his **heart is broken**. Then he says that his **bones** are disjointed, meaning that his mind is most painfully disturbed; what had been his most reliable asset has become weak and altogether feeble.

Then he compares himself to a drunk man. By this metaphor he infers that he was completely stunned and that all his senses were taken from him.

Because of the LORD and his holy words. He brings God before them as judge and avenger. This is like saying, "If they believe there is a God in heaven, it is a wonder that they are so brutish as to dare to boast of his name and yet silently to allow heaven and earth to be mixed together. Where, then, is their reason when they dare so heedlessly to profess a name so fearful and awful? Whenever God's name is mentioned, they should remember not only his goodness and mercy, but also his severity, and then his power, which is dreadful to all the wicked. These people dare to trifle with God in this way—so must not their stupidity be monstrous?" What the prophet means, then, is that it was a wonder that the prophets undertook their office and yet had no concern for the glory of God.

10. **The land is full of adulterers; because of the curse the land lies parched and the pastures in the desert are withered. The prophets follow an evil course and use their power unjustly.** Jeremiah now says why he was so horrified by the awareness that was lacking in the prophets. If things were in good order, or if at least they were tolerable, the prophets would have addressed the Jews more calmly. But with things in disorder and confusion, they had to be vehement.

The land lies parched and the pastures in the desert are withered. In other words, God's judgments are seen in the remotest places; it is not just in the plains, where most people lived, that the land mourns. If anyone climbs the mountains, where only shepherds with their sheep are to be found, even there God's wrath is visible. And the very mountains cry out that God is angry. Yet people still deluded themselves, while at the same time expounding the law. They were God's mouthpiece, and God had given them the job of reproving the people, but they were dumb.

11. **"Both prophet and priest are godless; even in my temple I find their wickedness," declares the LORD.** God through the prophet expands on what he had said about prophets' and priests' impiety. They corrupted the whole service of God, and the true prophets were derided by them. The priests' wickedness in the temple was that they engaged in a kind of trading under cover of the priesthood. So when the prophets trampled on God's service like this and corrupted and perverted the law in order to derive some financial benefit or to acquire power, their impiety was not only seen in the habits of daily life but also in the very temple of God, that is, with regard to the sacerdotal office.

12. **"Therefore their path will become slippery; they will be banished**

to darkness and there they will fall. I will bring disaster on them in the year they are punished," declares the LORD. Here he declares to false prophets and unfaithful priests that the Lord's judgment is close at hand because they have deceived the people.

13-14. "Among the prophets of Samaria I saw this repulsive thing: They prophesied by Baal and led my people Israel astray. And among the prophets of Jerusalem I have seen something horrible: They commit adultery and live a lie. They strengthen the hands of evildoers, so that no one turns from his wickedness. They are all like Sodom to me; the people of Jerusalem are like Gomorrah." These two verses should be read together. The prophet is comparing the false prophets, who had corrupted God's worship in the kingdom of Israel, with those in Jerusalem who wanted to appear more holy and perfect though they were not.

They commit adultery and live a lie. They strengthen the hands of evildoers. In other words, "When anyone is an adulterer, when anyone tries to deceive other people, that is, when anyone is fraudulent, they add to the strength of evildoers." Jeremiah shows how these men surpassed other prophets in impiety by dissimulating when they saw on one hand adulteries and on the other fraud, plundering, and perjury. In addition to this they had to contend with the patronage of the wicked, who strengthened the hands of the ungodly and added audacity to their madness. As fear weakens the hands, so does shame. As these prophets banished shame as well as fear from the wicked and ungodly, they strengthened their hands and gave them more confidence, so that they rushed headlong into every evil more freely and with greater liberty.

15. Therefore, this is what the LORD Almighty says concerning the prophets: "I will make them eat bitter food and drink poisoned water, because from the prophets of Jerusalem ungodliness has spread throughout the land." This verse is addressed to the prophets of the kingdom of Judah. It is like saying, "I will pursue them with every kind of punishment."

16. This is what the LORD Almighty says: "Do not listen to what the prophets are prophesying to you; they fill you with false hopes. They speak visions from their own minds, not from the mouth of the LORD." It must have seemed very severe and must have greatly offended the people for Jeremiah to tell them not to listen to the teaching of the prophets. He was not talking about magicians or impostors, strangers to God's people. He was not talking about Egyptians or Chaldeans or the prophets of Samaria, but of those people who appeared every day in the temple and boasted that they had been divinely chosen and were endued with the spirit of revelation and who professed to only say what God had committed to them. As Jeremiah forbade the people to listen to such men, they must have been very confused: "What does this mean? Why does God allow these unprincipled men to occupy a place in the temple and to exercise a prophetic office there though they are all cheats, perjurers, and impostors?"

17-18. "They keep saying to those who despise me, 'The LORD says: You will have peace.' And to all who follow the stubbornness of their hearts they say, 'No harm will come to you.' But which of them has stood in the council of the LORD to see or to hear his word? Who has listened and heard his word?" Jeremiah introduces another mark by which the false prophets may be distinguished from the true prophets—they flattered the ungodly and wicked people who despised God.

"But which of them has stood in the council of the LORD?" They doubtless spoke in this taunting way to the true prophets: "What! These people announce to you pestilence, war, and famine, as if they were angels sent by God from heaven. Have they stood in the council of God?"

19. "See, the storm of the LORD will burst out in wrath, a whirlwind swirling down on the heads of the wicked." The prophet now attacks the false prophets more vehemently. No people show such audacity as those who oppose God, except when they are totally blinded by Satan.

20. "The anger of the LORD will not turn back until he fully accomplishes the purposes of his heart. In days to come you will understand it clearly." The prophet teaches us that hypocrites will gain nothing from arrogantly opposing God, for they will discover, too late, that God has not spoken in vain.

21. "I did not send these prophets, yet they have run with their message; I did not speak to them, yet they have prophesied." The prophet again warns the Jews not to be perverted by the flattery of false teachers and not to disregard God's warnings.

22. "But if they had stood in my council, they would have proclaimed my words to my people and would have turned them from their evil ways and from their evil deeds." This verse explains the previous one. Its purpose was to convict the false teachers, so they would no longer boast in God's name and falsely pretend they were endued with the prophetic office and glory in that. The prophet says it was clear that they were not God's prophets because they did not faithfully teach what they ought to have derived from the law.

23-24. "Am I only a God nearby," declares the LORD, **"and not a God far away? Can anyone hide in secret places so that I cannot see him?"** declares the LORD. **"Do not I fill heaven and earth?"** declares the LORD. Here the prophet sharply rebukes the hypocrites who thought that they did not need to concern themselves with God, as is always the case with those who delude themselves in their sins. While they profess the truth that God is the judge of the world, they always think they themselves will somehow escape this and that God will forgive them.

25. "I have heard what the prophets say who prophesy lies in my name. They say, 'I had a dream! I had a dream!'" Whenever Jeremiah and those like him, who did their job faithfully, rebuked the people for their sins, these unprincipled men rose up against them and in the name of the prophets flattered the ungodly people who despised God.

26-27. "How long will this continue in the hearts of these lying prophets, who prophesy the delusions of their own minds? They think the dreams they tell one another will make my people forget my name, just as their fathers forgot my name through Baal worship." Here God reproves the false prophets and also promises his people what they especially desired, that he would cleanse his church from such pollution. He then shows that he would punish those false prophets, for they had abused his sacred name. The people kept thinking, "How is it that God permits this? Is it because he does not care about the safety of his people?" Hence God shows here that for a time he bore with the sacrilegious audacity that the false prophets practiced, but that he would at length punish it.

28. "Let the prophet who has a dream tell his dream, but let the one who has my word speak it faithfully. For what has straw to do with grain?" declares the LORD. This means, "Do not let the false prophets through their fallacies impede the course of God's servants, so that his Word should not be reverently heard."

For what has straw to do with grain? This was added because many people might have objected that they could not tell the difference between true and false prophets. God answers them here and says that the difference between true and false teaching was like the difference between **straw** and **grain.** By this comparison he shows how absurd it is for anyone to detract from the authority of the law by claiming that many people interpret it wrongly.

29. "Is not my word like fire," declares the LORD, "and like a hammer that breaks a rock in pieces?" He confirms what he said about straw and grain, using different words. He said that God's Word was grain because souls are nourished by it for a heavenly life. But now he declares it to be like **fire** and like **a hammer.** The Word, which itself is life-giving, is changed into **fire** that consumes and devours them, and it also becomes **a hammer** to break them into pieces and destroy them.

30-32. "Therefore," declares the LORD, "I am against the prophets who steal from one another words supposedly from me. Yes," declares the LORD, "I am against the prophets who wag their own tongues and yet declare, 'The LORD declares.' Indeed, I am against those who prophesy false dreams," declares the LORD. "They tell them and lead my people astray with their reckless lies, yet I did not send or appoint them. They do not benefit these people in the least," declares the LORD. The Lord through Jeremiah returns to the false teachers, who were the authors of all kinds of evils. They fascinated the people with their flatteries, so that all regard for heavenly teaching was squelched. When he adds the words, "They do not benefit these people in the least," he is telling the people to shun the false prophets like the plague.

33. "When these people, or a prophet or a priest, ask you, 'What is the oracle of the LORD?' say to them, 'What oracle? I will forsake you, declares the LORD.'" It is as if God said, "My Word tires you, and I will now avenge myself, for I am tired of putting up with you, for I see that you do not want to be healed. Previously I have been persistent in teaching you, but now I will leave you."

34. "If a prophet or a priest or anyone else claims, 'This is the oracle of the LORD,' I will punish that man and his household." We must note here the wickedness of the human mind. It is God's design to rebuke us in order to save us. This was the end intended by all the true prophets. But what is done by men? They despise this favor. And so God was constrained to warn them about false prophets.

35. "This is what each of you keeps on saying to his friend or relative: 'What is the LORD's answer?' or 'What has the LORD spoken?'" The meaning of this passage is that the Jews, renouncing their blasphemies, were to prepare themselves reverently to hear God's Word, so that no depraved feeling might prevent his Word from being believed. This is what the prophet means when he says, in essence, "You will later change your impious expression and will say, **'What is the LORD's answer?'** or **'What has the LORD spoken?'"** That is, they will come willingly to God's school and will be meek and teachable, so that nothing will stop them from embracing his Word.

36. "But you must not mention 'the oracle of the LORD' again, because every man's own word becomes his oracle and so you distort the words of the living God, the LORD Almighty, our God." Jeremiah continues with the same subject: Everyone should calmly and meekly listen to God speaking. It is as if he said, "Everyone seeks to be his own prophet; and as they all complain against God and will not accept his judgment, no matter how silent God's ministers may be, those false prophets who dare to rise up in this way against God give enough reason to be condemned."

37. "This is what you keep saying to a prophet: 'What is the LORD's answer to you?' or 'What has the LORD spoken?'" He repeats what he said in the previous verse. He means that if we want to benefit from God's school, we must take care that our minds are not preoccupied by any corrupt feeling.

38-39. "Although you claim, 'This is the oracle of the LORD,' this is what the LORD says: You used the words, 'This is the oracle of the LORD,' even though I told you that you must not claim, 'This is the oracle of the LORD.' Therefore, I will surely forget you and cast you out of my presence along with the city I gave to you and your fathers." Jeremiah shows that the Jews had made a great mistake. Their whole way of speaking came from a settled desire to be wicked. They wanted to pour scorn on God's Word, and so they acted in this disdainful way toward God himself. This is the meaning of these verses.

40. "I will bring upon you everlasting disgrace—everlasting shame that will not be forgotten." Although the Jews rightly gloried for a time in being God's special people, this would not benefit them since they had divested themselves of that honor by rejecting the true religion. He warns them that after God takes their glory away, they will stay in perpetual shame.

Jeremiah
Chapter 24

1-2. After Jehoiachin son of Jehoiakim king of Judah and the officials, the craftsmen and the artisans of Judah were carried into exile from Jerusalem to Babylon by Nebuchadnezzar king of Babylon, the LORD showed me two baskets of figs placed in front of the temple of the LORD. One basket had very good figs, like those that ripen early; the other basket had very poor figs, so bad they could not be eaten. This vision means there was no reason for the ungodly to flatter themselves if they continued in their wickedness, although God did bear with them for a time. King Jehoiachin (Jeconiah) had been carried away into exile along with leading men and the craftsmen. The condition of the king and those with him appeared much worse than that of the people who remained in the country, for they still kept alive the hope that the city would flourish again, even though it had been nearly emptied. For everything of any value had been removed by their conquerors, and we know that Nebuchadnezzar was full of avarice and rapacity. The Jews who were left in Jerusalem doubtless flattered themselves that God was dealing with them more kindly than with King Jeconiah. Had they really repented, they would indeed have given thanks to God for having spared them. But as they had abused his forbearance, they had to have set before them the contents of this chapter, since they concluded that God had been more propitious to them than to the rest.

This is shown by the vision. The prophet saw two baskets full of figs in front of the temple. The figs in one basket were sweet, but the figs in the other basket were bitter and could not be eaten. By the sweet figs God represented Jeconiah and the other exiles who had left their country. He compares them to ripe figs, for ripe figs have a sweet taste, while the other figs are rejected on account of their bitterness. In a similar way Jeconiah and the rest had, as it were, been consumed. But there were figs still left. And the prophet says that those whom God had punished in due time were better off than those who remained, as they were accumulating a heavier judgment by their obstinacy. For from the time that Nebuchadnezzar had ransacked the city, those who remained had not stopped adding sins to sins, so that there was a larger portion of divine vengeance ready to fall on them.

3-5. Then the LORD asked me, "What do you see, Jeremiah?" "Figs," I answered. "The good ones are very good, but the poor ones are so bad they cannot be eaten." Then the word of the LORD came to me: "This is what the LORD, the God of Israel, says: 'Like these good figs, I regard as good the exiles from Judah, whom I sent away from this place to the land of the Babylonians.'" Jeremiah remained in Jerusalem and knew how perverse the people left there were. As God had delayed his punishment, they supposed they had completely escaped. To break down this presumption, Jeremiah sets before them this vision, which he had been given from above.

6. "'My eyes will watch over them for their good, and I will bring them back to this land. I will build them up and not tear them down; I will plant them and not uproot them.'" God through Jeremiah confirms what he had said in the previous verse. Although God had punished the exiles severely, he planned to reconcile himself to them. From this it follows that their calamity was lighter than that which was in store for the rest, who resolutely despised God and his prophets.

7. "'I will give them a heart to know me, that I am the LORD. They will be my people, and I will be their God, for they will return to me with all their heart.'" Here is added the main benefit, that God would not only restore the exiles so that they might live in the Promised Land again, but also would change them inwardly.

By **all their heart** is meant sincerity and integrity. See Psalm 119:10-16 and Deuteronomy 4:29; 10:12. We are not being hypocritical toward God when we desire from the heart to give ourselves to him.

8. "'But like the poor figs, which are so bad they cannot be eaten,' says the LORD, 'so will I deal with Zedekiah king of Judah, his officials and the survivors from Jerusalem, whether they remain in this land or live in Egypt.'" God, having promised to deal kindly with the exiles, now declares that he would be more severe in his punishment of King Zedekiah and all the people who stayed in their country.

Whether they remain in this land or live in Egypt. The prophets rebuked them because they relied on Egypt to help them and took shelter under its protection. When they were attacked by their enemies, they fled to Egypt. But later on Nebuchadnezzar conquered Egypt also. So they were only out of danger for a short time.

9. "'I will make them abhorrent and an offense to all the kingdoms of the earth, a reproach and a byword, an object of ridicule and cursing, wherever I banish them.'" Here the prophet uses some words of Moses in order to lend weight to his prophecy. The people were ashamed to reject Moses, for they believed that the law of Moses came from God. They would at least have seen that it was an abominable thing to deny credit to the law. For in Deuteronomy and in other places Moses used this kind of language—that God would hand his people over as a reproach, a proverb, or a taunt to all the nations of the earth (see Deuteronomy 28:37; 1 Kings 9:7). It was as if the prophet said that a time was coming when the Jews would find that Moses' words had not been uttered in vain.

10. "'I will send the sword, famine and plague against them until they are destroyed from the land I gave to them and their fathers.'" Jeremiah confirms what he said in the previous verse—God would punish them severely by allowing the city of Jerusalem and the inhabitants who remained there to be given up to the will of their enemies.

Jeremiah
Chapter 25

1. The word came to Jeremiah concerning all the people of Judah in the fourth year of Jehoiakim son of Josiah king of Judah, which was the first year of Nebuchadnezzar king of Babylon. This prophecy doubtless preceded the vision we have just explained, which had just been presented to Jeremiah when Jehoiakim died and when Zedekiah reigned in the place of Jeconiah. Now Jeremiah relates the prophecy that he was commanded to proclaim in the fourth year of Jehoiakim, who reigned for eleven years. We conclude that Jeremiah's book was composed of various addresses, but that they were not always recorded in the same order in which they were presented. In short, this address means that when God found that the people could not be restored to a right mind through warnings, he pronounced final ruin on the Jews and on all the neighboring nations.

2. So Jeremiah the prophet said to all the people of Judah and to all those living in Jerusalem . . . Jeremiah gives himself the honorable title of **prophet**, implying that he came with the indubitable commands of God.

3-5. For twenty-three years—from the thirteenth year of Josiah son of Amon king of Judah until this very day—the word of the LORD has come to me and I have spoken to you again and again, but you have not listened. And though the LORD has sent you all his servants the prophets again and again, you have not listened or paid any attention. They said, "Turn now, each of you, from your evil ways and your evil practices, and you can stay in the land the LORD gave to you and your fathers for ever and ever."

Jeremiah does not simply accuse the Jews of being impious and ungrateful but adds the sin of perverseness, saying that they were like wild beasts who could not be tamed or corrected. He says that **from the thirteenth year of Josiah son of Amon king of Judah until this very day**, which was twenty-three years, he had not ceased faithfully to perform the office committed to him, but that had accomplished nothing. This shows how incorrigible was their wickedness. This passage teaches that we should immediately return to God when he invites us. Faith is known by its prompt action. As soon as God speaks, we must be attentive, following him at once.

For ever and ever. In other words, "I am prepared to do you good not only for one day or for a short time, but to be kind to you from age to age. It will then be your fault if you are not happy and if this happiness does not pass on from you to your children and grandchildren."

6. **"Do not follow other gods to serve and worship them; do not provoke me to anger with what your hands have made. Then I will not harm you."** The prophet mentions here one kind of sin. The Jews provoked God's wrath in very many ways, but it was their idolatrous superstitions that were responsible for their being severely punished.

"What your hands have made." In other words, "If the Jews are themselves nothing, the idols are less than nothing, for they are only the work of men's hands." In this way the prophet tried to shake the Jews out of their stupid ways. It is as if he said, "Do you not have one particle of right understanding in you? Do you not know that what you worship, you made with your own hands? And what can your hands do? For what are you yourselves?"

7. **"But you did not listen to me," declares the LORD, "and you have provoked me with what your hands have made, and you have brought harm to yourselves."** In other words, "What loss has God suffered by your perverseness? You have indeed tried to deprive him of his glory, for you have adorned your idols by spoils taken from him. But men do not have the power to take any of God's rights from him. He stays perfect forever. So it only turns out to your own ruin when you are rebellious."

8-9. **Therefore the LORD Almighty says this: "Because you have not listened to my words, I will summon all the peoples of the north and my servant Nebuchadnezzar king of Babylon," declares the LORD, "and I will bring them against this land and its inhabitants and against all the surrounding nations. I will completely destroy them and make them an object of horror and scorn, and an everlasting ruin."** Then follows a pronouncement of punishment. The prophet says that God will no longer deal in words but will take action.

"My servant Nebuchadnezzar." The Scriptures show that all mortals obey God whenever he plans to use them. This does not mean that they intend to serve God, but that he, through a secret influence, so rules them and their tongues, their minds and hearts, their hands and their feet, that they are constrained, willingly or unwillingly, to do his will and pleasure. It is in this sense that he calls Nebuchadnezzar **"my servant,"** for that cruel tyrant never meant to offer his service to God. But God used him as his instrument, as if he had been hired by him. And we will see that he is called God's servant elsewhere also.

"I will . . . make them an object of horror and scorn." When we hear about a moderate calamity we are indeed moved to pity; but when the greatness of the evil is beyond belief, we stand amazed, and all our senses are stunned. The prophet means that the calamity that God would bring on the Jews would be, as it were, monstrous and would amaze everyone who heard about it.

10. **"I will banish from them the sounds of joy and gladness, the voices of bride and bridegroom, the sound of millstones and the light of the lamp."** He confirms that the Jews will not be punished in a normal way but will be exposed to extreme distress. Even when everything does not go well for us, marriages may still be celebrated, and some joy may remain. We may still eat and drink and enjoy the necessities of life, even though we may not enjoy its pleasures. But the prophet shows here that the land would be so devastated that there would be no thoughts of marriage, that all hilarity and joy would end, that there would be no preparing food or grinding corn, and that, in short, candlelit feasts would no longer be celebrated.

11. **"This whole country will become a desolate wasteland, and these nations will serve the king of Babylon seventy years."** Here the Lord moderates the severity of their punishment. However grievously the Jews had sinned, God would only punish them for a limited time. After seventy years he would restore them to their own country and restore what they had lost, even living in the Promised Land, along with the holy city and the temple.

12. **"But when the seventy years are fulfilled, I will punish the king of Babylon and his nation, the land of the Babylonians, for their guilt,"** declares the LORD, **"and will make it desolate forever."** The prophet now shows more clearly why the time of exile had been defined. It was so the faithful might know that God would not forget his covenant, even though he deprived the people of the inheritance of the land for a time. These words were not addressed indiscriminately to all the people. The prophet intended them for the benefit of God's elect, who always retained a concern for true religion. If they had not been given this promise, they would have despaired a hundred times and more. This, then, was a special teaching intended as food for God's children.

13. **"I will bring upon that land all the things I have spoken against it, all that are written in this book and prophesied by Jeremiah against all the nations."** God confirms that he would **bring** all that he had **spoken** upon the Chaldeans. That is, he will give effect to all the prophecies, so that it will be evident that Jeremiah foretold nothing rashly, and that it was not for nothing that God had warned them through the mouth of his servant.

14. **"They themselves will be enslaved by many nations and great kings; I will repay them according to their deeds and the work of their hands."** We may again learn from the words of the prophet that God used

Nebuchadnezzar and others, though they did nothing worthy of praise. Had they been without fault, God would have not have been just to punish them. This passage teaches us that although the devil and reprobates carry out God's judgments, they do not deserve any praise for their obedience, for they have no worthy goal in mind.

15. This is what the LORD, the God of Israel, said to me: "Take from my hand this cup filled with the wine of my wrath and make all the nations to whom I send you drink it." There is nothing new here, except that the prophet is, as it were, the interpreter of his previous prophecy. Moreover, he relates a vision in order to lend weight to what is said. He says that he had been given a **cup** by God's **hand.** By this he shows that he had not chosen to come and frighten the Jews and other nations, but that he faithfully proclaimed what had been committed to him. He also intimates that God spoke nothing now except what he meant to carry out shortly.

The metaphor **this cup filled with the wine of my wrath** often occurs in the prophets, but in a different sense. God is sometimes said to make people drunk when he stupefies them and drives them to madness so they become like wild animals. But he is said also to make them drunk when he astonishes them with outward calamities. So now the prophet calls calamity the **cup** of **wrath,** even that calamity that, like fire, was to inflame the minds of all who received no benefit from punishments. Madness, indeed, means nothing but the despair of those who perceive God's hand stretched out against them and thus rage against and curse heaven and earth, themselves, and God. This is what we should understand by **wrath.** The Lord compares his wrath to **wine** because those who are smitten by his hand are carried away, as it were, beyond themselves and do not repent but hand themselves over to furious rage.

16. "When they drink it, they will stagger and go mad because of the sword I will send among them." The prophet says that the calamity of the nations with whom God was angry would be so atrocious that they would become stupefied and insane. They would become frantic, for despair would grip their minds and hearts. They would not be able to entertain any hope of deliverance or to submit to God but would, as is usual with reprobates, rise up against God and pour out blasphemies.

"Because of the sword I will send among them." God would send his sword, but he would extend it now to the Chaldeans, then to the Egyptians, now to the Assyrians, then to other nations, so that they would fight each other with the same sword, until at last it would prove to be the ruin of them all.

17. So I took the cup from the LORD's hand and made all the nations to whom he sent me drink it. The prophet now adds that he obeyed God's command. He intimates that he had no desire to do this, but that necessity was laid on him to do so. He then shows who these nations were.

18. Jerusalem and the towns of Judah, its kings and officials, to make them a ruin and an object of horror and scorn and cursing, as they are today. He begins with **Jerusalem**, just as it is said elsewhere that judgment would begin with the family of God (see 1 Peter 4:17). **As they are today**—the prophet is doubtless referring to the time of the city's destruction. It seems that he was trying to arouse the Jews from their complacency and to show them that in a short time all that he predicted would happen, and that they should not doubt this but think of the calamity as being already before their eyes.

19. Pharaoh king of Egypt, his attendants, his officials and all his people. It may be asked why he links **Pharaoh** with the Jews, mentioning the Egyptians first. The reason is clear—because the Jews expected deliverance from them. The reason for their irreclaimable obstinacy was that they could not be moved from that false confidence into which the devil had lulled them.

20. And all the foreign people there; all the kings of Uz; all the kings of the Philistines (those of Ashkelon, Gaza, Ekron, and the people left at Ashdod). Jeremiah, having spoken of his own nation and of the Egyptians, now mentions other nations that were probably only known by report to the Jews, for some of them were far away. His aim was to show that God's judgment was at hand and that it would extend to the whole world known to the Jews.

21. Edom, Moab and Ammon. He mentions the Idumeans, the descendants of Esau, and the Moabites, who were descendants of Lot, as also were the Ammonites.

22. All the kings of Tyre and Sidon; the kings of the coastlands across the sea. This refers to all those who were beyond the sea. **Tyre and Sidon** would be included in the punishment that was pronounced on both kings and people.

23. Dedan, Tema, Buz and all who are in distant places. He touches only briefly on these places as they were so far away.

24. All the kings of Arabia and all the kings of the foreign people who live in the desert. The prophet now mentions all the kings of Arabia who were the Jews' neighbors on one side. Although **Arabia** was divided into three parts, it was barren where it bordered on Judea and so might be said to be a **desert.**

25. All the kings of Zimri, Elam and Media. He now mentions nations that were more remote but whose fame was known among the Jews. We know that the Elamites, who lived between Media and Persia, were a people of great repute. As for **Media,** it was a very large kingdom and a wealthy one, abounding in many delicacies. **Zimri** was an obscure nation in comparison with the Elamites and the Medes. The prophet, however, intimates that every part of the earth, including the smallest kingdom known to the Jews, would be visited by God's judgment, so that the whole earth would witness that God sits in heaven as judge.

26. And all the kings of the north, near and far, one after the other—all the kingdoms on the face of the earth. The prophet now speaks about **the kings of the north**, who bordered on the king of Babylon.

And after all of them, the king of Sheshach will drink it too. This means that all these nations must drink God's judgment before it falls on Babylon.

27. "Then tell them, 'This is what the LORD Almighty, the God of Israel, says: Drink, get drunk and vomit, and fall to rise no more because of the sword I will send among you.'" Here the prophet returns to what he was saying earlier. He said that a cup was given to him by God's hand, so that he might give it to all nations to drink. He now repeats the same thing, but not in order to bring this message to all the nations. We have said that the benefit arising from these predictions belonged only to the Jews. Neither the Tyrians nor the Sidonians ever knew they were punished by God's hand when they were punished by their enemies. This never crossed their minds. The prophet had not been appointed to be their teacher but was only responsible for warning his own nation.

28. "But if they refuse to take the cup from your hand and drink, tell them, 'This is what the LORD Almighty says: You must drink it!'" In this verse the prophet shows that the nations will be forced to drink this **cup**. To present this in a striking way, he introduces them as refusing to drink the cup. People are indeed as wild as untamed horses, but God is powerful enough to quell such obstinacy.

29. "'See, I am beginning to bring disaster on the city that bears my Name, and will you indeed go unpunished? You will not go unpunished, for I am calling down a sword upon all who live on the earth, declares the LORD Almighty.'" The prophet says that God is now calling for a **sword** to fall on all the inhabitants of the earth. He had often chastised his own people in various ways, while the Gentiles were not in any danger and were free from troubles. But he now says he was calling for a **sword** to destroy all those whom he seemed to have forgiven.

30. "Now prophesy all these words against them and say to them: 'The LORD will roar from on high; he will lift his voice from his holy dwelling and roar mightily against his land. He will shout like those who tread the grapes, shout against all who live on the earth.'" The prophet uses hyperbole to present God speaking in a vehement way so that the complacent will be filled with terror. Those who tread the winepress encourage one another by shouting. One calls to another, and so they encourage each other in this way. So do sailors when they give their shouts. Although God would have no one to rouse him, he himself would be sufficient. "'He will shout like those who tread the grapes, shout against all who live on the earth.'"

31. "'The tumult will resound to the ends of the earth, for the Lord will bring charges against the nations; he will bring judgment on all mankind and put the wicked to the sword,' declares the LORD." Nothing detracts from God's power and authority, as we see when it says that he disputes or contends with people. This is how the clamors that the ungodly raise against him are checked. God condescends to assume the character of an opponent and proposes what is reasonable and just, like someone who tries to agree with his adversary in an attempt to prevent the matter from going to court. This is how God contends with us. Unless we are wholly irreclaimable, we can be restored to his favor, and reconciliation will be ready for us if only we allow him his rights.

32. This is what the LORD Almighty says: "Look! Disaster is spreading from nation to nation; a mighty storm is rising from the ends of the earth." God will not tire of summoning people to judgment but will include the most remote, who thought they were beyond danger. When a storm rises, it seems to threaten only a small part of the country, but it soon spreads itself and covers the whole heavens. God says that his vengeance will be like that, **spreading from nation to nation.**

33. At that time those slain by the LORD will be everywhere—from one end of the earth to the other. They will not be mourned or gathered up or buried, but will be like refuse lying on the ground. This verse explains the previous one. The prophet did not speak about one nation slaughtering another nation but says that God's wrath would spread like a storm to cover all nations and lands. God alone is acting, although elsewhere Jeremiah says that other nations acted as God's ministers in this respect.

34. Weep and wail, you shepherds; roll in the dust, you leaders of the flock. For your time to be slaughtered has come; you will fall and be shattered like fine pottery. The prophet now addresses his words to his own nation. He prophesied about God's judgments so the Jews would know that it would do them no good to look for impunity—the Lord would not pardon the ignorant and those who had no real knowledge, who might have pleaded their ignorance as an excuse. The godly would be comforted by the thought that the ungodly, involved in the same guilt as the other nations, would be subjected to the same judgment. Lastly, the Jews would see that they were different from the other nations, and so flee to God for his mercy.

35. The shepherds will have nowhere to flee, the leaders of the flock no place to escape. He had told the shepherds to wail and the leaders of the flock to roll in the dust. He now gives the reason for this: They would be unable to preserve their lives, even if they fled. It is indeed very miserable when anyone cannot save his life except by going into exile, where he will be poor and despised. But the prophet denies even this to the king and his counselors, as well as to the rich throughout the city and the whole land. They will have nowhere to flee, he says.

36. Hear the cry of the shepherds, the wailing of the leaders of the flock, for the LORD is destroying their pasture. Instead of just repeating the same thing in different words, he adds something even more dreadful: God will make their pastures desolate. He had used this comparison in speaking about the king's counselors and the priests, and he now does the same for others. By **pasture** he means the community, the people, in the city and in the country. It is as if he said that they had until now ruled over a land that was rich and fertile, and in which they enjoyed power and dignity, but now they would be deprived of all these benefits.

37. The peaceful meadows will be laid waste because of the fierce anger of the LORD. He continues with the same subject: Their previously peaceful life will be turned into turmoil and will be destroyed. The Jews had assumed that because they had not previously been disturbed, their future would remain undisturbed as well. But not so.

38. Like a lion he will leave his lair, and their land will become desolate because of the sword of the oppressor and because of the LORD's fierce anger. The prophet reminds us that the Jews' trust in God's protection was in vain, for he would forsake his own temple as well as the city. Hypocrites did not think God could remain faithful to his promises and at the same time allow them to be punished. They could not link these two things together—that God would always remember his covenant and that he would still judge his church. This is why the prophet now says that God, **like a lion**, would **leave his lair.** That is, God would leave his temple. God portrays his power like that of a **lion**, for the Jews would have been afraid if God had not been in control. But as they had expelled him by their vices, he no longer lived with them, and they were exposed to and would be plundered by all the nations. This passage says that as long as God lived in the temple he was **like a lion**, so that by his roaring alone he kept all nations away and defended the children of Abraham. But now, although he had not changed his nature, and although nothing was taken away from his power, the Jews would not be safe, for he would forsake them.

Jeremiah
Chapter 26

1-2. Early in the reign of Jehoiakim son of Josiah king of Judah, this word came from the LORD: "This is what the LORD says: Stand in the courtyard of the LORD's house and speak to all the people of the towns of Judah who come to worship in the house of the LORD. Tell them everything I command you; do not omit a word." This chapter contains a remarkable story, to which a very useful doctrine is annexed, for Jeremiah speaks of repentance, one of the main points of true religion, and he shows at the same time that the people were rejected by God because they perversely despised all warnings and could not be brought to a right mind by any means.

He says this word came to him **early in the reign of Jehoiakim.** This king is spoken about elsewhere, and Jeremiah related other discourses delivered in his reign. We conclude from this that the book of Jeremiah was not collated in chronological order but that different chapters were collected, and from them the volume was formed.

He adds, **"This is what the LORD says: Stand in the courtyard of the LORD's house"** (that is, the temple). People were not allowed to enter the temple, so the prophet was told to stay in the courtyard so everyone could hear him. He announced to all the people God's commands that are recorded here. He had to do this not only for the citizens of Jerusalem, but for *all* the Jews. It is specifically stated that he had to **speak to all the people of the towns of Judah who come to worship in the house of the LORD.** God seems to have anticipated the presumption of those who thought that wrong was being done to them when they were so severely reproved: "What! We have left our wives and our children and have come here to worship God. We have incurred great expense and have undertaken a tough journey in order to worship God. And yet you speak against us. Is that right? Does God reward his servants in such a way?"

3. "Perhaps they will listen and each will turn from his evil way. Then I will relent and not bring on them the disaster I was planning

151

because of the evil they have done." God shows in this verse why he sent his prophet. It would not have been enough for him to announce what he taught unless it was known to have been God's will. Here then God asserts that he will not be propitious to the people unless they comply with what he requires—that is, unless they repent. So he says this teaching will benefit them because it refers to their safety. God, when he saw the people rushing headlong in blind despair to all kinds of impiety, tested them to see if they could be healed. It is as if he said, "What are you doing, you miserable people? You are not yet finished. Just obey me, and that will be the remedy for all your evils." Now we see what God's purpose was: He wanted to give those Jews the hope of mercy, so that they might not reject what he taught when they heard it would be for their good.

From this we deduce a general doctrine. When God is especially displeased with us, it is evidence of his paternal kindness when he favors us with prophetic teaching. And it will bear fruit unless we hinder it. But at the same time it is clear that we are even more inexcusable if we reject that medicine that would certainly give us life. We must understand what the prophet is saying here: He was sent to see if the Jews would repent, for God was ready to receive them.

4-6. "Say to them, 'This is what the LORD says: If you do not listen to me and follow my law, which I have set before you, and if you do not listen to the words of my servants the prophets, whom I have sent to you again and again (though you have not listened), then I will make this house like Shiloh and this city an object of cursing among all the nations of the earth.'" The prophet now summarizes what he had been teaching the people, as he had been commanded to do by God. Unless the Jews walked in God's law and submitted to the prophets, final ruin would overtake the temple and the city.

"'If you do not listen to me and follow my law . . .'" God is saying that he requires obedience most of all, even more than sacrifices. (See 1 Samuel 15:22; Jeremiah 7:22-23.)

"'I will make this house like Shiloh.'" He says this in order to touch their hearts. God's ark had stayed at Shiloh for a long time; so that place might have been thought venerable. Jerusalem was indeed renowned, but Shiloh was so before it. But Shiloh was now forsaken. It presented a degraded spectacle. Jeremiah thus set before them an example of God's vengeance, which also awaited them.

7-8. The priests, the prophets and all the people heard Jeremiah speak these words in the house of the LORD. But as soon as Jeremiah finished telling all the people everything the LORD had commanded him to say, the priests, the prophets and all the people seized him and said, "You must die!" Here the prophet records what happened to him after he declared God's message and faithfully warned the people as God had commanded him.

9. **"Why do you prophesy in the LORD's name that this house will be like Shiloh and this city will be desolate and deserted?" And all the people crowded around Jeremiah in the house of the LORD.** Here is added the cause of Jeremiah's condemnation: He had dared to threaten the holy city and the temple with such severity. They did not ask if God had commanded that this should be done or whether he had any just reason for doing so. They assumed that God was being attacked when anything was said against his sacred city or temple. This is the argument the priests and prophets used to condemn Jeremiah.

10. **When the officials of Judah heard about these things, they went up from the royal palace to the house of the LORD and took their places at the entrance of the New Gate of the LORD's house.** The rulers were aroused by the clamor. Doubtless the king sent them to quell the commotion.

11. **Then the priests and the prophets said to the officials and all the people, "This man should be sentenced to death because he has prophesied against this city. You have heard it with your own ears!"** From this we conclude that the people assented to the sentence of the priests and prophets, even though they had not expressed their own judgment. So all classes of people condemned Jeremiah. It was as if the mob followed the directions of the priests and prophets, saying, "Yes, yes, we agree!" Jeremiah was condemned by **all the people** (verses 8, 11). But it must be seen that people are like the sea, which of itself is calm and tranquil, but as soon as any wind arises there is a great commotion, and waves crash into each other. In the same way the people were quiet and peaceful before they were stirred up. But sedition is easily raised when thoughtless people are excited.

12. **Then Jeremiah said to all the officials and all the people: "The LORD sent me to prophesy against this house and this city all the things you have heard."** Jeremiah simply pleads his own calling and God's command. In this way he refutes the preposterous charge they brought against him.

13. **"Now reform your ways and your actions and obey the LORD your God. Then the LORD will relent and not bring the disaster he has pronounced against you."** He not only confirms here what he had taught but also reproves the hardness and obstinate wickedness of the priests and prophets. Although he was addressing the rulers and the people, he doubtless intended for his message to hit home to all the ungodly people who opposed God.

14-15. **"As for me, I am in your hands; do with me whatever you think is good and right. Be assured, however, that if you put me to death, you will bring the guilt of innocent blood on yourselves and on** this city and on those who live in it, for in truth the LORD has sent me to you to speak all these words in your hearing." Jeremiah, after exhorting the rulers, the priests, and all the people to repent, now speaks about himself and warns them not to indulge their cruelty by carrying out their desire to kill him, for they had passed a death sentence on him. Jeremiah saw their rage as being so great that he almost despaired of his life. But he declares here that God will avenge him if they vent their fury on him.

16. Then the officials and all the people said to the priests and the prophets, "This man should not be sentenced to death! He has spoken to us in the name of the LORD our God." Jeremiah shows here that the sentence passed on him was soon changed. The priests and false prophets, in their blind rage, had condemned the holy prophet to death. He now says that he was acquitted by the rulers and the king's counselors, and also by the people.

17-18. Some of the elders of the land stepped forward and said to the entire assembly of people, "Micah of Moresheth prophesied in the days of Hezekiah king of Judah. He told all the people of Judah, 'This is what the LORD Almighty says: Zion will be plowed like a field, Jerusalem will become a heap of rubble, the temple hill a mound overgrown with thickets.'" What is recounted here is found in Micah 3:12. The prophet Micah had the same contest with the priests and prophets as Jeremiah had, for they said it was impossible for God to pour his vengeance on the holy city and the temple. They said, "Is not the Lord in the middle of us?" They also affirmed, "No evil will come on us." They were drunk with complacency and thought they were out of all danger. They ignored all the warnings of the prophets because they imagined that God was bound to them. We know that hypocrites have always relied on God's promise, "I dwell here." They took the words that God had uttered and twisted them, saying, "God lives in the midst of us, and therefore nothing bad will ever happen to us." But the prophet said, **"Zion will be plowed like a field, Jerusalem will become a heap of rubble, the temple hill a mound overgrown with thickets."**

19. "Did Hezekiah king of Judah or anyone else in Judah put him to death?" By the example of the pious King Hezekiah, they exhorted the people to show kindness and docility and showed that it honored both God and his prophets not to be angry about his warnings and reproofs. **"Did not Hezekiah fear the LORD and seek his favor? And did not the LORD relent, so that he did not bring the disaster he pronounced against them?"** They confirmed what Jeremiah had previously said: The only remedy was to submit themselves calmly to prophetic instruction and at the same time to flee to God's mercy. The **fear** of God here means true conversion. What else is fear of God other than submitting to his will because he is a Father and a Sovereign? Whoever acknowledges God like this will obey him. Therefore the elders meant that Hezekiah and all the people really turned to God.

20-23. (Now Uriah son of Shemaiah from Kiriath Jearim was another man who prophesied in the name of the LORD; he prophesied the same things against this city and this land as Jeremiah did. When King Jehoiakim and all his officers and officials heard his words, the king sought to put him to death. But Uriah heard of it and fled in fear to Egypt. King Jehoiakim, however, sent Elnathan son of Acbor to Egypt, along with some other men. They brought Uriah out of Egypt and took him to King Jehoiakim, who had him struck down with a sword and his body thrown into the burial place of the common people.) Another example is cited, which was similar but different: The king was different, but the prophet was the same. Uriah, who faithfully carried out his office, is mentioned here. But Jehoiakim could not stand his preaching and so killed him.

They brought Uriah out of Egypt. Something very shameful is set before us. Uriah was forced back to the land he had fled from and was brought before the king, who then cruelly killed him with a sword. Not satisfied with that barbarous act, the king made sure Uriah was buried ignominiously. All these details seem to show that these words may be applied to the holy men who defended the cause of Jeremiah rather than to his enemies.

24. Furthermore, Ahikam son of Shaphan supported Jeremiah, and so he was not handed over to the people to be put to death. An example of courage and perseverance is set before us. It is not enough to defend a good cause from a position of safety if we are not prepared to be ill-treated and despised and to accept all kinds of danger. We are also taught here how much influence one man wields when he boldly defends a good cause, risking everything for God and his ministers.

Jeremiah
Chapter 27

1-5. Early in the reign of Zedekiah son of Josiah king of Judah, this word came to Jeremiah from the LORD: This is what the LORD said to me: "Make a yoke out of straps and crossbars and put it on your neck. Then send word to the kings of Edom, Moab, Ammon, Tyre and Sidon through the envoys who have come to Jerusalem to Zedekiah king of Judah. Give them a message for their masters and say, 'This is what the LORD Almighty, the God of Israel, says: "Tell this to your masters: With my great power and outstretched arm I made the earth and its people and the animals that are on it, and I give it to anyone I please."'" This command was given to Jeremiah at the beginning of Jehoiakim's reign but was not carried out until the time of Zedekiah. It was God's plan to strengthen Jeremiah during this time, for he would have otherwise collapsed.

As kings are inflated with pride, the Lord uses this preface to say that he **"made the earth and its people and the animals that are on it."** He does not speak about heaven but only mentions that he made the earth and its people and animals by his great power and outstretched arm. He said this to remind people that the earth continues as it is only by God's power, which created it in the first place. The same power preserves men and animals, for nothing is safe unless God uses his secret, heavenly power. This is why these words are introduced here. God set his own arm and power in opposition to the pride of those who thought they stood in their own power and did not acknowledge that they were entirely dependent on God, who sustained them for as long as he pleased and then overthrew them and reduced them to nothing when it seemed good to him.

6-7. "'Now I will hand all your countries over to my servant Nebuchadnezzar king of Babylon; I will make even the wild animals subject to him. All nations will serve him and his son and his grandson until the time for his land comes; then many nations and great kings will subjugate him.'" God had claimed for himself the government of the whole earth and had shown that he has the power to elevate and crush the nations. He now decrees that he will make all the neighboring lands, including Tyre and Sidon, Moab, Ammon, Edom, and even Judah itself, subject to the king of Babylon. If Jeremiah had started off by saying that God had given King Nebuchadnezzar these lands, the prediction would not have been so readily accepted, for human pride would have been a barrier to this. But the preface served to show that they should not think they could stand against God's will. The Lord of heaven now declares that King Nebuchadnezzar will be lord over Judah as well as over the surrounding countries, for God would set him over these lands.

8. ""If, however, any nation or kingdom will not serve Nebuchadnezzar king of Babylon or bow its neck under his yoke, I will punish that nation with the sword, famine and plague, declares the LORD, until I destroy it by his hand."" God had issued his decree through the mouth of Jeremiah, and now he adds a warning himself, so that the Jews as well as others would accept willingly the yoke placed on them. The prophet had the Jews especially in mind here, but he extended it to apply to foreign nations. Now we see why this prediction about punishment was added. It should have been sufficient to say that Nebuchadnezzar was God's servant and that he would subdue Judah. But it was hard for the Jews to accept this enemy, let alone submit to him. So it was necessary to issue this warning: "Be alert about what you do, for you are not stronger than God." The people were so evil that they would have refused to accept Nebuchadnezzar's authority if they had not been warned like this.

9. ""So do not listen to your prophets, your diviners, your interpreters of dreams, your mediums or your sorcerers who tell you, 'You will not serve the king of Babylon.'"" Jeremiah had declared to the king, as well as to the citizens, that they would not escape the impending punishment, and now he shatters the vain confidence they placed in themselves.

10. ""They prophesy lies to you that will only serve to remove you far from your lands; I will banish you and you will perish."" This verse confirms that what God had to say through Jeremiah was meant for the Jews, for what is said here could not apply to godless nations. So what was said about **diviners . . . interpreters of dreams . . . mediums . . . sorcerers** in verse 9 also applied to the false prophets who deceived the miserable people.

""To remove you far from your lands."" Jeremiah now says in essence, "The false prophets only seek to drive you far away from your country. For they want you to think that you will be free from all punishment. But God is prepared to deal with you gently. Although he will not completely pass over all your vices, your punishment will be easy to bear, for you will remain in your own country. But if you believe these impostors, they will lead you into distant exile. For God says, **I will banish you, and you will perish.**"

11. ""**But if any nation will bow its neck under the yoke of the king of Babylon and serve him, I will let that nation remain in its own land to till it and to live there, declares the LORD.**"" When people submit to God's judgment, they receive his favor, so that heaven and earth and all the elements serve them. But the more people raise their horns of pride against God, the more enslaved they become. Their own chains bind them more firmly than anything else as they struggle with God and do not humble themselves under his mighty hand.

12. I gave the same message to Zedekiah king of Judah. I said, "Bow your neck under the yoke of the king of Babylon; serve him and his people, and you will live." This verse supports our view that what we have just expounded was spoken especially to the chosen people. For Jeremiah tells us here that he spoke to King Zedekiah, and in verse 16 he adds that he spoke to the priests and to the people. He was not sent as a teacher to the Moabites, the Tyrians, and other foreign nations. God had prescribed to him his limits, and he was to keep within them. That is why he says that he gave the same message to Zedekiah of Judah.

13. "Why will you and your people die by the sword, famine and plague with which the LORD has threatened any nation that will not serve the king of Babylon?" As they would not be moved by God's kindness, the prophet now adds, "Take note, for unless you receive the life offered to you, you must inevitably perish. Therefore you, Zedekiah, along with all your people, will be eternally destroyed if you continue to oppose God."

14. "Do not listen to the words of the prophets who say to you, 'You will not serve the king of Babylon,' for they are prophesying lies to you." This repetition is not superfluous, for he had a tough battle against the false prophets, who had acquired great authority. As Jeremiah alone attacked them all, most of them could have objected and said that in such complex matters nothing is clear or certain. So it was not easy to convince the Jews, who were inclined to believe the false prophets. It was necessary to repeat the same thing often.

15. "'I have not sent them,' declares the LORD. 'They are prophesying lies in my name. Therefore, I will banish you and you will perish, both you and the prophets who prophesy to you.'" The Lord confirms that Jeremiah has been sent by God. The prophet proclaims this to show the Jews that they should not accept mindlessly everything presented to them that claimed to come from God. They were to exercise discrimination and judgment. This passage should be carefully noted because the devil has always falsely assumed God's name.

16. Then I said to the priests and all these people, "This is what the LORD says: Do not listen to the prophets who say, 'Very soon

now the articles from the LORD's house will be brought back from Babylon.' They are prophesying lies to you." Jeremiah now adds this clear explanation—namely, that the Jews had been warned not to accept a false prophecy about the restoration of the vessels of the temple. To make the people believe their future was secure, the false prophets boasted, "The splendor of the temple will shortly be restored. The vessels that Nebuchadnezzar has taken away will return along with the exiles, and everything that has decayed will be restored." But Jeremiah said that what they had promised was false. "Do not believe them," he says, "when they say to you, 'Very soon now the articles from the LORD's house will be brought back from Babylon.' The king of Babylon will either be constrained to restore what he has taken away, or he will restore it of his own accord."

17. "Do not listen to them. Serve the king of Babylon, and you will live. Why should this city become a ruin?" In short, he declared to the Jews that a most awful condemnation awaited them if they allowed the city to perish through their own fault, and that they would be responsible for their own ruin if they did not submit to the yoke of the king of Babylon.

18. "If they are prophets and have the word of the LORD, let them plead with the LORD Almighty that the furnishings remaining in the house of the LORD and in the palace of the king of Judah and in Jerusalem not be taken to Babylon." Here the prophet laughs to scorn the foolish confidence with which the false prophets were taken when they promised nothing but happiness for the future. So he says they were not to be believed concerning the prosperity they prophesied but on the contrary should dread a most terrible punishment.

He says that if they are prophets and have the word of the Lord, let them plead with the Lord to keep what remained from being taken from Jerusalem. But in fact what still remained in the temple and in the king's palace and in the whole city would be taken off to Babylon. We now see what God's prophet is trying to say. He is comparing the future with the past and is showing that these impostors are foolish to promise a better state of things when God's heavy judgment is about to fall on them.

19-22. "For this is what the LORD Almighty says about the pillars, the Sea, the movable stands and the other furnishings that are left in this city, which Nebuchadnezzar king of Babylon did not take away when he carried Jehoiachin son of Jehoiakim king of Judah into exile from Jerusalem to Babylon, along with all the nobles of Judah and Jerusalem—yes, this is what the LORD Almighty, the God of Israel, says about the things that are left in the house of the LORD and in the palace of the king of Judah and in Jerusalem: 'They will be taken to Babylon and there they will remain until the day I come for them,' declares the LORD. 'Then I will bring them back and restore them to this place.'" He now repeats and confirms that what still stayed in Jerusalem will be taken away by their enemies, the Babylonians, who will attack them. Nebuchadnezzar had spared part of the temple and part of the city. He had taken away the most precious vessels but had not completely denuded the temple of all its decorations. Since some of its splendor still remained, the Jews should have seen that God had been kind to them. He now says that the temple and the city will be totally destroyed.

Jeremiah confirms that the people will remain in exile until the day of God's visitation—that is, for seventy years. When God says, **"Then I will bring them back and restore them to this place,"** he is referring to what later happened under Cyrus' command.

Jeremiah
Chapter 28

1-2. In the fifth month of that same year, the fourth year, early in the reign of Zedekiah king of Judah, the prophet Hananiah son of Azzur, who was from Gibeon, said to me in the house of the LORD in the presence of the priests and all the people: "This is what the LORD Almighty, the God of Israel, says: 'I will break the yoke of the king of Babylon.'" The prophet now relates how the haughty, false prophet Hananiah came forward to deceive the people.

The fourth year might be the beginning of Zedekiah's reign, as the first three years were so disturbed that the king possessed very little authority and hardly dared to ascend the throne.

3. "'Within two years I will bring back to this place all the articles of the LORD's house that Nebuchadnezzar king of Babylon removed from here and took to Babylon.'" We now see that what Hananiah had in mind was to promise impunity to the people, and not only this, but also to soothe them with false confidence, as if the people would soon have their king restored, together with the spoils the enemy had taken away.

4. "'I will also bring back to this place Jehoiachin son of Jehoiakim king of Judah and all the other exiles from Judah who went to Babylon,' declares the LORD, 'for I will break the yoke of the king of Babylon.'" Hananiah promises, as if to the king himself, what he has just predicted about the vessels of the temple and of the palace.

5-6. Then the prophet Jeremiah replied to the prophet Hananiah before the priests and all the people who were standing in the house of the LORD. He said, "Amen! May the LORD do so! May the LORD fulfill the words you have prophesied by bringing the articles of the LORD's house and all the exiles back to this place from Babylon." Jeremiah has been given a twofold message—to expose the vices of the people, and to show that the Jews were unworthy to inherit the land, for they had broken God's covenant and despised God and his law. He told them they would not be allowed to escape unpunished. All this greatly displeased the people. It was therefore Jeremiah's object to turn aside the false suspicion under which he labored, and he testified that he desired nothing more than the well-being of the people. So he said, "**Amen! May the LORD do so!**" "May it happen in this way. I would willingly retract, and that with shame, all that I have predicted so far, so great is my care and anxiety for the safety of the public. For I would prefer the welfare of all the people to my own reputation." But he later added that the promise of Hananiah was totally in vain, and that nothing would save the people from the calamity that was close at hand.

7-9. "**Nevertheless, listen to what I have to say in your hearing and in the hearing of all the people: From early times the prophets who preceded you and me have prophesied war, disaster and plague against many countries and great kingdoms. But the prophet who prophesies peace will be recognized as one truly sent by the LORD only if his prediction comes true.**" Jeremiah, having testified that he did not wish any harm on his own people but had goodwill toward them, now adds that what he predicted is yet more true. He shows that he wants nothing more than the welfare and the safety of his people, and yet it is not in his power, or in the power of any mortal, to change the heavenly decree that he pronounced. We see from this that God had so influenced the hearts and minds of his servants that they were not cruel or unfeeling. However, they did not allow themselves to be too influenced by people but boldly declared what God had commanded them.

Jeremiah's object was to show that all who predicted that something would happen that did not take place were guilty of falsehood. Such people were not sent by God. When therefore the prophets spoke of **peace**, that is, prosperity, or of **war, disaster and plague**, when experience proved true what they had said, their own authority was at the same time confirmed, as if God had shown that they had been sent by him.

10-11. Then the prophet Hananiah took the yoke off the neck of the prophet Jeremiah and broke it, and he said before all the people, "This is what the LORD says: 'In the same way will I break the yoke of Nebuchadnezzar king of Babylon off the neck of all the nations within two years.'" It was not enough for the impostor to resist the holy servant of God to his face, but he also had to lay sacrilegious hands on the visible symbol through which God had testified that the prophet's message was true.

At this, the prophet Jeremiah went on his way. The prophet's words intimate that he left the place because he was unwilling to dispute with such a violent person. Hananiah probably had great power in the temple, for his prophecies seemed plausible.

12-13. Shortly after the prophet Hananiah had broken the yoke off the neck of the prophet Jeremiah, the word of the LORD came to Jeremiah: "Go and tell Hananiah, 'This is what the LORD says: You have broken a wooden yoke, but in its place you will get a yoke of iron.'" Jeremiah had withdrawn from the crowd and was later sent by God. This was the reason he was silent for a short time.

14. "'This is what the LORD Almighty, the God of Israel, says: I will put an iron yoke on the necks of all these nations to make them serve Nebuchadnezzar king of Babylon, and they will serve him. I will even give him control over the wild animals.'" Nebuchadnezzar had indeed already subdued all these other nations. But the prophet means that the dominion of the king of Babylon would continue even though Hananiah had said it would only stand for two years. A long time is contrasted with a short time. It is as if he said, "Let the nations chafe and fret as much as they like—they will still be ruled by King Nebuchadnezzar. It will be pointless for them to try and extricate themselves, for God has delivered them into slavery."

15. Then the prophet Jeremiah said to Hananiah the prophet, "Listen, Hananiah! The LORD has not sent you, yet you have per-suaded this nation to trust in lies." This refutation should be remembered whenever we contend with Satan's ministers and false teachers. Whatever they may pretend, and however they mask their lies, this one thing should be enough to put an end to their boasting—they have not been sent by the Lord!

16. "Therefore, this is what the LORD says: 'I am about to remove you from the face of the earth. This very year you are going to die, because you have preached rebellion against the LORD.'" Here is added the punishment that confirmed Jeremiah's prophecy.

17. In the seventh month of that same year, Hananiah the prophet died. All those who had disregarded Jeremiah saw before their eyes God's judgment. No surer confirmation could have been expected by the Jews, had they a particle of understanding, than to see the impostor killed as predicted by the word of Jeremiah.

Jeremiah
Chapter 29

1. **This is the text of the letter that the prophet Jeremiah sent from Jerusalem to the surviving elders among the exiles and to the priests, the prophets and all the other people Nebuchadnezzar had carried into exile from Jerusalem to Babylon.** Here the prophet begins a new discourse. He not only spoke out constantly at Jerusalem, saying that the Jews who stayed there should repent, but he also comforted the exiles in their grief, exhorting them to hope for their return and to patiently endure the punishment they were experiencing. The prophet had two aims in mind as he did this. He not only wanted to encourage the exiles, but he also wanted to break down the obstinacy of his own nation, so that those who remained in Jerusalem and in Judea would link themselves to their other brethren.

2. **(This was after King Jehoiachin and the queen mother, the court officials and the leaders of Judah and Jerusalem, the craftsmen and the artisans had gone into exile from Jerusalem.)** He mentions the time when the letter was sent—after the calamity had happened, when King Jeconiah and his mother were driven into exile, and Zedekiah, his successor, was made governor in his place.

3-6. **He entrusted the letter to Elasah son of Shaphan and to Gemariah son of Hilkiah, whom Zedekiah king of Judah sent to King Nebuchadnezzar in Babylon. It said: This is what the LORD Almighty, the God of Israel, says to all those I carried into exile from Jerusalem to Babylon: "Build houses and settle down; plant gardens and eat what they produce. Marry and have sons and daughters; find wives for your sons and give your daughters in marriage, so that they too may have sons and daughters. Increase in number there; do not decrease."** This is the substance of the message, which the prophet undoubtedly explained in greater detail. He said he was sending his letter by the hand of the king's ambassadors.

God commanded the exiles to **"build houses"** in Chaldea, to **"plant**

167

gardens," and to **"marry and have sons and daughters,"** as if they were at home. It does not mean that it was God's purpose for them to set their hearts on Chaldea; on the contrary, they were always to keep their return in mind. But until the end of the seventy years, it was God's will that their minds should continue to be quiet and to live as if they were in their own country.

7. "Also, seek the peace and prosperity of the city to which I have carried you into exile. Pray to the LORD for it, because if it prospers, you too will prosper." Jeremiah goes further. He implies that the Jews had been led to Babylon in order to give willing obedience to the authority of King Nebuchadnezzar and to testify to this by their prayers. He not only tells them to patiently endure the punishment laid on them but also to be faithful subjects to their conqueror.

8-9. Yes, this is what the LORD Almighty, the God of Israel, says: "Do not let the prophets and diviners among you deceive you. Do not listen to the dreams you encourage them to have. They are prophesying lies to you in my name. I have not sent them," declares the LORD. Almost everyone's mind was taken up with the vain and false confidence they had imbibed from false prophecies—namely, that they would return after two years. The prophet reminds them to beware of such impostures.

10. This is what the LORD says: "When seventy years are completed for Babylon, I will come to you and fulfill my gracious promise to bring you back to this place." In order to expose the dreams by which the false prophets had made people drunk, the Lord through Jeremiah repeats what he had already said, that the end of their exile could not be expected until the end of seventy years. This method of teaching should be particularly observed, for God's truth will always dissipate the mists in which Satan never ceases to envelop the pure truth.

11. "For I know the plans I have for you," declares the LORD, "plans to prosper you and not to harm you, plans to give you hope and a future." There is here an implied contrast between the certain counsel of God and the vain imaginations in which the Jews indulged themselves. See Isaiah 55:9. They were used to measuring God by their own ideas.

Plans to give you hope and a future. It was no small trial when the Jews were deprived of the land that was God's dwelling place. It was as if all hope had been cut off. But here God declares that he will put an end to their exile, for it is to last only for a limited time. From this we infer that the people did not perish when they were led into exile but were only being chastised by God's hand.

12. "Then you will call upon me and come and pray to me, and I will listen to you." God promises to listen to them when they begin to pray.

13. "You will seek me and find me when you seek me with all your heart." There is no doubt that the Jews groaned a thousand times every year when oppressed by the Chaldeans, for they had to bear all kinds of reproaches, and they had nothing safe or secure. So they would have become harder than iron if they had not offered up prayers. But God shows that the right time would not come until their prayers proceeded from a right feeling; this is what he means by **with all your heart.** Of course, people never turn to God with their whole heart, nor is the whole heart engaged in prayer as much as it should be. But the prophet contrasts the whole heart with the double heart. So we should understand here not perfection (which can never be found in human beings) but integrity and sincerity.

14. **"I will be found by you,"** declares the LORD, **"and will bring you back from captivity. I will gather you from all the nations and places where I have banished you,"** declares the LORD, **"and will bring you back to the place from which I carried you into exile."** We may deduce a helpful doctrine from this. God in a wonderful way gathers his church when scattered, to make it into one body, even though for a time he may obliterate its name and even its very appearance. Thus we see that this prophecy has not just been fulfilled once. God has often manifested the grace that is here set forth, and he still manifests it in gathering his church.

15-17. **You may say, "The LORD has raised up prophets for us in Babylon,"** but this is what the LORD says about the king who sits on David's throne and all the people who remain in this city, your countrymen who did not go with you into exile—yes, this is what the LORD Almighty says: **"I will send the sword, famine and plague against them and I will make them like poor figs that are so bad they cannot be eaten."** Jeremiah urges the exiles not to allow themselves to be led astray. Indirectly he is reproving them because they could not bear a condition that was better than the others still in the land. To put it another way, "Why are you being so unreasonable? All your ways are closed up against you, and the power of your conqueror is so great that you cannot move a finger without his approval, and yet you think you will be set free in two years! If you used to be foolishly secure and confident, your calamities ought to make you humble. But your brethren, who seem still to enjoy freedom because they live in Jerusalem, suffer more than you do."

The prophet has addressed the exiles and now turns his attention to King Zedekiah and the Jews who are still in their own country. From this the exiles will see how foolish they have been to promise themselves they will return to their land when they had been driven to a remote land and when final ruin is about to fall on the king and people remaining in Jerusalem.

18-19. **"I will pursue them with the sword, famine and plague and will make them abhorrent to all the kingdoms of the earth and an object of cursing and horror, of scorn and reproach, among all the nations where I drive them. For they have not listened to my words,"** declares the LORD, **"words that I sent to them again and again by** my servants the prophets. And you exiles have not listened either," declares the LORD. God through Jeremiah continues with the same subject—namely, that God will go on consuming them with pestilence, famine, and the sword until he totally destroys them, according to what we find in Jeremiah 24. He repeats what is said in that chapter, but the words are taken from Deuteronomy 28—29. The prophets, we know, drew the substance of their doctrine from the fountain of the law and, strictly speaking, introduced nothing new but accommodated the teaching of Moses to the circumstances of the time in which each lived.

20-21. **Therefore, hear the word of the LORD, all you exiles whom I have sent away from Jerusalem to Babylon. This is what the LORD Almighty, the God of Israel, says about Ahab son of Kolaiah and Zedekiah son of Maaseiah, who are prophesying lies to you in my name: "I will hand them over to Nebuchadnezzar king of Babylon, and he will put them to death before your very eyes."** Jeremiah announces a special prophecy but confirms his previous doctrine. His object is still the same—to stop the exiles' listening to flatteries and to make them feel sure that they are to bear their exile until the end of seventy years. But he speaks in this passage of three impostors. He links two of them together and mentions the third one on his own (verse 24). He directs his discourse especially to all the exiles; he is not addressing those who professed to be God's enemies and sold themselves to the devil in order to deceive people; it is useless to waste time on them. Rather he addresses the whole people and at the same time foretells what will happen to the two false prophets **Ahab** and **Zedekiah.**

The meaning of the prophecy is that a judgment will soon overtake them, for they will be killed by King Nebuchadnezzar. They were in exile, but such madness had possessed them that they did not hesitate to provoke the wrath of the tyrant whom they knew to be cruel and bloodthirsty. Jeremiah declares that since they have deceived the people, they will soon be punished—Nebuchadnezzar will kill them. Doubtless Nebuchadnezzar saw how he could benefit from this. These false prophets did not stop encouraging the hope of a speedy return, and unless this was checked, it was bound to end in frequent disturbances. Therefore Nebuchadnezzar, as is usual with earthly kings, saw how he could use the situation to his own advantage. At the same time he was unknowingly God's servant, for these two impostors, who had promised that the people would return, were to be exposed to contempt. Their death revealed their vanity, for that event showed they were not sent by God. It is indeed true that God's faithful servants are often treated cruelly and are even killed by the ungodly. But it was a different matter in the case of these two. They were not killed because they made some unpopular prophecy but because they said that the people would soon return to their own country. From their death it could be concluded that whatever they had promised about the return of the people was false.

22. "Because of them, all the exiles from Judah who are in Babylon will use this curse: 'The LORD treat you like Zedekiah and Ahab, whom the king of Babylon burned in the fire.'" If Jeremiah had only spoken about their death, the Jews might still have doubted that Jeremiah's words were a genuine prophecy. But now that he adds how they would be punished, and that this punishment would be most unusual, so they would see that Jeremiah's prophecy was genuine. If the king had ordered the exiles to be killed with the sword, people would not have thought anything unusual had taken place. But it never occurred to anyone that they would be **burned in the fire.** We see here that God left no room for doubt in the perverse minds of the people, for he specified the exact death they would undergo.

23. "For they have done outrageous things in Israel; they have committed adultery with their neighbors' wives and in my name have spoken lies, which I did not tell them to do. I know it and am a witness to it," declares the LORD. We see why the prophet mentions the reason for their death. It was so that the Jews would not merely see the event according to their own thoughts but would be sure God was taking vengeance on the impiety of those who had falsely prophesied in his name. Often when we focus on the immediate cause of an event, we neglect to take into account God's judgments. To correct this evil, Jeremiah again repeats that Zedekiah and Ahab were not being punished by the king of Babylon but by God himself, **"for they have done outrageous things in Israel."**

24-27. Tell Shemaiah the Nehelamite, "This is what the LORD Almighty, the God of Israel, says: You sent letters in your own name to all the people in Jerusalem, to Zephaniah son of Maaseiah the priest, and to all the other priests. You said to Zephaniah, 'The LORD has appointed you priest in place of Jehoiada to be in charge of the house of the LORD; you should put any madman who acts like a prophet into the stocks and neck-irons. So why have you not reprimanded Jeremiah from Anathoth, who poses as a prophet among you?'" Here Jeremiah prophesies about a third person, who had written a letter to the priests and to all the people against the prophet. This person expostulated with the chief priests and with others because Jeremiah had, with impunity, urged the people to suffer their long exile. Shemaiah had not only encouraged the people, as others did, to hope for a speedy return but had tried to put Jeremiah in such a bad light that he would be killed as a false prophet, as an enemy of the public good, as well as of the law and the temple.

28-29. "'He has sent this message to us in Babylon: It will be a long time. Therefore build houses and settle down; plant gardens and eat

what they produce.'" Zephaniah the priest, however, read the letter to Jeremiah the prophet.

The crime Jeremiah was accused of was that he made the exiles indifferent to their captivity and disregarded their own country. But Jeremiah's purpose was quite different: He wanted the people to look forward to their eventual return to their land. So Jeremiah was reproached, as if he were indifferent to the long delay.

30-32. Then the word of the LORD came to Jeremiah: "Send this message to all the exiles: 'This is what the LORD says about Shemaiah the Nehelamite: Because Shemaiah has prophesied to you, even though I did not send him, and has led you to believe a lie, this is what the LORD says: I will surely punish Shemaiah the Nehelamite and his descendants. He will have no one left among this people, nor will he see the good things I will do for my people, declares the LORD, because he has preached rebellion against me.'" Here Jeremiah declares that this impostor will not escape punishment, because he has claimed to speak in God's name and yet is directly opposed to Jeremiah. In sum, Shemaiah will not see God's favor, and none of his descendants will remain alive. (It was well known that a person who died childless was cursed under the law; see Deuteronomy 28:18.) This prophecy was intended to benefit the people in exile, to lead them to repentance, no matter how late in the day it was. This is the import of the passage.

Jeremiah
Chapter 30

1-3. This is the word that came to Jeremiah from the LORD: "This is what the LORD, the God of Israel, says: 'Write in a book all the words I have spoken to you. The days are coming,' declares the LORD, 'when I will bring my people Israel and Judah back from captivity and restore them to the land I gave their forefathers to possess,' says the LORD." This chapter, and the next one, contain a most important truth. To make the people more attentive to it, God introduces these prophecies with a preface.

Ungodly people always run to extremes. At one moment they are inflated with pride, and the next moment they are totally disheartened and fall into the abyss of despair. God saw that this would be the case with the people if he did not come to their aid. So he proposes here the best remedy—that the prophet, as he had not effected anything through his speaking, should as it were convert what he had said into writing and deeds or acts, so that after two years they might be encouraged and afterwards acknowledge that they had been deceived by unprincipled men and then turn to God.

Understanding the purpose of God, let us learn that when we go astray we should not throw away our hope of salvation. For we see that God here stretches out his hand to those who had erred.

"'The days are coming,' declares the LORD, 'when I will bring my people Israel and Judah back from captivity and restore them to the land I gave their forefathers to possess,' says the LORD." We see why he says, "The days are coming," for after two years all hope would have been extinguished if God had not intervened.

"I will bring my people Israel and Judah back from captivity and restore them to the land." The ten tribes had already been led into exile. Only the tribe of Judah and the half tribe of Benjamin remained. Hence the ten tribes, the whole kingdom of Israel, are mentioned first. The exile of Israel was much longer than that of Judah.

4-6. These are the words the LORD spoke concerning Israel and Judah: "This is what the LORD says: 'Cries of fear are heard—terror, not peace. Ask and see: Can a man bear children? Then why do I see every strong man with his hands on his stomach like a woman in labor, every face turned deathly pale?'"

Cries of fear are heard. This means that although the people were asleep in their sins, God's warnings to them about repentance would not be in vain. It is as if he said, "Deride and scoff as you please, or remain unaware of your delusions—God will still drag this confession from you, this voice of trembling and fear."

Terror, not peace. This is added most emphatically so that the prophet might shake the people out of their complacency and the foolish delusions they had caught from the false prophets. So he says that it was no good for them to keep hoping for peace, for they could not run away from **terror** and **fear**. The prophet speaks about a dreadful thing here. He asks ironically, **"Can a man bear children?"** because God would make all men suffer intense pain and agony as if they were women giving birth. As women exert every nerve and writhe in anguish during childbirth, so men, all the men, would have their hands on their lower abdomens because of their **terror** and dread.

Every face turned deathly pale. That is, God would frighten them all.

7. In this verse the prophet continues to describe the terrible punishment about which the people felt no concern, since they disregarded all God's warnings. This is why he emphasizes this denunciation and exclaims, **"'How awful that day will be!'"**

"'None will be like it.'" It was a dreadful spectacle to see the city destroyed and the temple partly pulled down and partly consumed by fire. The king and all the nobility were driven into exile; the king's eyes were put out and his children killed. He was later taken away in such a degraded manner that it would have been better to have died a hundred times than to endure such indignity. The prophet said this to stir the people out of their false beliefs. They thought that the holy city, which God had chosen to live in, could not fall, nor could the temple perish.

"'It will be a time of trouble for Jacob'"—that is, for the people. But at the end of the verse he gives them hope and points them to God's mercy, even deliverance from this distress: **"'but he will be saved out of it.'"**

8. **"'In that day,'** declares the LORD Almighty, **'I will break the yoke off their necks and will tear off their bonds; no longer will foreigners enslave them.'"** He says, **"'In that day'"**—that is, when the appointed day arrived. The false prophets inflamed the people with false expectation, as if their deliverance would take place after two years. God tells them to wait patiently and not to be in a hurry. He had assigned a day for them, and that was the seventieth year.

174

"'I will break the yoke off their necks'"—that is, the yoke of the king of Babylon. Another way of saying the same thing was that he would "'tear off their bonds.'" The yoke was what Nebuchadnezzar laid on the Jews, and their chains or bonds were the ways in which Nebuchadnezzar had bound them. At last the prophet adds, "'no longer will foreigners enslave them'"; that is, they will not rule over them and oppress them.

We now see the prophet's purpose. He urges the Jews to be patient and shows that their exile will be long, but their deliverance will be certain.

9. "'Instead, they will serve the LORD their God and David their king, whom I will raise up for them.'" We can now see how the prophet comforted the faithful. He not only promised them freedom but said that their happiness would be complete, for God would rule over them. "'They will serve the LORD their God.'" The phrase "And David their king" means God planned that his people would be governed by a king—not that the king would sit in the place of God, but he would serve as God's minister. This was said a long time after the death of David, for he died many years before Jeremiah was born. He did not live again to rule over the people. But the name of David here stands for anyone who succeeds him.

"'Whom I will raise up for them.'" It was the office and work of God to raise up Christ. We must always come to the fountain of God's mercy if we want to enjoy the blessings of Christ. We will find in Christ whatever is necessary for our salvation. This is why the prophet specifically says that God will "'raise up for them'" a king to rule over his people.

10. "'So do not fear, O Jacob my servant; do not be dismayed, O Israel,' declares the LORD. 'I will surely save you out of a distant place, your descendants from the land of their exile. Jacob will again have peace and security, and no one will make him afraid.'" The prophet reinforces his teaching with an exhortation. It would not be enough simply to assure us of God's paternal love and goodwill unless we were encouraged to hope for it, because experience teaches us how backward and slow we are to embrace God's promises. This is why the prophet encourages the faithful to entertain hope.

He speaks to **Jacob** and to **Israel**, but they mean the same thing, as in other places. These duplicates, as they are called, are common, we know, in the Hebrew language. Words are repeated for the sake of emphasis. So in this passage there is more force when Jeremiah mentions two names than if he had just said, "Fear not, O Jacob, and do not be afraid."

"'So do not fear, O Jacob my servant; do not be dismayed, O Israel.'" He says this so that the Jews might remember that God had not just been propitious to their father Jacob on one occasion but many times.

My servant. This should not be understood as implying the merits of the people, for their obedience is not being commended here; it is not as if they had faithfully responded to God's call. He is merely extolling their unmerited adoption.

"'Jacob will again have peace and security, and no one will make him afraid.'" A return to their own country would not have been very important if they could not live in it quietly. Thus God promises them his constant blessing.

11. "'I am with you and will save you,' declares the LORD. 'Though I completely destroy all the nations among which I scatter you, I will not completely destroy you. I will discipline you but only with justice; I will not let you go entirely unpunished.'" He repeats in other words what he has already said, to lend further support to trembling and wavering minds. God promises that he will be present with his people to save them. As this could not easily be believed, and as the Jews could only despair because of the state they were in, the prophet added this comparison between them and the Gentiles. The Chaldeans and the Assyrians flourished seventy years in every kind of wealth, in luxuries, in honor; in short, they possessed everything necessary for earthly happiness. The Jews must have thought that unbelievers and God's enemies were happy, while they were miserable, being oppressed by hard slavery, living in poverty, and being treated like sheep destined for slaughter. These things were plain before their eyes; so their minds were full of despair. In this verse God anticipates this objection.

12. "This is what the LORD says: 'Your wound is incurable, your injury beyond healing.'" The purpose of the prophet should first of all be noticed. He was fighting against the impostors who gave the people hope of returning in a short time, while in reality it would take seventy years. The prophet then wanted to show the people how foolish they were to hope for an end to their evils in so short a time. This needs to be carefully observed, for the prophet dwelt on this point at length. Nothing is more difficult than to lead people to a serious acknowledgment of God's judgment.

The prophet speaks here about their evils not because the Israelites were unaware of them, but because they had been too quick to believe in and were still hoping for a return. They were deceiving themselves with false comfort.

13. "'There is no one to plead your cause, no remedy for your sore, no healing for you.'" The prophet speaks plainly at first, then illustrates the simple truth by a metaphor. He says there was no one to **plead [their] cause**; in other words, they were devoid of all help. This was already partly evident, but the people nevertheless indulged in false hopes every day. Then Jeremiah declared what had already happened and what was still to happen. In this way he showed the folly of the people who still flattered themselves while they were involved in evil. "You think," he says, "there is no one to stretch out a hand to you or who is ready to help you. And yet you still think you will soon be free. But this is all a vain expectation."

He then comes to the metaphor: "'There is . . . no remedy for your sore, no healing for you.'" In one sentence he includes the whole first chapter of Isaiah, who handles the subject in more detail. But there is nothing obscure when the prophet says there was no one to heal the evils of the people.

14. "'All your allies have forgotten you; they care nothing for you. I have struck you as an enemy would and punished you as would the cruel, because your guilt is so great and your sins so many.'" The prophet repeats that nothing remained for Israel from men—no one offered to bring help.

God calls himself **an enemy** and compares himself to someone **cruel** who was punishing them. By this it must not be understood that the covenant had been abolished through which he had adopted the children of Abraham as his own. In his mercy he always reserved a remnant. As the prophet here addresses the faithful, there is no doubt that God is calling himself **an enemy** because, according to the state of things at that time, the Jews could only have thought God was angry with them.

15. "'Why do you cry out over your wound, your pain that has no cure? Because of your great guilt and many sins I have done these things to you.'" Here God frees himself from the false charges of the people and shows that those who grumbled acted unjustly, not considering what they deserved, for they should have received the heaviest punishment.

16. "'But all who devour you will be devoured; all your enemies will go into exile. Those who plunder you will be plundered; all who make spoil of you I will despoil.'" There is teaching here that we find throughout the prophets: God, after starting his church, becomes the judge of all nations. If he does not even spare his elect, his own family, how can he leave foreigners unpunished? It is the church's constant consolation that although God uses the wicked to punish his people, the condition of those wicked does not improve, for after they have triumphed for a moment, God soon judges them. There is, therefore, no reason for the faithful to envy their enemies when those faithful are punished by God's hand and when their enemies exult in their pleasures. Their enemies' prosperity will soon come to an end, and God will punish them as a reward for the wrong they have done to his people.

17. "'But I will restore you to health and heal your wounds,' declares the LORD, 'because you are called an outcast, Zion for whom no one cares.'" Once God was reconciled to his people, he would **heal the wounds** he had inflicted. Only he who inflicts wounds on us can heal us. He exercises judgment in punishing but afterwards acts as a doctor, delivering us from our evils. It is, therefore, as though the prophet said, "When the right time passes, which God has fixed for his people, deliverance will definitely arrive. For the Lord has decreed that he will punish his people only for a time, and not completely destroy them."

18. "This is what the LORD says: 'I will restore the fortunes of Jacob's tents and have compassion on his dwellings; the city will be rebuilt on her ruins, and the palace will stand in its proper place.'" The city had been destroyed in such a way that some ruins and some vestiges of the walls still remained. It is as if he said that however splendid and wealthy the city had been before, it would be restored so that its dignity would be no less than then. But he speaks of its extent when he says it would be **rebuilt on her ruins**—that is, on her ancient foundations.

In short, he promises such a restoration of the city and kingdom that no less favor from God was to be expected in the second state of the church than it had had before. God would obliterate all memory of calamities when the church flourished again, the kingdom becoming so eminent in wealth, honor, power, and other excellencies that it would be clear that God had only been displeased with his church for a time.

19. "'From them will come songs of thanksgiving and the sound of rejoicing. I will add to their numbers, and they will not be decreased; I will bring them honor, and they will not be disdained.'" The prophet intimates that although the Jews would be in sorrow for a time and would groan and mourn, their condition would not be permanent. God would at length comfort them, so that they would not only rejoice but also proclaim his mercy when they were freed.

20. "'Their children will be as in days of old.'" I am sure this is a reference to the kingdom of David. It is like saying that the state of the church would be no less prosperous and happy under Christ than it had been previously under David. Although the kingdom, with all its dignity, was to become extinct through a dreadful devastation, the Jews would still, through Christ, recover what they had lost because of their sins of ingratitude and perverseness.

"'Their community will be established before me; I will punish all who oppress them.'" God confirms again the promise of the lasting nature of the church. That is why he says that **"their community will be established before"** him, telling the Jews to look upwards, for in the world they would find nothing but despair. God calls the attention of the Jews to himself.

21. "'Their leader will be one of their own; their ruler will arise from among them. I will bring him near and he will come close to me, for who is he who will devote himself to be close to me?' declares the LORD."** Since the people rejected God, he rightly complains about their impiety, as if he were in a state of wonder and amazement. Had he simply said, "Who is he who comes to me?" the meaning, because of brevity, would have been obscure. But God here clearly distinguishes between two kinds of access. The first was when freedom was given to the people by the decree of Cyrus and permission was given to build the city and the temple. God, therefore, caused them then to draw near that they might come to him. This was the first access.

But he now adds that the Jews did not form or prepare their heart. He indeed speaks of the future but accuses them of ingratitude, which later became apparent. So he says in effect, "Who is this that he comes to me?" That is, "I will make them unite again in one body, call on me, and enjoy their inheritance. I will do this so that they may come to me. But many will prefer to live in their own evil ways and will choose Chaldea and other countries instead of the temple and religion. Many, then, will not change heart and come to me."

22. "'So you will be my people, and I will be your God.'" As this verse and the first verse of chapter 31 are materially the same, they will be explained together here. God says that the Jews would become a **people** to him and that he would become a **God** to them. We find this way of speaking everywhere in the prophets. It is very expressive and incorporates true happiness. For where is there life unless we become the people of God? See Psalm 144:15. This confirms that a happy life is complete in all its parts when God promises to be a God to us and takes us as his people. That is why the prophets often inculcate this truth. Until we feel assured that God is a Father to us and that we are his people, whatever happiness we may have will only end in misery.

23. See, the storm of the LORD will burst out in wrath, a driving wind swirling down on the heads of the wicked. The prophet seems to speak abruptly. Nothing could be more delightful than the promise that God gives, to be a Father to the people. But Jeremiah immediately adds that **a driving wind** would arrive, **swirling down on the heads of the wicked.** At first sight these things seem to contradict each other. But the latter sentence should be applied to the heathen or to any enemies of the church. Whenever God appears as the Saviour of his people, his vengeance goes forth and is poured on the wicked. So, in short, the prophet teaches here that God's vengeance would be fatal to all the wicked.

24. The fierce anger of the LORD will not turn back until he fully accomplishes the purposes of his heart. In days to come you will understand this. He confirms the last sentence and compares the wrath or vengeance of God to a messenger or a minister who is sent to carry a message or to carry out what he has been commanded. In the book of Isaiah the Lord says, "My word that goes out of my mouth . . . will not return to me empty" (55:11). This means that whatever God threatens or promises *will* take place. Those who say this means that the Word of God does not return empty because it brings forth fruit are wrong, for he is speaking about the effect of the Word, whether for salvation or for perdition. So now also God declares through Jeremiah that his vengeance, when it has gone out, will not return until it fulfills what has been commanded.

Jeremiah
Chapter 31

1-2. "At that time," declares the LORD, "I will be the God of all the clans of Israel, and they will be my people." This is what the LORD says: "The people who survive the sword will find favor in the desert; I will come to give rest to Israel." I mentioned verse 1 under Jeremiah 30:22. This is what the prophet is saying in verse 2: There was no reason to fear that God would not, in due time, deliver his people. It was well known that when he had liberated them previously, his power was seen in many ways. He cared for his people for forty years in the desert; their leaving Egypt was like a resurrection. So there was no doubt that God would deliver them now in a wonderful way and make his power known, as he had done for their fathers.

3. The LORD appeared to us in the past, saying: "I have loved you with an everlasting love; I have drawn you with loving-kindness." He says that as he had embraced Israel with perpetual love, he had therefore drawn out or extended his mercy. From the time he delivered his people from the tyranny of Pharaoh and fed them for forty years in the desert, he had lavished on them many benefits. He had given them many victories and often had pity on them. Since that time when God stretched out his hand to them, he did not cease to have mercy on them. In this sense he drew them with his **loving-kindness.** This was not just for one day or one year; he showed himself to be the same for 400, 500, even 600 years.

4. "I will build you up again and you will be rebuilt, O Virgin Israel. Again you will take up your tambourines and go out to dance with the joyful." In this verse Jeremiah continues with the same subject. Although it would take seventy years, God would be the liberator of his church. Joy is here contrasted with the grief that the people in exile experienced. But Jeremiah expresses their joy and gladness in a figurative way: **take up your tambourines and go out to dance.** When the prophets announce God's vengeance, they are likely to say, "All joy will leave you. You will no longer play your harp or any other musical instrument." Here

Jeremiah says that they will **again . . . take up** their **tambourines and . . . dance** when God restores them to their own country. By **tambourines and . . . dance**, he means holy joy—not a kind of licentiousness, but the joy that is linked to the praises of God and to the sacrifice of thanksgiving.

5. **"Again you will plant vineyards on the hills of Samaria; the farmers will plant them and enjoy their fruit."** The **hills of Samaria** were rich in vines. So when the vines there were cut down, there was a dreadful devastation. When, therefore, the prophet says that **the farmers will plant** them, he is saying the land will be desolate only for a time. He is reminding the Jews that they had to bear God's judgment while they could see nothing but desolation throughout the land.

6. **"There will be a day when watchmen cry out on the hills of Ephraim, 'Come, let us go up to Zion, to the LORD our God.'"** The prophet here amplifies the kindness of God, who will not only restore the tribe of Judah but also the ten tribes who had been led into exile previously. The Lord promises here a full and complete restoration of the church.

7. This is what the LORD says: **"Sing with joy for Jacob; shout for the greatest of the nations. Make your praises heard, and say, 'O LORD, save your people, the remnant of Israel.'"** The prophet here confirms the previous verse. He added this because what he had just said seemed to be almost incredible. He therefore enlarged on it.

This is what the LORD says. This preface is expressed in order to lend weight to his message. Jeremiah indeed adduced nothing except what he had learned from God, through the revelation of his Spirit. But it was necessary to say this repeatedly on account of his hearers' dullness.

"Sing with joy." God not only seeks to ease their sorrow but also to fill them with spiritual joy, that they might always be hopeful and cheerfully bear their calamities, for he promised to be propitious to them.

8. The prophet confirms the same truth but amplifies it. This oracle not only has a preface stating that it comes from God, but to make it more powerful, God himself is introduced as the speaker.

"See, I will bring them from the land of the north and gather them from the ends of the earth." Babylon, of course, was north of Judea, and whenever the prophets speak about the deliverance of the people, they always specify the north. When they warn the people, they say that an army or calamity will come from the north. The prophet now says that God had power to liberate them from the land of the north.

"Among them will be the blind and the lame, expectant mothers and women in labor; a great throng will return." Jeremiah adopts another way of speaking to show that nothing can exceed God's power when his purpose is to deliver his people. **The blind** cannot move a step without stumbling or falling, and they are in no fit state to undertake a journey. **The lame** cannot make any progress. But God promises that such will be their deliverance that both **the lame** and **the blind** will participate in it. He then mentions that **expectant mothers and women in labor** will return with the rest. It is as if he said there was no need to fear that God would restore his church, because his power was superior to all the impediments of the world.

9. **"They will come with weeping; they will pray as I bring them back. I will lead them beside streams of water on a level path where they will not stumble, because I am Israel's father, and Ephraim is my firstborn son."** Jeremiah points out that the reason for their deliverance was because God desired to be reconciled to his people. He also says that the cause of the exile, and of all the evils that had been and would be, was that they had provoked God by their sins. When the Jews were expelled from their inheritance, it was simply because they were wholly alienated from God. He was therefore no Father to them at that time; that is, he did not appear to be so, although he did prove himself to be a Father when the people returned to their own country, because God's favor then shone out after having been gone, so to speak, for a time.

10. **"Hear the word of the LORD, O nations; proclaim it in distant coastlands: 'He who scattered Israel will gather them and will watch over his flock like a shepherd.'"** The prophet dwells for a long time on the redemption that everyone believed would be impossible, especially since so many years had elapsed. The people, as it were, had been buried in their graves for seventy years. The length of time alone was enough to cut off all hope. No wonder then that our prophet sets forth in a lofty way the return of the people.

"'He who scattered Israel will gather them and will watch over his flock like a shepherd.'" The prophet shows here that God's favor would not be momentary; rather, their freedom would be the beginning of a deliverance that would continue to the end. It is very important to know this, for how will it benefit us if we are only delivered by God once? If that was the case, our salvation would quickly fail. But when we hear that we are delivered by God from the tyranny of our enemies so that he may continue to show us his favor and may become our permanent guardian and shepherd, this is a solid ground for confidence. This is why the prophet, after speaking about the deliverance of his people, adds that God will be their **shepherd**; he will perpetually guard and preserve his people.

11. **"For the LORD will ransom Jacob and redeem them from the hand of those stronger than they."** He continues with the same subject. He had said before that it would not be difficult or arduous for God to deliver his people. He now says that **"the LORD will ransom Jacob and redeem them from the hand of those stronger than they."** Jeremiah again removes the doubt that might have dejected the godly. For they kept on thinking: "How can God redeem us? He could have restrained the Chaldeans, but now they rule over all of the east. This

monarchy is like a gulf in which the whole world is swallowed up. Since God has so exalted the Chaldean power, we are totally without hope." They might have despaired when they compared this evil with all the remedies that might occur to them. But the prophet here confirms what he has just stated: God would show himself to be more powerful than the Chaldeans and all other enemies. This is like saying, "Although your enemies are strong, and you are like sheep in the jaws of wolves, nothing will stop God from redeeming you."

12. **"They will come and shout for joy on the heights of Zion; they will rejoice in the bounty of the LORD—the grain, the new wine and the oil, the young of the flocks and herds. They will be like a well-watered garden, and they will sorrow no more."** He says they will "come and shout for joy on the heights of Zion." By this the Lord through Jeremiah promises the restoration of the temple, for otherwise the return of the Jews to their own country would have been of no great importance.

"They will rejoice in the bounty of the LORD—the grain, the new wine and the oil, the young of the flocks and herds." Something better and more excellent than food is promised here. The language conveys something spiritual: The people would by degrees ascend to the spiritual kingdom of Christ, which was as yet in shadow and obscurity.

"They will be like a well-watered garden." Their abundance will be perpetual. God promises that their souls will be like watered gardens because they will not just be satisfied for a short time but will never be exposed to want or famine.

"They will sorrow no more." He means that when God's people are set free, God's blessing will continue with them, so that the faithful will not be subject to the common miseries of humanity.

13. **"Then maidens will dance and be glad, young men and old as well. I will turn their mourning into gladness; I will give them comfort and joy instead of sorrow."** This is a confirmation of the previous verse. He says that joy will be common to young women and young men, and also to the old. He has spoken about the permanence of joy, but now he extends this joy to both sexes and to all ages.

14. **"I will satisfy the priests with abundance, and my people will be filled with my bounty," declares the LORD.** This verse is connected with the previous one. What the prophet has said generally about the whole people, he now specifically declares about the priests. For the priests were, so to speak, the heart of the people. By this promise God gave further evidence of his favor. This is why the Scripture, in setting forth God's blessing to his chosen people, speaks especially about the priests, as we see in many passages.

15-16. This is what the LORD says: **"A voice is heard in Ramah, mourning and great weeping, Rachel weeping for her children and** refusing to be comforted, because her children are no more." This is what the LORD says: "Restrain your voice from weeping and your eyes from tears, for your work will be rewarded," declares the LORD. "They will return from the land of the enemy." Here, in the first place, the prophet describes the desolation of the land when deprived of all its inhabitants. In the second place he adds some comfort: God will restore the captives from exile, that the land might be inhabited. But there is here what is called a personification, that is, an imaginary person introduced. The prophet raises up Rachel from the grave and portrays her as lamenting. Rachel was weeping and could receive no consolation, for her posterity was destroyed and had become extinct in the land. But a promise follows that makes the calamity less grievous. The two verses should be read together, for they complement one another. "Although Rachel is weeping for her children and has at present no grounds for consolation, God will yet console her."

17. "So there is hope for your future," declares the LORD. "Your children will return to their own land." The whole country would lament for a time, and then their tears would be turned to laughter and their sorrow to joy. In short, Jeremiah teaches here that God's people should bear patiently the grievous time during which he would afflict them

18. "I have surely heard Ephraim's moaning: 'You disciplined me like an unruly calf, and I have been disciplined. Restore me, and I will return, because you are the LORD my God.'" The Jews always complained, "Why does not God spare us and forgive us? Why does he not deal more gently with us?" The prophet therefore shows that God cared about the well-being of his people when he punished them. Had he indulged them in their sins, their pride and perverseness would have increased.

The intention of these words is so the Jews might know that all their punishment, which otherwise would have been bitter and grievous, was a sort of medicine by which their spiritual diseases were to be healed.

"'Because you are the LORD my God.'" By this clause the prophet means that God favors only his elect with such privilege. In other words, not everyone repents and submits to God when he punishes them for their sins; this is a benefit peculiar to his chosen people.

19. "'After I strayed, I repented; after I came to understand, I beat my breast. I was ashamed and humiliated because I bore the disgrace of my youth.'" When we see that God cares about our salvation while treating us somewhat roughly, our sorrow is lessened, especially when experience proves that punishment is good for us.

"I repented." This word, meaning turning or conversion, includes the renewal of the whole soul. This means they were not touched by the true fear of God before they were endued with a right mind; but at the same time he testifies that this has been obtained through the special favor of God. From this we learn that the prophet, in the name of the ten tribes, acknowledges that nothing depended on people's free will, but that a sound mind and a right feeling of the heart is the work of the Spirit of God.

20. **"Is not Ephraim my dear son, the child in whom I delight? Though I often speak against him, I still remember him. Therefore my heart yearns for him; I have great compassion for him," declares the** LORD. Here God ascribes to himself human feelings. We sigh and groan deeply when we are weighed down by great sorrow. Similarly, when God expresses the feelings of a tender father, he means that he has great compassion on his people.

21. **"Set up road signs; put up guideposts. Take note of the highway, the road that you take. Return, O Virgin Israel, return to your towns."** He now describes what mercy will do: God will at length restore the captives and bring them back from exile and into their own country. God's favor had been mentioned earlier so we would know that the people were restored for no other reason but because God had mercy on them.

"Return, O Virgin Israel, return to your towns." In other words, "Although the land has been deserted for a time and reduced to solitude, yet the cities remain and will be inhabited again. The land still waits for its people, through God's wonderful favor."

22. **"How long will you wander, O unfaithful daughter? The** LORD **will create a new thing on earth—a woman will surround a man."** As the prophet had promised the people would return, he now reproves the Israelites who looked here and there but would not accept the word of God alone. These Israelites were looking forward to what might happen and could not entertain any hope of their return except when some appearance of hope was presented to them; and the prophet reproves them for this.

23. **This is what the** LORD **Almighty, the God of Israel, says: "When I bring them back from captivity, the people in the land of Judah and in its towns will once again use these words: 'The** LORD **bless you, O righteous dwelling, O sacred mountain.'"** The prophet deliberately used this way of speaking, for we know that Jerusalem was entirely overthrown, and the temple was pulled down and even set afire. As this was such a dreadful spectacle, Jeremiah describes here a wonderful transformation. Zion would again be the **sacred mountain**, and Jerusalem the **righteous dwelling**, even though it was then desolated. This passage deserves to be carefully noted, so that we may know that God restores his church as if he drew it up out of hell itself.

24. **"People will live together in Judah and all its towns—farmers and those who move about with their flocks."** He speaks here about the

restoration of the church, saying that its restored state will be in no way inferior to its previous state. Its inhabitants in the villages and country places will not be less secure than those in the cities.

25. "I will refresh the weary and satisfy the faint." Although Israel would be hungry and thirsty, God would bring relief to them, for he had the power and the will to satisfy their hunger and thirst.

26. At this I awoke and looked around. My sleep had been pleasant to me. The prophet, by his own example, encourages the faithful to be confident, to rely on God's promise as if they already possessed it, even though it was incredible.

I awoke and looked around. In darkness people lose the ability to see things, and so the prophet confesses that he was for a time, as it were, lifeless. He then says that he **awoke**—that is, when God's favor shone forth in this prophecy.

27. "The days are coming," declares the LORD, "when I will plant the house of Israel and the house of Judah with the offspring of men and of animals." The prophet is not saying anything new but is only encouraging the Jews concerning their deliverance and return. Yet he uses another illustration: God would again **plant** Judah in the land, that he might produce more people, more cattle, and more animals. God had condemned the land to desolation and solitude, but the prophet now says that God will make it inhabited again by both men and animals.

28. "Just as I watched over them to uproot and tear down, and to overthrow, destroy and bring disaster, so I will watch over them to build and to plant," declares the LORD. Here we see the Holy Spirit's purpose. God sets himself forth as the judge who had punished them for their sins, so that he might convince them that he will also become their doctor. It is as if he said, "I who have inflicted your wound am the one who can heal you." See 1 Samuel 2:6.

29-30. "In those days people will no longer say, 'The fathers have eaten sour grapes, and the children's teeth are set on edge.' Instead, everyone will die for his own sin; whoever eats sour grapes—his own teeth will be set on edge." Ezekiel showed that people believed they suffered for the sins of their fathers. Horace, a heathen who despised God, also said, "O Roman, you suffer undeservedly for the faults of your father." So the arrogance of the Jews was that they claimed to be innocent when God punished them.

31-32. "The time is coming," declares the LORD, "when I will make a new covenant with the house of Israel and with the house of Judah. It will not be like the covenant I made with their forefathers when I took them by the hand to lead them out of Egypt, because they broke my covenant, though I was a husband to them," declares the LORD. Jeremiah continues with the same subject but shows more clearly that God's favor toward them was even richer than before. The Lord promises not simply the restoration of the dignity and greatness they had lost, but something better and more excellent. So we see that this passage refers to the kingdom of Christ, for without Christ the people could have not have hoped for anything superior to the law.

From this we conclude that the prophet predicts the coming of Christ's kingdom. This passage is also quoted by the apostles (see Romans 11:27; Hebrews 8:8-12; 10:16). God made **a new covenant** when he accomplished through his Son what had been foreshadowed under the law. For the sacrifices could not of themselves pacify God, as is well known, and whatever the law taught about expiation was of itself useless and of no importance. The **new covenant** was made when Christ appeared with water and blood and really fulfilled what God had exhibited in the form of types, so that the faithful might have salvation.

But the coming of Christ would not have been sufficient if new birth through the Holy Spirit had not been added. It was in some respects a new thing when God regenerated the faithful by his Spirit. Under the Gospel, says Paul, the veil is removed, and God in the face of Christ presents himself so we can see him.

33. "This is the covenant I will make with the house of Israel after that time," declares the LORD. "I will put my law in their minds and write it on their hearts. I will be their God, and they will be my people." Jeremiah shows here the difference between the law and the Gospel, for the Gospel brings with it the grace of regeneration. Its doctrine, therefore, is not that of the letter; rather, it penetrates into the heart and reforms all the inner faculties, so that we are obedient to the righteousness of God.

Jeremiah says the same thing in two ways. He says that God will put his law in their minds and write it on their hearts. We know that the Scriptures say we cannot be Christ's disciples unless we both renounce the world and deny ourselves (see Matthew 16:24; Luke 14:26-27). Similarly, the prophet is not content with just one statement on this subject.

34. "No longer will a man teach his neighbor, or a man his brother, saying, 'Know the LORD,' because they will all know me, from the least of them to the greatest," declares the LORD. "For I will forgive their wickedness and will remember their sins no more." When God says, **"they will all know me, from the least of them to the greatest,"** he does not mean that everyone will have the same degree of knowledge. Experience indeed proves this to be false. And we also know that God has testified from the beginning, as Paul also reminds us (Romans 12:2-3), that the measure of his gifts is according to his good pleasure. God's message through the prophet means that those who are lowest or least among God's people will be endued with so much light of knowledge that they will be almost like teachers. Joel 2:28 expresses a similar thought. This is why Christ says, "He who is least in the kingdom of heaven is greater than he [John the Baptist]" (Matthew 11:11). John the Baptist was, in his office, exalted above all the prophets, and he excelled them in knowledge. And yet the least of those who profess the Gospel and bear testimony to it is greater, says Christ, than John the Baptist.

35-36. This is what the LORD says, he who appoints the sun to shine by day, who decrees the moon and stars to shine by night, who stirs up the sea so that its waves roar—the LORD Almighty is his name: "Only if these decrees vanish from my sight," declares the LORD, "will the descendants of Israel ever cease to be a nation before me." God says through Jeremiah, "I am he who created the sun, the moon, and the stars. The regular order of things in creation still continues, for the sun rises and sets and so does the moon. And I am still faithful to Israel."

37. This is what the LORD says: "Only if the heavens above can be measured and the foundations of the earth below be searched out will I reject all the descendants of Israel because of all they have done," declares the LORD. He had said before that God's covenant with Abraham's children could no more fail than the laws of nature. He now says that if anyone can measure the heavens and investigate the foundations of the earth, then, he says, **"will I reject all the descendants of Israel."** But God brings before us these strange and impossible things so that we may know that he will at length be reconciled to his people after having justly punished them.

We now see the prophet's purpose. He has the faithful in mind, who might have been overwhelmed with despair, thinking they had no hope of a return. The prophet reassures them that God cares for them and would gather his scattered seed.

38-40. "The days are coming," declares the LORD, "when this city will be rebuilt for me from the Tower of Hananel to the Corner Gate. The measuring line will stretch from there straight to the hill of Gareb and then turn to Goah. The whole valley where dead bodies and ashes are thrown, and all the terraces out to the Kidron Valley on the east as far as the corner of the Horse Gate, will be holy to the LORD. The city will never again be uprooted or demolished." The prophet now speaks about the rebuilding of the city. I am sure he did this to show them that the size and splendor of the city, after the return of the people, would be no less than it had been under David.

When the prophet says, **"this city will be rebuilt for me,"** that is, to the Lord, he mentions what the Jews especially expected—that the city would be holy again. Merely flourishing in wealth and power like other cities would have been of little comfort to the Israelites. He points out here the difference between Jerusalem and all ungodly cities. God was the architect of that city (see Psalm 87:5), and God would again care for that city, for the temple would become, as it were, his royal throne and earthly sanctuary.

When the prophet affirms that the extent of the city will not be less than it was before, we see that this prophecy must refer to Christ's king-dom. For although Jerusalem before Christ's coming was eminent and surrounded by a triple wall, and although it was esteemed in all the East, it nevertheless never achieved the greatness it enjoyed under David and Solomon. So we must focus on the spiritual state of the city and explain the promise as the grace that came through Christ.

But we must especially notice that the text says the city will be **holy to the LORD** and that there will no longer be fear of destruction. The prophet here promises that the city and all within its vicinity will be holy to God because God would cleanse it from all the defilements by which it had been polluted. God claims that this will be his own work, for sancti-fication is a work that only God can perform.

Jeremiah
Chapter 32

1-3. This is the word that came to Jeremiah from the LORD in the tenth year of Zedekiah king of Judah, which was the eighteenth year of Nebuchadnezzar. The army of the king of Babylon was then besieging Jerusalem, and Jeremiah the prophet was confined in the courtyard of the guard in the royal palace of Judah. Now Zedekiah king of Judah had imprisoned him there, saying, "Why do you prophesy as you do? You say, 'This is what the LORD says: I am about to hand this city over to the king of Babylon, and he will capture it.'" The prophet declares here that although he was in prison, the Word of God was not bound, and he himself was in that sense as free as if he could roam the streets and lanes of the city. So he did not stop doing his prophetic work just because he was in prison. From this we see that the work of heavenly truth cannot be impeded, no matter how much the world may speak against all its ministers and silence them. We also see the perseverance of the prophet, for he was not overcome by fear although he was in prison and in great danger. We find that even there he continued prophesying.

Jeremiah points out the circumstances of that time. He says that he was put in prison during **the tenth year of Zedekiah** and the eighteenth year of Nebuchadnezzar. In the middle of the siege of Jerusalem, God told Jeremiah to prophesy the future return of the people. But the people could not be restored before they had been driven into exile. This was indeed a dreadful instance of obduracy. Having been scourged so often, they did not benefit at all. They had experienced God's heavy judgment under Jehoiakim and also under Jeconiah. But the memory of these calamities soon vanished, and they lived as complacently as if they had never heard a word from the mouth of Jeremiah. And Jeremiah was not the only person who warned them, for Isaiah and others had done so before him, and Ezekiel had done so at the same time as him. This indicates the great obstinacy of the people.

4. "'Zedekiah king of Judah will not escape out of the hands of the

Babylonians but will certainly be handed over to the king of Babylon, and will speak with him face to face and see him with his own eyes.'" When the king saw that he would not be exempt from the common judgment, he was especially displeased with Jeremiah. Kings try to exempt themselves from all laws, and they like to exclude themselves when the people are reproved. But Jeremiah classed King Zedekiah with all the rest of the people, and the proud king could not endure such a thing. So he imprisoned Jeremiah and became implacable, even when God's hand was laid on him.

5. "He will take Zedekiah to Babylon, where he will remain until I deal with him, declares the LORD. If you fight against the Babylonians, you will not succeed.'" Here the prophet answers the Jews' foolish ideas that made them refuse to submit to God. There were still many men in the city, which still had strong fortifications, and they placed their confidence in those fortifications. The prophet attacks this foolishness by saying, "If you fight against the Babylonians, you will be unsuccessful, for God will cut you down before your enemies."

The summary of this introduction is that Jeremiah was in prison and the king continued being insubordinate to God, although he was hard-pressed by God. In this situation the prophet boldly attacked the king and the city and declared that God's judgment was at hand. The king would be taken into exile and the city taken and plundered by their enemies.

6-15. These verses should be read together, for the prophet explains how and by what symbol this prophecy had been confirmed. His purpose here is to show that after a long time the Jews would return to their own country, for God would restore them, and their captivity would come to an end. God's design, then, was to give them hope of deliverance; but they were admonished to wait patiently for the end of their exile.

Jeremiah said, "The word of the LORD came to me: Hanamel son of Shallum your uncle is going to come to you and say, 'Buy my field at Anathoth, because as nearest relative it is your right and duty to buy it.' Then, just as the LORD had said, my cousin Hanamel came to me in the courtyard of the guard and said, 'Buy my field at Anathoth in the territory of Benjamin. Since it is your right to redeem it and possess it, buy it for yourself.' I knew that this was the word of the LORD; so I bought the field at Anathoth from my cousin Hanamel and weighed out for him seventeen shekels of silver. I signed and sealed the deed, had it witnessed, and weighed out the silver on the scales. I took the deed of purchase—the sealed copy containing the terms and conditions, as well as the unsealed copy—and I gave this deed to Baruch son of Neriah, the son of Mahseiah, in the presence of my cousin Hanamel and of the witnesses who had signed the deed and of all the Jews sitting in the courtyard of the guard. In their presence I gave Baruch these instructions: 'This is what the LORD Almighty, the God of Israel, says:

Take these documents, both the sealed and unsealed copies of the deed of purchase, and put them in a clay jar so they will last a long time.'"

Now we come to consider the external symbol. The prophet was commanded to buy a field from his uncle's son. This seemed strange, for the enemies had possessed that part of the country, and no Jews could venture out into their fields. The prophet must have seemed insane to buy a field that was then in the possession of the enemy. But this was the way God intended to show that after the Jews had been deprived of the possession of the land for a time, they would go back to it, so that everyone would return to his own property; and thus everything would be totally their own, after God had shown them mercy.

"'For this is what the LORD Almighty, the God of Israel, says: Houses, fields and vineyards will again be bought in this land.'" God's purpose was that his servant should hand over his money, paying no attention to his own benefit, so that he might through this act encourage the faithful to hope for the time of restoration. What is said here was thought incredible, for no one thought this change could ever come about—the Jews being allowed to return to their own country! The power of the Babylonians was thought to be invincible, and they would have to be totally overthrown before God's people could be set free. This vision was given so the Jews would know that their calamity would not last forever, for God planned to restore the people and their land.

Fields means all possessions, for the prophet mentions not only **houses, but fields and vineyards.**

16-18. "After I had given the deed of purchase to Baruch son of Neriah, I prayed to the LORD: Ah, Sovereign LORD, you have made the heavens and the earth by your great power and outstretched arm. Nothing is too hard for you. You show love to thousands but bring the punishment for the fathers' sins into the laps of their children after them." If you did not bear in mind the context of this passage, you might think the prophet was rambling here, apparently not linking his sentences to each other; his prayer seems to be incoherent. But the prophet knew that people speak about God's deeds too freely, so he prepared them for what he had to say before he came to his subject. He gives a kind of introduction: "O Lord, it is not right for me to fight with you, nor it is right for me to ask you to give me a reason for doing what you do. For **'you have made the heavens and the earth by your great power and outstretched arm.'"** A contrast is implied here between God and mortals. "Who am I to dare to summon you to any contest? Your power is rightly to be dreaded by us. When we raise up our eyes to heaven, when we look on the earth, there is nothing that ought not to fill us with admiration of your power, for its immensity appears above and below." So we see that the prophet extols God's power to keep himself meek and humble and not to presume to pass any judgment on what he does.

"O great and powerful God, whose name is the LORD Almighty."
Again he declares the greatness of God's power, that he might restrain
himself and not indulge in idle speculations and call God to account,
as if he had summoned him to appear before a tribunal where he might
be found guilty. Because human nature is so insolent and arrogant, the
prophet surrounds himself with barriers here, that he might keep within
the bounds of humility.

19. "Great are your purposes and mighty are your deeds. Your eyes
are open to all the ways of men; you reward everyone according to
his conduct and as his deeds deserve." Jeremiah continues to express his
wonder at God's judgments. He first declares that God's purposes are
great and his deeds mighty. By **purposes** he means the wisdom of God,
which is beyond all our thinking. He adds that his **eyes are open to all
the ways of men.** By this Jeremiah means that God is the judge of the
whole world. This means that God's providence extends to all parts of
the world, so that no one's deeds can be hidden from him, and nobody
can escape from him. The Lord will **reward everyone according to his
conduct and as his deeds deserve.**

20-22. "You performed miraculous signs and wonders in Egypt
and have continued them to this day, both in Israel and among all
mankind, and have gained the renown that is still yours. You brought
your people Israel out of Egypt with signs and wonders, by a mighty
hand and an outstretched arm and with great terror. You gave them
this land you had sworn to give their forefathers, a land flowing with
milk and honey." The prophet remembers God's kindness in showing
his fatherly goodness to his church. He says that the **miraculous signs
and wonders** that God did **in Egypt** were for the sake of his people.
He adds, **"in Israel"**; he thus not only extols God's power in miracles,
but especially the mercy he showed to his chosen people. He also cites
the renown that is still yours. This does not mean that God performed
miracles in every age, but that his miracles deserve to be remembered all
the time, throughout all ages. God did indeed perform miracles at certain
times, but he performed them so that they might be remembered in all
ages, and so that posterity might acknowledge how wonderfully God had
acted toward their fathers.

23. "They came in and took possession of it [the land], but they
did not obey you or follow your law; they did not do what you commanded them to do. So you brought all this disaster upon them."
Jeremiah states in this verse that God's vengeance was just when the
people were thrown out of the land and driven into exile, because the
people did not obey God's voice. The sight of the land ought to have
made the people obey God. They could not have eaten a crumb of bread
without being reminded about where their food came from, for God
had expelled the Gentiles from that land. When, therefore, they were

filled with all kinds of good things and at the same time despised God, they had no excuse. That is why the prophet links two things together: the Israelites **took possession of** the land, and they **did not do what you commanded them.**

24-25. "See how the siege ramps are built up to take the city. Because of the sword, famine and plague, the city will be handed over to the Babylonians who are attacking it. What you said has happened, as you now see. And though the city will be handed over to the Babylonians, you, O Sovereign LORD, say to me, 'Buy the field with silver and have the transaction witnessed.'" Jeremiah confirms that the destruction of the city came about through God's judgment. So he adds, **"What you said has happened."** So the city was not destroyed by chance, for God only used his servants to foretell things that he had decreed and resolved to do. The ruin of Jerusalem was the work of God, prophesied through his servants. God's mouth and God's hand should be thought of together. The prophet shows that the destruction of the city was God's righteous judgment, because the prophets had previously spoken about it.

26-27. Then the word of the LORD came to Jeremiah: "I am the LORD, the God of all mankind. Is anything too hard for me?" When something happens to Jeremiah that seems to be inconsistent with God's will, Jeremiah throws his anxiety, as it were, into God's heart. Then God, in order to relieve him, says that nothing is difficult for him, because he is God of all mankind.

28-29. "Therefore, this is what the LORD says: I am about to hand this city over to the Babylonians and to Nebuchadnezzar king of Babylon, who will capture it. The Babylonians who are attacking this city will come in and set it on fire; they will burn it down, along with the houses where the people provoked me to anger by burning incense on the roofs to Baal and by pouring out drink offerings to other gods." God says that although he will end their seventy years of exile, hypocrites should not be encouraged by this, for it will not apply to them. So God speaks here, in the first place, about his vengeance, in order to fill those who despised the law with fear, and to intimate that they were excluded from the favor of redemption. He goes on to add that he will at length be merciful to the exiles, but this favor is confined to the elect and faithful alone.

30. "The people of Israel and Judah have done nothing but evil in my sight from their youth; indeed, the people of Israel have done nothing but provoke me with what their hands have made, declares the LORD." Jeremiah exposes the sins of the people and says that they never left their vices. He mentions the ten tribes of **Israel** and the tribe of **Judah.** The ten tribes, as we know, had stopped engaging in the pure worship of God, the true religion being practiced in Jerusalem. By mentioning the people of Judah, the prophet doubtless aggravated their guilt, intimating that they had fallen along with the Israelites, though for a time they had been preserved. When Scripture links Israel with Judah, Israel means the ten tribes; for either honor or reproach the house of Judah is sometimes referred to separately from the kingdom of Israel. But when Israel alone is mentioned, it includes all the children of Abraham without exception. In this place Jeremiah says that **the people of Israel and Judah** had done nothing but **provoke** God. Later he mentions only **Israel** and includes the twelve tribes.

31. **"From the day it was built until now, this city has so aroused my anger and wrath that I must remove it from my sight."** Nothing new is said in this verse, but as it was something so difficult to believe, the prophet dwells on it and says, speaking for God, that the city of Jerusalem has **"so aroused my anger and wrath that I must remove it from my sight."** It is as if he said that the Jews had never stopped sinning, so it was high time that they were punished. For the people had not only begun to sin in the wilderness, but they persisted in this way, and never stopped sinning.

32. **"The people of Israel and Judah have provoked me by all the evil they have done—they, their kings and officials, their priests and prophets, the men of Judah and the people of Jerusalem."** This verse is linked to the previous one. God had complained that the city had been so perverse that it seemed to have been founded for the purpose of seeking its own ruin by its sins. He confirms that declaration by adding, **"The people of Israel and Judah have provoked me by all the evil they have done."** By **all the evil** he means that they had only been doing evil and that they had abandoned themselves to impiety.

33. **"They turned their backs to me and not their faces; though I taught them again and again, they would not listen or respond to discipline."** Here the prophet expresses more clearly the perverseness of the people, as though he was saying that they had deliberately rejected every instruction and had shown no regard for God. The person who turns his back on us does so deliberately, intending to show contempt. So God complains that the Jews had not fallen away through ignorance but, as it were, through premeditated obstinacy.

34. **"They set up their abominable idols in the house that bears my Name and defiled it."** Here was extreme wickedness, for the Jews had profaned the temple itself. It was a serious offense to hold private services at home, where they burned incense on the roofs and poured libations to foreign gods. When impiety had gone so far that even the temple itself was polluted with idols, what hope was there of repentance?

35. **"They built high places for Baal in the Valley of Ben Hinnom to sacrifice their sons and daughters to Molech, though I never commanded, nor did it enter my mind, that they should do such a detestable thing and so make Judah sin."** After complaining about

the profanation of his own temple, God now says that the Jews had
sinned through another superstition—the valley of the son of Hinnom
had become their temple instead of the true one. In the law, God had
forbidden sacrifices to be offered except where he had appointed (see
Deuteronomy 12:4-5). As God then had specifically said that sacrifices
were not acceptable to him except in one temple and on one altar, he
shows here that the lawful worship had been corrupted by the Jews,
because they had made their sons and daughters pass through the fire
in honor of Molech. (He also calls him Baal; so it appears that the word
Baal includes all kinds of idols.)

36-37. "**You are saying about this city, 'By the sword, famine and
plague it will be handed over to the king of Babylon'; but this is what
the LORD, the God of Israel, says: I will surely gather them from all
the lands where I banish them in my furious anger and great wrath;
I will bring them back to this place and let them live in safety.**" Now
we see the purpose of the prophet. This is a truth that should be carefully
noted. For we will misunderstand the prophets' doctrine unless we know
that after threatening the wicked and those who despised God, they then
address the elect, encouraging them to bear their punishment patiently.
Jeremiah did this himself when he urged the faithful to lay in the dust and
patiently wait for God, although for a time he would hide his face from
Jacob—that is, from his church.

38. "They will be my people, and I will be their God." When the
prophet spoke about the restoration of the people, he spoke of the chief
and most desirable thing—that is, to know that God was reconciled to
them, and that they thus became his people.

**39. "I will give them singleness of heart and action, so that they will
always fear me for their own good and the good of their children after
them."** He now explains the previous verse more clearly, mentioning
the effects of God's favor. God declares that he will be our God, for he
adopts us as his children. From this comes the certainty of our heavenly
inheritance and of his mercy, which is better than life. Nothing more can
be desired than this benefit. God offers himself to us and deigns to receive
and embrace us as his people.

**40. "I will make an everlasting covenant with them: I will never stop
doing good to them, and I will inspire them to fear me, so that they
will never turn away from me."** He continues on the same subject. But
the repetition is intended to recommend the grace of God emphatically,
for we know how people always try and withhold the praise due to his
grace, because of their pride. God, on the other hand, celebrates his grace,
in case people should deliberately obscure it.

First he says, "**I will make an everlasting covenant with them.**"
Note the contrast between the covenant of the law and the covenant
about which the prophet now speaks. In chapter 31 he called it "a new

covenant"—because their fathers had fallen away so quickly after the law had been proclaimed, and because the law's doctrine was of the letter, and deadly. But now he calls it **an everlasting covenant.** Because of what people did, the covenant of the law became void and of no benefit to them. God says that when his doctrine is presented to people it has no effect, for it sounds in their ears but does not penetrate their hearts. So the grace of the Holy Spirit is needed. Unless God speaks within and touches our hearts, the sound will be of no avail. We now see why the covenant that God promises is called an **everlasting** one.

41. **"I will rejoice in doing them good and will assuredly plant them in this land with all my heart and soul."** When God says he will take pleasure in doing good to his people, he adopts a human expression, for parents rejoice when they can do good to their children. God used this illustration because his parental love for his people could not have been expressed in any other way. Also, note the contrast here: God rejoiced when he punished his people for their wickedness. God delights in judgment as well as in mercy. For a time, then, God rejoiced when he punished the people; since his judgment is right, he delights in it. But now he says he will show his parental affection as he takes pleasure in doing them good.

"I will . . . plant them in this land." He had indeed planted them when, through Joshua, the land was given to them (see Psalm 80:8). But later the people were plucked up by the roots. So the first possession of the land until the time of the Exile was not, strictly speaking, a planting, for the people did not strike firm roots then. So when God speaks here of planting, he is promising something new and unusual.

This planting depends on the covenant. Since the **covenant** is **everlasting,** this planting will endure. We now understand what the prophet means when he compares the restoration of the people after their return from exile to a planting.

42. **"This is what the LORD says: As I have brought all this great calamity on this people, so I will give them all the prosperity I have promised them."** God shows his prophet again here that exile would be temporary for the remnant. We know that most of the people had been wholly rejected, but it pleased the Lord that his church should survive, although it would be very small. So this promise is not to be extended indiscriminately to all the twelve tribes but refers especially to the elect, as the event proved, and as Paul also faithfully interpreted. This should be carefully borne in mind, because hypocrites always steal for themselves whatever God promises to his faithful people. Let us understand God's purpose: He wanted to support his chosen people in case despair should make them stop praying. Since, then, some of the people remained, this promise was fulfilled, so that the church might not be completely cut off.

43-44. **"Once more fields will be bought in this land of which you** say, 'It is a desolate waste, without men or animals, for it has been handed over to the Babylonians.' Fields will be bought for silver, and deeds will be signed, sealed and witnessed in the territory of Benjamin, in the villages around Jerusalem, in the towns of Judah and in the towns of the hill country, of the western foothills and of the Negev, because I will restore their fortunes, declares the LORD." He confirms the prediction about the return of the people and applies the vision that he had been given. He had been commanded to buy a field in the land of Benjamin. God now links that sign to the prophecy. The purpose of signs is to secure faith in doctrine. True doctrine deserves to be believed on its own account and is fully authentic, but as a concession to our weakness, signs are given to us, so that the promises are more firmly fixed in our hearts.

To show more clearly what is said in the preceding verse, he adds, "Fields will be bought for silver, and deeds will be signed, sealed and witnessed in the territory of Benjamin." The prophet then mentions all the boundaries that surrounded Jerusalem. We know part of the city was given to Benjamin, and one gate is named after him. The prophet promises that God is going to restore to the exiles the land they had previously possessed.

Jeremiah
Chapter 33

1-6. While Jeremiah was still confined in the courtyard of the guard, the word of the LORD came to him a second time: "This is what the LORD says, he who made the earth, the LORD who formed it and established it—the LORD is his name: 'Call to me and I will answer you and tell you great and unsearchable things you do not know.' For this is what the LORD, the God of Israel, says about the houses in this city and the royal palaces of Judah that have been torn down to be used against the siege ramps and the sword in the fight with the Babylonians: 'They will be filled with the dead bodies of the men I will slay in my anger and wrath. I will hide my face from this city because of all its wickedness. Nevertheless, I will bring health and healing to it; I will heal my people and will let them enjoy abundant peace and security.'"

This prophecy refers to the same subject as previously. It was God's purpose to confirm by many prophecies what he had once testified about the restoration of the people. But he had a special care for the faithful, that they might not grow faint and succumb under their many trials. And the people who were to return to their own country needed special support, so that they might confidently rely on God's mercy for seventy years. We now see why God repeated this teaching about the return of the people.

While Jeremiah was still confined in the courtyard of the guard, the word of the LORD came to him a second time. Jeremiah had been subjected to great cruelty as he faithfully carried out his prophetic office. Yet he is told to comfort the people who had imprisoned him.

7. "I will bring Judah and Israel back from captivity and will rebuild them as they were before." By the word **rebuild**, God means they will return to their own country and remain secure in it. This promise was very necessary, for the Jews were surrounded on every side by enemies. All their neighbors had united against them and never stopped creating more trouble for them. So the prophet mentions that God **will rebuild**

them. The prosperity of the city would be lasting, for it would be founded in such a way that it would not totter or fall under any kind of assault.

8. "I will cleanse them from all the sin they have committed against me and will forgive all their sins of rebellion against me." First, he says he will **cleanse them from all the sin they have committed** and then that he will be propitious despite **all their sins of rebellion.** These words are not superfluous, for the Jews needed to be reminded that they had many vices, of which they were conscious even though they did not repent. Since they were perversely following their own will, the prophet had to prick them sharply, so that they might know they faced eternal destruction if God's mercy did not come to their rescue. He presents the greatness of their sins, so that he might extol the mercy of God.

9. "Then this city will bring me renown, joy, praise and honor before all nations on earth that hear of all the good things I do for it; and they will be in awe and will tremble at the abundant prosperity and peace I provide for it." God uses these words to exhort everyone to be grateful to him. Whenever God's blessings are pointed out to us, we should not be indifferent to them but should be stimulated to give thanks to God for them. When therefore God declares that the redemption of his people will **bring him renown . . . before all the nations,** he is showing the godly that they should not be torpid but should proclaim his goodness. God mentions his own **renown** so the Jews will continue to be hopeful, no matter how guilty they had been and no matter how much they deserved eternal destruction.

10-11. "This is what the LORD says: 'You say about this place, "It is a desolate waste, without men or animals." Yet in the towns of Judah and the streets of Jerusalem that are deserted, inhabited by neither men nor animals, there will be heard once more the sounds of joy and gladness, the voices of bride and bridegroom, and the voices of those who bring thank offerings to the house of the LORD, saying, "Give thanks to the LORD Almighty, for the LORD is good; his love endures forever." For I will restore the fortunes of the land as they were before,' says the LORD."

These two verses are linked to each other and should never have been separated. Jeremiah continues to teach the return of the people. It is little wonder that he speaks often about that favor that was thought to be impossible. Its memory might not have been fixed in the hearts of the faithful if he had not often repeated it.

12-13. "This is what the LORD Almighty says: 'In this place, desolate and without men or animals—in all its towns there will again be pastures for shepherds to rest their flocks. In the towns of the hill country, of the western foothills and of the Negev, in the territory of Benjamin, in the villages around Jerusalem and in the towns of Judah,

flocks will again pass under the hand of the one who counts them,' says the LORD." Jeremiah continues the same subject. But he speaks here of the settled happiness of the people, as if saying there was no reason for the Israelites to fear that God would not open for them a way back to their own country and preserve and protect them after their return. In describing their quiet and peaceful condition, he speaks of **shepherds**. We know it is a sure sign of peace when flocks and herds are led into fields in security. To show that the Jews would enjoy peaceful conditions, God says, **"There will again be pastures for shepherds to rest their flocks."**

Someone not familiar with Scripture might ask, Is this promise confined to shepherds? The promise is a general one though expressed in this particular way. God would be the guardian of his people, so that shepherds could drive their flocks here and there in perfect safety.

14. "'The days are coming,' declares the LORD, 'when I will fulfill the gracious promise I made to the house of Israel and to the house of Judah.'" Jeremiah shows why God had promised there would be quiet **pastures for shepherds.** This was meant to show that no one would be able to take the flocks away by force. God declares that his promise would not be void, for its effects would soon be evident, when his mercy was known by the ten tribes and by the kingdom of Judah. He says, **"The days are coming,"** for it was necessary for the faithful to look beyond their immediate situation. They were exposed to slaughter, and the unbelieving still entertained vain hopes; but the children of God saw thousands of people killed. This terror nearly brought them to despair. And in their exile they saw that they were taken away from their own country, without any hope of return. In order to support these people, the prophet tells them to think about the future. It is as if he said that the favor he predicts could not be grasped unless the faithful took their minds off the present situation and patiently waited for their promised deliverance.

15. "'In those days and at that time I will make a righteous Branch sprout from David's line; he will do what is just and right in the land.'" This passage should doubtless be understood to refer to Christ. We know that commonly among the Jews, whenever the prophets promised them the seed of David, their attention was directed to Christ. This was a way of teaching familiar to the Jews. The prophets, indeed, sometimes mentioned David himself, and not his son: "I will place over them one shepherd, my servant David" (Ezekiel 34:23). Now David was dead, and his body was reduced to dust and ashes; but in the person of David the prophets exhibited Christ. It is certain that Jeremiah is here celebrating the grace of deliverance because a Redeemer would come.

He calls this one **a righteous Branch** to contrast him with the children of David who had become degenerate. God had almost deemed them accursed, for most of the kings did not possess God's grace. There was, then, but one **righteous Branch,** Christ.

16. "'In those days Judah will be saved and Jerusalem will live in safety. This is the name by which it will be called: The LORD Our Righteousness.'" In chapter 23 this name is given to Christ, and to him alone it rightly belongs. But it is here transferred to the church, for whatever belongs to the head is made common to all the members. Indeed, we know that Christ holds nothing as his own. As he is made righteousness, it belongs to us, as Paul says: "Christ Jesus . . . has become for us . . . our righteousness, holiness, and redemption" (1 Corinthians 1:30). As, then, the Father conferred righteousness on his own Son for our sake, it is no wonder that what is in his power is transferred to us.

17-18. "For this is what the LORD says: 'David will never fail to have a man to sit on the throne of the house of Israel, nor will the priests, who are Levites, ever fail to have a man to stand before me continually to offer burnt offerings, to burn grain offerings and to present sacrifices.'" The prophet had spoken about the restoration of the church; he now confirms the same truth, promising that the kingdom and the priesthood will be everlasting. The safety of the people, of course, was secured by these two things. Without a king they were like an imperfect body, and without a priesthood there was nothing but ruin. The priest was, so to speak, the mediator between God and the people, and the king represented God. We now see why the prophet speaks about both the kingdom and the priesthood here, for the people had no other ground to stand on. He therefore declares that the people would be safe because there would always be some of the descendants of David who would succeed to govern them, and there would always be some of the descendants of Levi to offer sacrifices.

19-21. The word of the LORD came to Jeremiah: "This is what the LORD says: 'If you can break my covenant with the day and my covenant with the night, so that day and night no longer come at their appointed time, then my covenant with David my servant—and my covenant with the Levites who are priests ministering before me—can be broken and David will no longer have a descendant to reign on his throne.'" He confirms the same thing with an illustration. He shows that God's covenant with the people of Israel will be no less strong than the settled order of nature. The sun, moon, and stars are constant in their progress. This settled state of things is so fixed that in a great variety of circumstances there is no change. We have rain and then fair weather, and we have the various seasons, but the sun continues its daily course. The moon is new every month, and the revolving of day and night, which God has appointed, never ceases (see Psalm 19). The prophet sets the order of nature before us and says that God's covenant with his church will be no less fixed and unchangeable.

22. "'I will make the descendants of David my servant and the Levites who minister before me as countless as the stars of the sky and as measureless as the sand on the seashore.'" God through Jeremiah shows that he will be true and faithful in his promise, so that his church will increase and be as numerous as **the stars of the sky** and the sands of the sea.

23-24. **The word of the LORD came to Jeremiah: "Have you not noticed that these people are saying, 'The LORD has rejected the two kingdoms he chose'? So they despise my people and no longer regard them as a nation."** God now says why he has spoken so much about the deliverance of the people and their everlasting preservation—because unbelievers thought the blessing promised by God was uncertain. In addition to this, God not only reminds his prophet why he told him to repeat the same thing so often, but he speaks for the sake of the people, so that they might know this was not pointless repetition but was necessary to contend against their perverse wickedness. For they had so filled their hearts and minds with despair that they rejected all God's promises, and there was no room left for hope or faith.

25-26. **"This is what the LORD says: 'If I have not established my covenant with day and night and the fixed laws of heaven and earth, then I will reject the descendants of Jacob and David my servant and will not choose one of his sons to rule over the descendants of Abraham, Isaac and Jacob. For I will restore their fortunes and have compassion on them.'"** Here God contrasts the constancy of his faithfulness with their perverse grumbling. He uses the same illustration as before. "If I have not fixed my covenant, or if there is no covenant concerning the day and night, if there are no laws about the heavens and the earth, then I will now cast aside the descendants of Jacob and David. But if my constancy is always as clear as the laws of nature, why do you not give me the honor I deserve? I am the same God who created the heavens and the earth, who fixed all the laws of nature that remain unchangeable, and who also has made a covenant with my church. If my faithfulness concerning the laws of nature does not change, why should it change concerning the sacred covenant that I have made with my chosen people?"

Jeremiah
Chapter 34

1-2. **While Nebuchadnezzar king of Babylon and all his army and all the kingdoms and peoples in the empire he ruled were fighting against Jerusalem and all its surrounding towns, this word came to Jeremiah from the LORD: "This is what the LORD, the God of Israel, says: Go to Zedekiah king of Judah and tell him, 'This is what the LORD says: I am about to hand this city over to the king of Babylon, and he will burn it down.'"** Jeremiah first says this word came to him from the LORD. Second, he says when it happened. If he had reproved Zedekiah when peace prevailed and when there was no danger, the king might have opposed what the prophet said. But when he saw the city surrounded by such a large and powerful army and still refused to listen, he was forced to acknowledge that this was God's just vengeance and clear evidence of that man's extreme blindness. But God had blinded him in this way because he planned to bring extreme punishment on the people. The blindness, then, and the madness of the king were evidences of God's wrath toward all the people. Zedekiah might have appeased God if he had repented. It was God's will, then, that he should have such an intractable disposition, so that his perversity might bring ruin on himself.

3. **"'You will not escape from his grasp but will surely be captured and handed over to him. You will see the king of Babylon with your own eyes, and he will speak with you face to face. And you will go to Babylon.'"** As Zedekiah saw the people still doing their duty, he despised his enemy. The city was very strongly fortified, and he hoped to preserve it a little longer. So he entertained these false hopes of deliverance, thinking that the enemy would become tired and return to Chaldea. He was deceived in this expectation. The prophet attacked him and declared that he would become a captive, which Zedekiah indeed deserved because of his ingratitude. For Nebuchadnezzar had put him in the place of his nephew when Jeconiah was taken away into Babylon. He later rebelled against the king of Babylon, to whom he had pledged his faith and to

whom he paid tribute. But the prophet did not pay attention to these intermediate causes but to the primary cause—the people had not stopped sinning. So God, resolving to inflict extreme punishment on a people so perverse and desperate, blinded their king, which brought destruction on himself, the city, and the whole country. God passed over the intermediate causes that are apparent to us; but he had his hidden purpose, which he achieved through external means.

4-5. "'Yet hear the promise of the LORD, O Zedekiah king of Judah. This is what the LORD says concerning you: You will not die by the sword; you will die peacefully. As people made a funeral fire in honor of your fathers, the former kings who preceded you, so they will make a fire in your honor and lament, "Alas, O master!" I myself make this promise, declares the LORD.'" Here Jeremiah adds some comfort— namely, that Zedekiah himself will not be killed by the sword but will die in bed. It was indeed some mitigation of punishment that God prolonged his life and did not allow him to be killed immediately. And yet if we look at all the circumstances, it would have been a lesser evil to be put to death at once than to prolong life on the condition of being doomed to pine away in constant misery. When the eyes are put out (as his were by the Babylonians; see 2 Kings 25:7 and Jeremiah 39:7; 52:11), we know that a major part of life is lost. When, therefore, this punishment was inflicted on Zedekiah, would not death be considered desirable? Further, not only was he deprived of his royal dignity, but he was also bereaved of his own children and was later bound in chains. What remained for him was not at all desirable, and he would have preferred to die. God, however, meant it as a favor that he would **not die by the sword.**

6-7. Then Jeremiah the prophet told all this to Zedekiah king of Judah, in Jerusalem, while the army of the king of Babylon was fighting against Jerusalem and the other cities of Judah that were still holding out—Lachish and Azekah. These were the only fortified cities left in Judah. He repeats again that Jerusalem was then surrounded by the army of the king of Babylon, as were the other cities he names, **Lachish** and **Azekah.** He seems, therefore, indirectly to be reproving Zedekiah for his arrogance, for that monarch still retained his high spirits even though he was reduced to such straits. It is clear from this that Zedekiah rushed headlong to his own ruin like a wild beast devoid of reason.

8-22. The word came to Jeremiah from the LORD after King Zedekiah had made a covenant with all the people in Jerusalem to proclaim freedom for the slaves. Everyone was to free his Hebrew slaves, both male and female; no one was to hold a fellow Jew in bondage. So all the officials and people who entered into this covenant agreed that they would free their male and female slaves and no longer hold them in bondage. They agreed, and set them free. But afterward they changed their minds and took back the slaves they had freed and enslaved them again.

Then the word of the LORD came to Jeremiah: "This is what the LORD, the God of Israel, says: I made a covenant with your forefathers when I brought them out of Egypt, out of the land of slavery. I said, 'Every seventh year each of you must free any fellow Hebrew who has sold himself to you. After he has served you six years, you must let him go free.' Your fathers, however, did not listen to me or pay attention to me. Recently you repented and did what is right in my sight: Each of you proclaimed freedom to his countrymen. You even made a covenant before me in the house that bears my Name. But now you have turned around and profaned my name; each of you has taken back the male and female slaves you had set free to go where they wished. You have forced them to become your slaves again.

"Therefore, this is what the LORD says: You have not obeyed me; you have not proclaimed freedom for your fellow countrymen. So I now proclaim 'freedom' for you, declares the LORD—'freedom' to fall by the sword, plague and famine. I will make you abhorrent to all the kingdoms of the earth. The men who have violated my covenant and have not fulfilled the terms of the covenant they made before me, I will treat like the calf they cut in two and then walked between its pieces. The leaders of Judah and Jerusalem, the court officials, the priests and all the people of the land who walked between the pieces of the calf, I will hand over to their enemies who seek their lives. Their dead bodies will become food for the birds of the air and the beasts of the earth.

"I will hand Zedekiah king of Judah and his officials over to their enemies who seek their lives, to the army of the king of Babylon, which has withdrawn from you. I am going to give the order, declares the LORD, and I will bring them back to this city. They will fight against it, take it and burn it down. And I will lay waste the towns of Judah so no one can live there."

Although it does not say that what the prophet relates here was done by God's command, yet we may easily gather that Zedekiah the king had been admonished to free the slaves as the law stipulated: "If you buy a Hebrew servant, he is to serve you six years. But in the seventh year, he shall go free, without paying anything" (Exodus 21:2). It was God's will that some difference should be made between the people he had adopted and other nations. For God had chosen the descendants of Abraham as his special treasure, and other nations were in this respect aliens. It was therefore his will to establish his law among the people of Israel, so that servitude would not be forever unless a person chose to bind himself for his whole life. (See Deuteronomy 15:16-17.) When a person deprived himself of the benefit of this law, his master bored his ear with an awl. Having this mark on him, he could no longer become free, except perhaps if he lived to the jubilee year. From the words of the prophet we learn that this command of the law had been disregarded, for at the end of the seventh year the servants were not granted their freedom. Since King Zedekiah had been warned about this, he called the people together and, with everybody's consent, proclaimed freedom to the slaves as God had commanded. But this was done in bad faith, for soon afterwards the slaves were taken back into slavery, and so treachery was added to cruelty. From this we see that they not only wronged their own brethren by imposing on them perpetual slavery, but they also wickedly profaned the sacred name of God, for they were violating a solemn oath.

Jeremiah
Chapter 35

1-10. This is the word that came to Jeremiah from the LORD during the reign of Jehoiakim son of Josiah king of Judah: "Go to the Recabite family and invite them to come to one of the side rooms of the house of the LORD and give them wine to drink." So I went to get Jaazaniah son of Jeremiah, the son of Habazziniah, and his brothers and all his sons—the whole family of the Recabites. I brought them into the house of the LORD, into the room of the sons of Hanan son of Igdaliah the man of God. It was next to the room of the officials, which was over that of Maaseiah son of Shallum the doorkeeper. Then I set bowls full of wine and some cups before the men of the Recabite family and said to them, "Drink some wine." But they replied, "We do not drink wine, because our forefather Jonadab son of Recab gave us this command: 'Neither you nor your descendants must ever drink wine. Also you must never build houses, sow seed or plant vineyards; you must never have any of these things, but must always live in tents. Then you will live a long time in the land where you are nomads.' We have obeyed everything our forefather Jonadab son of Recab commanded us. Neither we nor our wives nor our sons and daughters have ever drunk wine or built houses to live in or had vineyards, fields or crops. We have lived in tents and have fully obeyed everything our forefather Jonadab commanded us."

The example of the Recabites is used, not so their obedience may be commended, but so that the prophet might reprove the Jews for giving less honor to the living God than the Recabites did to their dead father.

Jonadab did not forbid his descendants from drinking wine or sowing seed or planting vineyards in order to set up something new in worshiping God. He did it because he thought it would be good for his descendants to live in the land in this way, so that they might not become attached to their possessions, and so that in the midst of many changes they might be less anxious and be prepared, as it were, to move elsewhere when prudent. It was not the main aim of Jonadab's precept to demand from his descendants abstinence from wine; it was for a totally different reason. What is commanded for a different end is not necessary, but neither is it necessarily opposed to the Word of God. Their freedom of conscience was not taken away, and it was not Jonadab's aim to claim for himself the authority of God, as if he were some spiritual lawgiver. His precept only referred to a civil or social matter.

The Recabites are not commended for obeying their father as God but for obediently receiving what their father had commanded, which was only a civil precept. He therefore had an ulterior object in mind, and he did not require abstinence from wine and other things for its own sake. Paul, in one sentence, has settled this controversy. When he exhorts children to obey their parents, he modifies his exhortation by saying, "in the Lord" (Ephesians 6:1). Paul commands children to obey their parents not in everything, but so that God who is the Sovereign and the only Father of all may still retain his authority, and so that earthly parents may not claim for themselves the authority that would make them lawgivers to souls.

11. "But when Nebuchadnezzar king of Babylon invaded this land, we said, 'Come, we must go to Jerusalem to escape the Babylonian and Aramean armies.' So we have remained in Jerusalem." From this we can see what Jonadab had in mind when he forbade his posterity to use wine: He foresaw what dreadful revolution was at hand. He wanted to train up his posterity so that when difficulties arose they would not collapse under the burden but could patiently bear trouble that others would have found intolerable. So when the Israelites were held back by their fields and domestic possessions, the Recabites went to Jerusalem and were free from danger.

12-16. Then the word of the LORD came to Jeremiah, saying: "This is what the LORD Almighty, the God of Israel, says: Go and tell the men of Judah and the people of Jerusalem, 'Will you not learn a lesson and obey my words?' declares the LORD. 'Jonadab son of Recab ordered his sons not to drink wine and this command has been kept. To this day they do not drink wine, because they obey their forefather's command. But I have spoken to you again and again, yet you have not obeyed me. Again and again I sent all my servants the prophets to you. They said, "Each of you must turn from your wicked ways and reform your actions; do not follow other gods to serve them. Then you will live in the land I have given to you and your fathers." But you have not paid attention or listened to me. The descendants of Jonadab son of Recab have carried out the command their forefather gave them, but these people have not obeyed me.'"

Jeremiah now applies the example he had related. God's complaint is linked to it—his people took less notice of him than the descendants of

Jonadab did of Jonadab. To make the reproof more effective the prophet introduces God as the speaker. God wanted his reproof to the Jews conveyed in his own name and as it were in his own person. "'Will you not learn a lesson and obey my words?' declares the LORD." "I require only," he says in essence, "that you obey me. The rule of meekness that I demand from you is lovely. Since I demand nothing except what children should willingly give to their fathers, why is this moderation so displeasing to you?"

17. "Therefore, this is what the LORD God Almighty, the God of Israel, says: 'Listen! I am going to bring on Judah and on everyone living in Jerusalem every disaster I pronounced against them. I spoke to them, but they did not listen; I called to them, but they did not answer.'" The prophet, having shown that the Jews were condemned by the example of the Recabites and that there was no defense for them, adds that since the Word of God had been useless to them, it would now be effective against them.

18-19. Then Jeremiah said to the family of the Recabites, "This is what the LORD Almighty, the God of Israel, says: 'You have obeyed the command of your forefather Jonadab and have followed all his instructions and have done everything he ordered.' Therefore, this is what the LORD Almighty, the God of Israel, says: 'Jonadab son of Recab will never fail to have a man to serve me.'" The prophet affects the Jews deeply by promising a reward to the sons of Jonadab for obeying their father. For this he promises them a blessing from God. This is hardly surprising, for this commandment, as Paul says, "is the first commandment with a promise" (Ephesians 6:2). There is nothing odd, then, about God promising the Recabites a reward for following their father's command, for God had promised that in the law.

Jeremiah
Chapter 36

1-2. In the fourth year of Jehoiakim son of Josiah king of Judah, this word came to Jeremiah from the LORD: "Take a scroll and write on it all the words I have spoken to you concerning Israel, Judah and all the other nations from the time I began speaking to you in the reign of Josiah till now." The prophet relates a most helpful story in this chapter. He says that he wrote down, at God's command, what he had previously taught in the temple, and also that he sent Baruch to recite that summary in the temple. He says that news of this reached the king's counselors, who then summoned Baruch. When they discovered what was written, they told Baruch to hide, and also Jeremiah, in case the king was angry. This indeed did happen. The king was immediately filled with rage and ordered Baruch and Jeremiah to be taken so they could be killed. But they were hidden and protected by God's goodness.

3. "Perhaps when the people of Judah hear about every disaster I plan to inflict on them, each of them will turn from his wicked way; then I will forgive their wickedness and their sin." Here God explains his purpose. He gave the Jews another test to see if they wanted to be healed, in which case the prophet's teaching would have led to their salvation.

4-6. So Jeremiah called Baruch son of Neriah, and while Jeremiah dictated all the words the LORD had spoken to him, Baruch wrote them on the scroll. Then Jeremiah told Baruch, "I am restricted; I cannot go to the LORD's temple. So you go to the house of the LORD on a day of fasting and read to the people from the scroll the words of the LORD that you wrote as I dictated. Read them to all the people of Judah who come in from their towns." Here the prophet declares that he dictated to Baruch, God's servant, what he had previously taught. There is no doubt that God brought to the prophet's mind anything that he might have forgotten. Jeremiah then stood, as it were, between God and Baruch. God, by his Spirit, presided over and guided the mind and tongue of the prophet. So the prophet, with the Spirit as his guide and teacher, recited what God had commanded. Baruch wrote this down and then proclaimed the summary of what the prophet had taught.

7. **"Perhaps they will bring their petition before the LORD, and each will turn from his wicked ways, for the anger and wrath pronounced against this people by the LORD are great."** Jeremiah, after dictating to the scribe Baruch what he had previously preached to the people, repeats why he did this. It was God's will to test the people, to see if they would be restored to a sound mind.

8. **Baruch son of Neriah did everything Jeremiah the prophet told him to do; at the LORD's temple he read the words of the LORD from the scroll.** Here Baruch's prompt action is commended; he did not disobey God's prophet but willingly undertook the office delegated to him. His office was not without danger, for his message was not at all popular; but he knew he had to carry out this work. Jeremiah then says that **Baruch son of Neriah did everything Jeremiah the prophet told him to do** and **read the words of the LORD** in the temple. A little later on, in verse 10, he calls them **the words of Jeremiah,** but the two phrases mean the same thing. God is represented by his ministers, and he often transfers to them what belongs particularly to himself (see Romans 2:16; 16:25; 2 Timothy 2:8). What is called the teaching of Jeremiah is, strictly speaking, the teaching of God. In the same way Paul called the Gospel that he preached and witnessed to his Gospel, even though he had not composed the Gospel but had received it from Christ and passed it on faithfully.

9-10. **In the ninth month of the fifth year of Jehoiakim son of Josiah king of Judah, a time of fasting before the LORD was proclaimed for all the people in Jerusalem and those who had come from the towns of Judah. From the room of Gemariah son of Shaphan the secretary, which was in the upper courtyard at the entrance of the New Gate of the temple, Baruch read to all the people at the LORD's temple the words of Jeremiah from the scroll.** The prophet adds a fuller explanation here of what he had just said. He had said that Baruch read the words of God in the temple as he had been commanded, but now he relates when and how that was done. He says the book was read when a fast was proclaimed **in the fifth year of Jehoiakim.** The Jews were doubtless aware that some terrible calamity was imminent, for this was a most unusual proclamation. When some calamity was about to happen, they usually resorted to this action. Fasting was not in itself pleasing to God, but it was a symbol of humility, and it also prepared people for prayer.

11-13. **When Micaiah son of Gemariah, the son of Shaphan, heard all the words of the LORD from the scroll, he went down to the secretary's room in the royal palace, where all the officials were sitting: Elishama the secretary, Delaiah son of Shemaiah, Elnathan son of Acbor, Gemariah son of Shaphan, Zedekiah son of Hananiah, and all** the other officials. After Micaiah told them everything he had heard Baruch read to the people from the scroll . . . We do not know why Micaiah came to the princes and the king's counselors. He may have reported to them because he was perverse or perhaps because he was genuinely filled with wonder at what he heard. We have no way of knowing.

14. All the officials sent Jehudi son of Nethaniah, the son of Shelemiah, the son of Cushi, to say to Baruch, "Bring the scroll from which you have read to the people and come." So Baruch son of Neriah went to them with the scroll in his hand. These men should have gone at once to the temple. Although they were not totally irreligious, they showed their pride by not humbling themselves immediately, for they did not wish to mix with ordinary people. Therefore they sent for Baruch.

15-16. They said to him, "Sit down, please, and read it to us." So Baruch read it to them. When they heard all these words, they looked at each other in fear and said to Baruch, "We must report all these words to the king." They did not want to offend the king, so they referred the matter to him. This is the religion of the court—to fear God but not to lose favor with the king. The prophet gives us here a summary of the religion of the king's counselors. Their minds were eaten up with worldly ambition, and they gave more attention to a mortal king than to the only true King of heaven.

17-18. Then they asked Baruch, "Tell us, how did you come to write all this? Did Jeremiah dictate it?" "Yes," Baruch replied, "he dictated all these words to me, and I wrote them in ink on the scroll." The king's counselors were doubtless astonished when they heard that these warnings had been written down as the prophet dictated them. They could hardly believe that these words had been delivered by memory.

19. Then the officials said to Baruch, "You and Jeremiah, go and hide. Don't let anyone know where you are." The king's counselors told Baruch to hide himself, along with Jeremiah, for they realized what danger those two men would be in if they did not immediately flee.

20-23. After they put the scroll in the room of Elishama the secretary, they went to the king in the courtyard and reported everything to him. The king sent Jehudi to get the scroll, and Jehudi brought it from the room of Elishama the secretary and read it to the king and all the officials standing beside him. It was the ninth month and the king was sitting in the winter apartment, with a fire burning in the firepot in front of him. Whenever Jehudi had read three or four columns of the scroll, the king cut them off with a scribe's knife and threw them into the firepot, until the entire scroll was burned in the fire. Here Jeremiah shows how little he had achieved. The king did not just set the scroll to one side, but he tore it into pieces and then, wanting to erase it from memory, threw it into the fire. This trial must have greatly moved the mind of the prophet. He had dictated that scroll by God's command, but all his labor had been in vain. But God calls his servants to speak to the deaf and to bring light to the blind.

24. The king and all his attendants who heard all these words showed no fear, nor did they tear their clothes. They did not rip their clothes, and they showed no fear when they heard such dreadful warnings. It must be seen as a terrible thing when people show contempt at such warnings from above, since they show that they do not fear being instantly destroyed.

25. Even though Elnathan, Delaiah and Gemariah urged the king not to burn the scroll, he would not listen to them. The prophet highlights the king's wickedness by indicating that three of his men opposed his actions, even though this put them in great danger. They saw that the king was carried away by his violent temper. As he resisted God in such an insolent way, what would he not have dared to do to them?

26. Instead, the king commanded Jerahmeel, a son of the king, Seraiah son of Azriel and Shelemiah son of Abdeel to arrest Baruch the scribe and Jeremiah the prophet. But the LORD had hidden them. Jeremiah doubtless accepted the advice he was given, and so his life was protected. However, he acknowledges that he was preserved by God's kindness.

27-28. After the king burned the scroll containing the words that Baruch had written at Jeremiah's dictation, the word of the LORD came to Jeremiah: "Take another scroll and write on it all the words that were on the first scroll, which Jehoiakim king of Judah burned up." The prophet shows what the ungodly gain by contending against God. No matter how hard-hearted they are, they will be broken down by God's power. This happened to King Jehoiakim.

29-30. "Also tell Jehoiakim king of Judah, 'This is what the LORD says: You burned that scroll and said, "Why did you write on it that the king of Babylon would certainly come and destroy this land and cut off both men and animals from it?" Therefore, this is what the LORD says about Jehoiakim king of Judah: He will have no one to sit on the throne of David; his body will be thrown out and exposed to the heat by day and the frost by night.'" There is a double warning here. The first applies to kings and to those who are wealthy and powerful on earth. They are warned to submit reverently to God's Word and not to think they are above it or exempt from its demands. The other admonition applies to teachers: They are to do whatever God commands, without showing any deference to anyone. They are not to fear the consequences of such actions, even in the face of a king, a drawn sword, or any other danger.

31. "'I will punish him and his children and his attendants for their wickedness; I will bring on them and those living in Jerusalem and the people of Judah every disaster I pronounced against them, because

they have not listened.'" The prophet points out their dreadful iniquity in not listening to the warnings by which God had tried to rescue them from the impending ruin.

32. So Jeremiah took another scroll and gave it to the scribe Baruch son of Neriah, and as Jeremiah dictated, Baruch wrote on it all the words of the scroll that Jehoiakim king of Judah had burned in the fire. And many similar words were added to them. Here the prophet tells us that he faithfully obeyed God in writing another book. His perseverance in this matter deserves special praise.

Jeremiah
Chapter 37

1-2. Zedekiah son of Josiah was made king of Judah by Nebuchadnezzar king of Babylon; he reigned in place of Jehoiachin son of Jehoiakim. Neither he nor his attendants nor the people of the land paid any attention to the words the LORD had spoken through Jeremiah the prophet. The prophet tells us here that after King Jehoiachin (Jeconiah) had been taken into exile, the Jews had still not repented. Likewise, Zedekiah, who had succeeded Jeconiah, rejected sound teaching and did not obey the counsel of the prophet.

    3-8. King Zedekiah, however, sent Jehucal son of Shelemiah with the priest Zephaniah son of Maaseiah to Jeremiah the prophet with this message: "Please pray to the LORD our God for us." Now Jeremiah was free to come and go among the people, for he had not yet been put in prison. Pharaoh's army had marched out of Egypt, and when the Babylonians who were besieging Jerusalem heard the report about them, they withdrew from Jerusalem. Then the word of the LORD came to Jeremiah the prophet: "This is what the LORD, the God of Israel, says: Tell the king of Judah, who sent you to inquire of me, 'Pharaoh's army, which has marched out to support you, will go back to its own land, to Egypt. Then the Babylonians will return and attack this city; they will capture it and burn it down.'"

    Jeremiah had briefly explained the state of the city and the land, that although the people had been severely punished by God they remained obstinate in their wickedness. He now adds that messengers were sent to him by King Zedekiah when danger came from the Babylonians. They were expecting help from the Egyptians but were anxious, as the ungodly always are, and so sent a messenger to Jeremiah. They were fearful, although they tried to shake off their fear.

    9-10. "This is what the LORD says: Do not deceive yourselves, thinking, 'The Babylonians will surely leave us.' They will not! Even if you were to defeat the entire Babylonian army that is attacking you and only wounded men were left in their tents, they would come out and burn this city down." Jeremiah took it for granted that the destruction of the city of Jerusalem would not be effected by the forces of King Nebuchadnezzar or by his power or the number of his soldiers, but by God's judgment. Because of this he says that if only wounded men were left in their tents, even if they lay half-dead, they [the Babylonians] would come out and burn this city down. Jeremiah intimates that even if the contest were only with shadows, they would not escape the extreme vengeance that God had threatened.

11-14. After the Babylonian army had withdrawn from Jerusalem because of Pharaoh's army, Jeremiah started to leave the city to go to the territory of Benjamin to get his share of the property among the people there. But when he reached the Benjamin Gate, the captain of the guard, whose name was Irijah son of Shelemiah, the son of Hananiah, arrested him and said, "You are deserting to the Babylonians!" "That's not true!" Jeremiah said. "I am not deserting to the Babylonians." But Irijah would not listen to him; instead, he arrested Jeremiah and brought him to the officials.

Jeremiah relates here how, and on what occasion, he was thrown into prison. It was a miracle that he did not die in the dungeon they put him in. This happened when the Babylonian army went out to meet the Egyptians. He was then free to leave the city. Before this no one could go out of the city, for the gates were closed and the city was surrounded by enemies. It was then, he says, that he went out, in order to go to the territory of Benjamin to get his share of the property.

15. They were angry with Jeremiah and had him beaten and imprisoned in the house of Jonathan the secretary, which they had made into a prison. Jeremiah continues the same narrative and shows how unjustly he was treated, for he received no justice from the hands of the princes. Jeremiah complains that he was oppressed because the princes boiled with rage, so that they did not even allow him the opportunity to speak and make any defense.

16. Jeremiah was put into a vaulted cell in a dungeon, where he remained a long time. We must note the circumstances of the case. It was cruel enough that an innocent man, having been beaten, should be thrown into prison. But being put into a dark and deep place was an additional burden. Since the holy prophet was treated so atrociously, we should not think it strange that the same thing is endured by God's children today. It happens for the same reason—because they give witness to celestial truth. The length of time increased the evil, for the prophet was not kept in prison for a few days or for a month, but until the city was taken—not, indeed, in that prison, for the king moved him into the court of the prison, and he was thrown into a filthy prison for a second time, as if he were destined to die.

17. Then King Zedekiah sent for him and had him brought to the palace, where he asked him privately, "Is there any word from the LORD?" "Yes," Jeremiah replied, "you will be handed over to the king of Babylon." From these words we learn that king Zedekiah, although he had not obeyed good and wise counsels, or God and his truth, did at least call the prophet to him to find out if there was any way in which he could appease God.

18. Then Jeremiah said to King Zedekiah, "What crime have I committed against you or your officials or this people, that you have put me in prison?" Although the prophet's words had displeased the king, Jeremiah also complains that wrong had been done to him since he had been thrown into prison. In this way he shows that he had been unjustly condemned for having threatened ruin to the city and destruction to the kingdom, for he was constrained to do this by the obligations of his office. So the prophet shows that he had not sinned in this but had proclaimed God's commands, however bitter they were to the king and to the people.

19. "Where are your prophets who prophesied to you, 'The king of Babylon will not attack you or this land'?" Here Jeremiah becomes confident and advances the argument to higher ground. He condemns Zedekiah's folly in listening to false prophets and their flatteries. He did this to show how innocent he was. It is as if he said, "I indeed am blamed because I warned against the ruin of the city and temple. But what if the Lord had constrained me to do this? It is clear that I was commissioned by God, for what I have declared has always happened; events have proven that I was sent from above—I told you what would happen. But where are your prophets? They have always been flattering you. Because of their false prophecies you have not returned to the right way. There was still time for you to be reconciled to God when I first warned you. All my efforts were used for this purpose, so that you might be willing to turn to God in repentance. Since your own prophets have deceived you, and the event now clearly proves this, know, O king, that I have been sent from above."

20. "But now, my lord the king, please listen. Let me bring my petition before you: Do not send me back to the house of Jonathan the secretary, or I will die there." This verse shows that Jeremiah was not devoid of human feelings, for he, like other men, dreaded death. But he was so able to control himself that no fear made him neglect his duty. He did not disregard his circumstances, however; and as far as he could, he sought relief from his evils. So he asked for some alleviation from the king. From this we see that the prophets were not logs of wood and did not have iron hearts. Yet, although they were subject to human feelings, they elevated themselves to an invincible courage in order to carry out their work.

21. King Zedekiah then gave orders for Jeremiah to be placed in the courtyard of the guard and given bread from the street of the bakers each day until all the bread in the city was gone. So Jeremiah remained in the courtyard of the guard. Jeremiah tells us he remained in the courtyard of the guard in order to show that God tested his patience, for a prison was a place of degradation. The prophet was exposed to everyone's abuse; so God did not wholly deliver him at this time.

Jeremiah
Chapter 38

1-4. Shephatiah son of Mattan, Gedaliah son of Pashhur, Jehucal son of Shelemiah, and Pashhur son of Malkijah heard what Jeremiah was telling all the people when he said, "This is what the LORD says: 'Whoever stays in this city will die by the sword, famine or plague, but whoever goes over to the Babylonians will live. He will escape with his life; he will live.' And this is what the LORD says: 'This city will certainly be handed over to the army of the king of Babylon, who will capture it.'" Then the officials said to the king, "This man should be put to death. He is discouraging the soldiers who are left in this city, as well as all the people, by the things he is saying to them. This man is not seeking the good of these people but their ruin."

The prophet was again dragged from the court of the prison to the inner part (verse 6), which was dark, filthy, and like a grave. He states the reason for this: It was because four of the princes had heard his words. Probably many of the people had come to listen to the prophet, and he had received a message and delivered it to everyone who visited him. Although he was in prison, the Word of God was not bound. (See 2 Timothy 2:9.) So the prison was intended to hold prophetic truth captive. But the king and his counselors were mistaken, for Jeremiah was no less free in the prison courtyard than if he had walked through the city all day accompanied by many heralds.

5. "He is in your hands," King Zedekiah answered. "The king can do nothing to oppose you." Zedekiah doubtless knew that wrong was being done to the holy prophet. And although he wanted him to remain a prisoner, he also knew that the prophet had not threatened the people out of ill will. So Zedekiah was conscious that he had to face God and was not just dealing with a mortal man. He knew that Jeremiah was no danger to public order as the princes had alleged. The king may even have wanted to deliver Jeremiah from their hands, but he submitted to their anger. For he was divested of all regal power and had become, as it were, a slave to his own counselors, on whom depended the government of the kingdom.

6. So they took Jeremiah and put him into the cistern of Malkijah, the king's son, which was in the courtyard of the guard. They lowered Jeremiah by ropes into the cistern; it had no water in it, only mud, and Jeremiah sank down into the mud. The extreme cruelty of the princes is here portrayed. They threw the holy prophet into a pit, where he sank into the mud. Not to spare so excellent a servant of God was evidence of hardened impiety. It was also sheer savage cruelty, for they had no reason to be so full of anger—Jeremiah had obeyed God and had faithfully carried out the office committed to him.

7-9. But Ebed-Melech, a Cushite, an official in the royal palace, heard that they had put Jeremiah into the cistern. While the king was sitting in the Benjamin Gate, Ebed-Melech went out of the palace and said to him, "My lord the king, these men have acted wickedly in all they have done to Jeremiah the prophet. They have thrown him into a cistern, where he will starve to death when there is no longer any bread in the city." Jeremiah relates here how he was rescued from death, for he could not have lived long in the mud. He would have died from lack of food, cold, and suffocation in the filth of the dungeon. But God rescued him in a wonderful way through the help of Ebed-Melech, a Cushite. He was a foreigner, and this is stated so that we might know that none of the king's counselors resisted this great wickedness. Only a Cushite was found to come to the help of God's prophet.

10. Then the king commanded Ebed-Melech the Cushite, "Take thirty men from here with you and lift Jeremiah the prophet out of the cistern before he dies." Jeremiah's rescue was indeed from above, from the Lord. The king, full of fear, had recently given over the holy prophet to the cruelty of the princes. Since the king had not dared to stand up to his princes, how was it that he now ventured to extricate Jeremiah from the pit? We see that the king's mind had been changed. Previously he had been in the grip of fear and did not dare to plead the cause of the holy man. But now he commanded Ebed-Melech to have Jeremiah taken out of the cistern. It is clear that divine power had overruled.

11-13. So Ebed-Melech took the men with him and went to a room under the treasury in the palace. He took some old rags and worn-out clothes from there and let them down with ropes to Jeremiah in the cistern. Ebed-Melech the Cushite said to Jeremiah, "Put these old rags and worn-out clothes under your arms to pad the ropes." Jeremiah did so, and they pulled him up with the ropes and lifted him out of the cistern. And Jeremiah remained in the courtyard of the guard. Whenever God relieves our miseries, and yet does not completely free us at once, let us bear them patiently and call to mind this example of Jeremiah. God indeed manifested his power in delivering him, and yet it was his will that his prophet should continue in prison. Even through this God was working out his purpose. If the full splendor of God's grace does not shine on us, or if our deliverance is

226

not yet complete, let us allow God to proceed a small step at a time. The least alleviation should be enough for comfort and patience.

14-15. Then King Zedekiah sent for Jeremiah the prophet and had him brought to the third entrance to the temple of the LORD. "I am going to ask you something," the king said to Jeremiah. "Do not hide anything from me." Jeremiah said to Zedekiah, "If I give you an answer, will you not kill me? Even if I did give you counsel, you would not listen to me." King Zedekiah sent for Jeremiah to come to him in **the temple** (that is, in the court of the temple, for it was unlawful for the king to enter the sanctuary, and the court is often called the temple). Zedekiah, in order to have a private conversation with Jeremiah, went to **the third entrance of the temple** and there asked the prophet to explain to him faithfully what he had received from God.

16. But King Zedekiah swore this oath secretly to Jeremiah: "As surely as the LORD lives, who has given us breath, I will neither kill you nor hand you over to those who are seeking your life." The king, wanting some new revelation, assured Jeremiah of his safety. He then said that he would not take revenge on him, even if he was displeased with the prophet's answer.

17-18. Then Jeremiah said to Zedekiah, "This is what the LORD God Almighty, the God of Israel, says: 'If you surrender to the officers of the king of Babylon, your life will be spared and this city will not be burned down; you and your family will live. But if you will not surrender to the officers of the king of Babylon, this city will be handed over to the Babylonians and they will burn it down; you yourself will not escape from their hands.'" The prophet gave the king the hope of pardon. But as hypocrites are not easily moved when God woos them by the sweetness of his promises, Jeremiah added the warning, **"But if you will not surrender to the officers of the king of Babylon, this city will be handed over to the Babylonians."**

19. King Zedekiah said to Jeremiah, "I am afraid of the Jews who have gone over to the Babylonians, for the Babylonians may hand me over to them and they will mistreat me." Zedekiah had good reason to be anxious, and the simple way he expressed this to Jeremiah seemed to give some hope that he was going to be obedient to God. But succeeding events would show that he was bound by fear and that he refused the counsel of God and the prophet.

20-22. "They will not hand you over," Jeremiah replied. **"Obey the LORD by doing what I tell you. Then it will go well with you, and your life will be spared. But if you refuse to surrender, this is what the LORD has revealed to me: All the women left in the palace of the king of Judah will be brought out to the officials of the king of Babylon. Those women will say to you: 'They misled you and overcame you—those trusted friends of yours. Your feet are sunk in the mud; your friends have deserted you.'"** Once again Jeremiah encourages Zedekiah by saying that at least his punishment would be light. He then promised Zedekiah that he would be safe from all the insults he feared. **"They will not hand you over,"** he says; or in other words, "Leave this to God's providence, resign yourself to God, and do not doubt that he will keep you safe." God, in his kindness, allows the faithful to cast their cares on him. But at the same time if they disobey him, that is a sign of deliberate wickedness, and such perverseness puts out all the light of grace. Zedekiah was so dull in heart that he did not accept this second promise. He did well to confess his fear, but he should also have received the remedy.

23. **"All your wives and children will be brought out to the Babylonians. You yourself will not escape from their hands but will be captured by the king of Babylon; and this city will be burned down."** Jeremiah continues the same subject, showing the seriousness of the situation. The king was at least frightened and so might submit to the right counsel. When we hear that death is close at hand, that fills us with horror. When many evils are mentioned, we are moved. This is doubtless what the prophet looked for in Zedekiah. Then he says that Zedekiah would come into the hands of his enemies and that all his **wives and children will be brought out to the Babylonians.** Had Zedekiah been in his right mind, he would have preferred to die a hundred times. From this we see the prophet's purpose. He saw that Zedekiah could not be moved to action just by presenting him with his own death; so he added other circumstances that were calculated to affect him more strongly.

24-26. **Then Zedekiah said to Jeremiah, "Do not let anyone know about this conversation, or you may die. If the officials hear that I talked with you, and they come to you and say, 'Tell us what you said to the king and what the king said to you; do not hide it from us or we will kill you,' then tell them, 'I was pleading with the king not to send me back to Jonathan's house to die there.'"** The miserable state of the king is seen here. He chose a life of trembling rather than immediately being free from care and anxiety. He acknowledged that what the prophet said was true, but he declined to do anything about it.

27. **All the officials did come to Jeremiah and question him, and he told them everything the king had ordered him to say. So they said no more to him, for no one had heard his conversation with the king.** The prophet says that he did as the king commanded him, but he does not commend what he had done. We see that even God's servants have sometimes spoken evasively, when oppressed with extreme fear. So we are reminded to seek resolute firmness from God, for he alone can sustain us to cope with the fear of danger.

28. **And Jeremiah remained in the courtyard of the guard until the day Jerusalem was captured.** The city was taken just as God had declared to him. He now starts to narrate historically the destruction and the burning of the city.

Jeremiah
Chapter 39

38:28b—39:2. This is how Jerusalem was taken: In the ninth year of Zedekiah king of Judah, in the tenth month, Nebuchadnezzar king of Babylon marched against Jerusalem with his whole army and laid siege to it. And on the ninth day of the fourth month of Zedekiah's eleventh year, the city wall was broken through. Jeremiah seems to take the role of historian rather than prophet here. But he confirms his previous prophecies and at the same time shows that he had said nothing thoughtlessly.

3-4. Then all the officials of the king of Babylon came and took seats in the Middle Gate: Nergal-Sharezer of Samgar, Nebo-Sarsekim a chief officer, Nergal-Sharezer a high official and all the other officials of the king of Babylon. When Zedekiah king of Judah and all the soldiers saw them, they fled; they left the city at night by way of the king's garden, through the gate between the two walls, and headed toward the Arabah. It is shown here that Jeremiah's prophecy was fulfilled. It became evident that he had not spoken unadvisedly but from the mouth of God.

5. But the Babylonian army pursued them and overtook Zedekiah in the plains of Jericho. They captured him and took him to Nebuchadnezzar king of Babylon at Riblah in the land of Hamath, where he pronounced sentence on him. The Babylonians pursued the fugitive king, doubtless from a hidden impulse from above. It is probable that Zedekiah was betrayed by his own people. But he might have escaped if he had not been given up by the hand of God.

6. There at Riblah the king of Babylon slaughtered the sons of Zedekiah before his eyes and also killed all the nobles of Judah. The prophet now tells us how cruelly Nebuchadnezzar treated Zedekiah. It was surely a sad spectacle to see a king, who came from a noble family and who was a type of Christ, lying prostrate at the feet of a proud conqueror. But much worse than this was to see his own sons killed before his eyes.

Nebuchadnezzar wanted to remove all hope by killing the royal family and the nobles.

7. Then he put out Zedekiah's eyes and bound him with bronze shackles to take him to Babylon. Here was an accumulation of misery. The king had his eyes put out after he had seen his own sons killed.

8. The Babylonians set fire to the royal palace and the houses of the people and broke down the walls of Jerusalem. Here the prophet shows that whatever he had predicted was fulfilled, so that nothing was lacking to render faith sure and strong. He had said that if Zedekiah surrendered, the houses in the city would not be burned. Zedekiah thought this was idle talk and refused to listen to it. He now heard, although he was blind, that everything that God declared through Jeremiah's mouth came about, for his palace was burned along with all the other houses.

9. Nebuzaradan commander of the imperial guard carried into exile to Babylon the people who remained in the city, along with those who had gone over to him, and the rest of the people. The prophet now recounts what happened to those who remained in the city, whom Nebuchadnezzar and his army spared. He says they were carried into exile to Babylon.

10. But Nebuzaradan the commander of the guard left behind in the land of Judah some of the poor people, who owned nothing; and at that time he gave them vineyards and fields. The prophet now adds that some were left to inhabit the land, the poor people who owned nothing. He says these were made, as it were, the lords of the land when the Babylonians returned to their own nation.

11-12. Now Nebuchadnezzar king of Babylon had given these orders about Jeremiah through Nebuzaradan commander of the imperial guard: "Take him and look after him; don't harm him but do for him whatever he asks." The prophet now shows God's fatherly care, which he experienced in the preservation of his life and safety.

13-14. So Nebuzaradan the commander of the guard, Nebushazban a chief officer, Nergal-Sharezer a high official and all the other officers of the king of Babylon sent and had Jeremiah taken out of the court-yard of the guard. They turned him over to Gedaliah son of Ahikam, the son of Shaphan, to take him back to his home. So he remained among his own people. Jeremiah states that he was released from prison at Nebuchadnezzar's command.

15-18. While Jeremiah had been confined in the courtyard of the guard, the word of the LORD came to him: "Go and tell Ebed-Melech the Cushite, 'This is what the LORD Almighty, the God of Israel, says: I am about to fulfill my words against this city through disaster, not prosperity. At that time they will be fulfilled before your eyes. But I will rescue you on that day, declares the LORD; you will not be handed over to those you fear. I will save you; you will not fall by the

sword but will escape with your life, because you trust in me, declares the LORD.'" The prophet says that God remembered Ebed-Melech the Cushite, by whom he was preserved, although he was a foreigner from an uncivilized nation. The prophet says that man will be rewarded for his exceptional courage and service. In his very danger he experienced God's favor and was protected and delivered from peril.

Jeremiah
Chapter 40

1-4. The word came to Jeremiah from the LORD after Nebuzaradan commander of the imperial guard had released him at Ramah. He had found Jeremiah bound in chains among all the captives from Jerusalem and Judah who were being carried into exile to Babylon. When the commander of the guard found Jeremiah, he said to him, "The LORD your God decreed this disaster for this place. And now the LORD has brought it about; he has done just as he said he would. All this happened because you people sinned against the LORD and did not obey him. But today I am freeing you from the chains on your wrists. Come with me to Babylon, if you like, and I will look after you; but if you do not want to, then don't come. Look, the whole country lies before you; go wherever you please." Jeremiah now expands on what he has just recounted. He tells us that some of the Babylonian generals were sent to release him from prison. He adds that he had been placed in the care of Gedaliah, who had been set over the poor of the land. He now tells us that he was brought to Ramah still bound in chains.

5. However, before Jeremiah turned to go, Nebuzaradan added, "Go back to Gedaliah son of Ahikam, the son of Shaphan, whom the king of Babylon has appointed over the towns of Judah, and live with him among the people, or go anywhere else you please." Then the commander gave him provisions and a present and let him go. Jeremiah continues, telling how Nebuzaradan dealt bountifully with him and allowed him to go wherever he wanted. From this we conclude that Nebuchadnezzar was completely convinced about Jeremiah's honesty. He was invited to Babylon, but he was also allowed to remain in his own country.

6. So Jeremiah went to Gedaliah son of Ahikam at Mizpah and stayed with him among the people who were left behind in the land. Jeremiah's firm resolve is seen here. He did not hesitate to reject Nebuzaradan's kind offer so that he would not give any offense.

7-8. When all the army officers and their men who were still in the open country heard that the king of Babylon had appointed Gedaliah son of Ahikam as governor over the land and had put him in charge of the men, women and children who were the poorest in the land and who had not been carried into exile to Babylon, they came to Gedaliah at Mizpah—Ishmael son of Nethaniah, Johanan and Jonathan the sons of Kareah, Seraiah son of Tanhumeth, the sons of Ephai the Netophathite, and Jaazaniah the son of the Maacathite, and their men. The prophet now tells us that the leaders of the forces went to Gedaliah.

9-10. Gedaliah son of Ahikam, the son of Shaphan, took an oath to reassure them and their men. "Do not be afraid to serve the Babylonians," he said. "Settle down in the land and serve the king of Babylon, and it will go well with you. I myself will stay at Mizpah to represent you before the Babylonians who come to us, but you are to harvest the wine, summer fruit and oil, and put them in your storage jars, and live in the towns you have taken over." It was a great thing when Gedaliah said that he would **represent** the people. It was as if he said he would be a surety for them and nothing terrible would happen to them. He was not thinking about himself, but he used the power given to him for the public good.

11-12. When all the Jews in Moab, Ammon, Edom and all the other countries heard that the king of Babylon had left a remnant in Judah and had appointed Gedaliah son of Ahikam, the son of Shaphan, as governor over them, they all came back to the land of Judah, to Gedaliah at Mizpah, from all the countries where they had been scattered. And they harvested an abundance of wine and summer fruit. The prophet shows here that if inner wickedness had not arisen, the condition of the people would have been endurable until the time of exile had elapsed.

13-14. Johanan son of Kareah and all the army officers still in the open country came to Gedaliah at Mizpah and said to him, "Don't you know that Baalis king of the Ammonites has sent Ishmael son of Nethaniah to take your life?" But Gedaliah son of Ahikam did not believe them. This is a sad story, from which we may conclude that God's wrath against the people had not been appeased by the destruction of the city and the burning of the temple. It was some token of mercy when Gedaliah was set over the remnant of the people and the poor who had been allowed to stay in the land. But Gedaliah would soon be killed (41:1-2), and the people would be scattered. The king of Babylon became angry, for the Babylonian guards were also killed. It was God's purpose to execute his judgment also on this remnant.

15-16. Then Johanan son of Kareah said privately to Gedaliah in Mizpah, "Let me go and kill Ishmael son of Nethaniah, and no one will know it. Why should he take your life and cause all the Jews who are gathered around you to be scattered and the remnant of Judah to perish?" But Gedaliah son of Ahikam said to Johanan son of Kareah, "Don't do such a thing! What you are saying about Ishmael is not true." We see here that the holy man acted like a blind man, for he not only disregarded the counsel given to him, but he also rejected the help offered to him.

Jeremiah
Chapter 41

1-3. In the seventh month Ishmael son of Nethaniah, the son of Elishama, who was of royal blood and had been one of the king's officers, came with ten men to Gedaliah son of Ahikam at Mizpah. While they were eating together there, Ishmael son of Nethaniah and the ten men who were with him got up and struck down Gedaliah son of Ahikam, the son of Shaphan, with the sword, killing the one whom the king of Babylon had appointed as governor over the land. Ishmael also killed all the Jews who were with Gedaliah at Mizpah, as well as the Babylonian soldiers who were there. It was particularly cruel of Ishmael to kill Gedaliah, for Gedaliah had shown Ishmael kindness and entertained him. Even ungodly nations have always deemed hospitality as something sacred. To violate it has always been thought of as committing a great atrocity.

4-7. The day after Gedaliah's assassination, before anyone knew about it, eighty men who had shaved off their beards, torn their clothes and cut themselves came from Shechem, Shiloh and Samaria, bringing grain offerings and incense with them to the house of the LORD. Ishmael son of Nethaniah went out from Mizpah to meet them, weeping as he went. When he met them, he said, "Come to Gedaliah son of Ahikam." When they went into the city, Ishmael son of Nethaniah and the men who were with him slaughtered them and threw them into a cistern. The prophet shows here that after Ishmael had assassinated Gedaliah, he continued his violent acts. This is how wicked men become hardened. Ishmael flattered and enticed innocent men, pretended to be kind to them, and then killed them.

8. But ten of them said to Ishmael, "Don't kill us! We have wheat and barley, oil and honey, hidden in a field." So he let them alone and did not kill them with the others. We see that Ishmael's violent deeds were linked to greed. He killed the innocent like a madman. But when he was offered the hope of gain, he spared some of them. So in one man we see there were many monsters; if he hated all those who favored Gedaliah, why did he allow these ten men to escape? It was because his avarice prevailed.

9. Now the cistern where he threw all the bodies of the men he had killed along with Gedaliah was the one King Asa had made as part of his defense against Baasha king of Israel. Ishmael son of Nethaniah filled it with the dead. The prophet tells us that the cistern he used to deposit the bodies of those he killed had been dug by King Asa as a fortification for the city.

10. Ishmael made captives of all the rest of the people who were in Mizpah—the king's daughters along with all the others who were left there, over whom Nebuzaradan commander of the imperial guard had appointed Gedaliah son of Ahikam. Ishmael son of Nethaniah took them captive and set out to cross over to the Ammonites. The prophet now tells us that Ishmael made captives of all the rest of the people. After he had killed Gedaliah, his barbarity frightened everyone, and thus many people sided with him. They made him their leader, and so he was able to capture all these people and take them to the Ammonites.

11-12. When Johanan son of Kareah and all the army officers who were with him heard about all the crimes Ishmael son of Nethaniah had committed, they took all their men and went to fight Ishmael son of Nethaniah. They caught up with him near the great pool in Gibeon. Here the prophet informs us that Ishmael did not succeed in his plans. He had hoped to sell the people to the king of Ammon, but he was prevented from doing this.

13-14. When all the people Ishmael had with him saw Johanan son of Kareah and the army officers who were with him, they were glad. All the people Ishmael had taken captive at Mizpah turned and went over to Johanan son of Kareah. The people were glad to go over to Johanan and his army because Johanan and the other leaders came with arms and were trained to fight. So Ishmael had made plans for himself, but God frustrated them. Yet it was God's will that he should remain alive.

15. But Ishmael son of Nethaniah and eight of his men escaped from Johanan and fled to the Ammonites. Let us learn not to make judgments merely on the basis of appearances. Rather, let us patiently wait while God makes known to us the various ways in which he punishes the wicked. This should help to strengthen our faith when we see godly people cruelly killed and wicked people surviving. From this it follows that we are to look for a judgment of God that does not yet appear.

16-18. Then Johanan son of Kareah and all the army officers who were with him led away all the survivors from Mizpah whom he had recovered from Ishmael son of Nethaniah after he had assassinated Gedaliah son of Ahikam: the soldiers, women, children and court officials he had brought from Gibeon. And they went on, stopping

at Geruth Kimham near Bethlehem on their way to Egypt to escape the Babylonians. They were afraid of them because Ishmael son of Nethaniah had killed Gedaliah son of Ahikam, whom the king of Babylon had appointed as governor over the land. The prophet now shows that although some kind of virtue appeared in Johanan son of Kareah, he did not possess a sound mind. He was an energetic and discreet man, but he showed his lack of belief when he led the remnant of the people into Egypt, though the prophet had forbidden such a thing. This passage shows us that the leaders who put Ishmael to flight were courageous, but they lacked faith. They lacked what is most important—piety and a fear of God.

Jeremiah
Chapter 42

1-3. Then all the army officers, including Johanan son of Kareah and Jezaniah son of Hoshaiah, and all the people from the least to the greatest approached Jeremiah the prophet and said to him, "Please hear our petition and pray to the LORD your God for this entire remnant. For as you now see, though we were once many, now only a few are left. Pray that the LORD your God will tell us where we should go and what we should do." They asked Jeremiah to pray that they would know God's will about where they should go. They did this because they wanted to flatter the prophet after all the wrong they had done. Had they spoken from the heart, they would have allowed themselves to be guided by what God had already told them, but as it was they just showed how hypocritical they were, as we shall see in the coming verses.

4. "I have heard you," replied Jeremiah the prophet. "I will certainly pray to the LORD your God as you have requested; I will tell you everything the LORD says and will keep nothing back from you." In order to prepare them to obey, the prophet says that he will be God's faithful messenger. The prophet suspected their motives.

5-6. Then they said to Jeremiah, "May the LORD be a true and faithful witness against us if we do not act in accordance with everything the LORD your God sends you to tell us. Whether it is favorable or unfavorable, we will obey the LORD our God, to whom we are sending you, so that it will go well with us, for we will obey the LORD our God." From this it appears that the people understood that Jeremiah wanted to assure them of his faithfulness and sincerity before he consulted God. But they soon betrayed their true colors when they heard that what they had intended to do did not please God. They had not only rejected God's counsel and that of his prophet, but they had treated him insolently, as if he had told them something that was untrue. Their hypocrisy ought to be a lesson to us.

7-10. Ten days later the word of the LORD came to Jeremiah. So he called together Johanan son of Kareah and all the army officers who were with him and all the people from the least to the greatest. He said to them, "This is what the LORD, the God of Israel, to whom you sent me to present your petition, says: 'If you stay in this land, I will build you up and not tear you down; I will plant you and not uproot you, for I am grieved over the disaster I have inflicted on you.'" Jeremiah recounts the answer God gave him. He passes this on, in God's name, to the leaders and to all the people. The answer is that they should remain in the land, as this would be for their good. But they had deceitfully asked for God's counsel and had resolved not to obey God.

11-12. "'Do not be afraid of the king of Babylon, whom you now fear. Do not be afraid of him, declares the LORD, for I am with you and will save you and deliver you from his hands. I will show you compassion so that he will have compassion on you and restore you to your land.'" Although Nebuchadnezzar had been offended and might avenge the wrong done to him, God promised to prevent this and declared that he would not allow him to harm the Jews. God says in effect, "You fear Nebuchadnezzar, but you do not need to." He adds, **"For I am with you and will save you and deliver you from his hands."** He tells the Jews to be hopeful because as long as they rely on God's protection, they will be safe. (See Psalm 23:4; 37:3.) We should be fully convinced that God's help is above all the aid any human beings can ever give us. So if the whole world rises up against us, we can look down on the situation from a secure height without fear. This is the summary of what is said here. It is in line with Christ's saying, "My Father, who has given them to me, is greater than all" (John 10:29).

13-17. "However, if you say, 'We will not stay in this land,' and so disobey the LORD your God, and if you say, 'No, we will go and live in Egypt, where we will not see war or hear the trumpet or be hungry for bread,' then hear the word of the LORD, O remnant of Judah. This is what the LORD Almighty, the God of Israel, says: 'If you are determined to go to Egypt and you do go to settle there, then the sword you fear will overtake you there, and the famine you dread will follow you into Egypt, and there you will die. Indeed, all who are determined to go to Egypt to settle there will die by the sword, famine and plague; not one of them will survive or escape the disaster I will bring on them.'" God had promised that his advice to the Jews would be good and safe. Now he warns them that if they disobey him, everything they do will end in misery. They had not specifically asked if it would be for their good if they went to Egypt or if that would please God. But God, who penetrates all hidden motives, anticipated their thoughts and declared that they would be unhappy if they went to Egypt. From this we see how the prophet, or rather God himself who spoke through his servant, tried every possible means to keep them on the path of duty.

18. "This is what the LORD Almighty, the God of Israel, says: 'As my anger and wrath have been poured out on those who lived in Jerusalem, so will my wrath be poured out on you when you go to Egypt. You will be an object of cursing and horror, of condemnation and reproach; you will never see this place again.'" In other words, "You know how God's anger has been poured out on the inhabitants of Jerusalem. In the same way it will be poured upon those who flee to Egypt."

19-21. "O remnant of Judah, the LORD has told you, 'Do not go to Egypt.' Be sure of this: I warn you today that you made a fatal mistake when you sent me to the LORD your God and said, 'Pray to the LORD our God for us; tell us everything he says and we will do it.' I have told you today, but you still have not obeyed the LORD your God in all he sent me to tell you." Here the prophet explains their sin in more detail. Their punishment might have seemed extreme if their impiety had not been clearly exposed. He says that the Jews had continually despised God's counsel. They had pretended that they would obey God's will as soon as they knew it. But they showed that they never had any intention of doing this. They had no desire to obey God.

22. "So now, be sure of this: You will die by the sword, famine and plague in the place where you want to go to settle." The prophet now concludes his discourse, having mentioned why God dealt with them so severely. He tells them what awaited them in Egypt and that they had no hope of being safe there.

"You will die by the sword, famine and plague." This was a common way of speaking among the prophets, as is well known. When they say it is no good for ungodly people to hope for impunity, they represent God as having at his command all kinds of punishment.

Jeremiah
Chapter 43

1-3. When Jeremiah finished telling the people all the words of the LORD their God—everything the LORD had sent him to tell them—Azariah son of Hoshaiah and Johanan son of Kareah and all the arrogant men said to Jeremiah, "You are lying! The LORD our God has not sent you to say, 'You must not go to Egypt to settle there.' But Baruch son of Neriah is inciting you against us to hand us over to the Babylonians, so they may kill us or carry us into exile to Babylon." The prophet continues with the narrative. He says he has not only spoken in God's name, but as he knew their hardness, he adds protestations that might have moved even stones. But he addresses the deaf; and so it appears that they were completely fascinated by the devil. From this we learn not to mock God or to be deceitful when we ask for his guidance. We must be ruled by his Word.

4. So Johanan son of Kareah and all the army officers and all the people disobeyed the LORD's command to stay in the land of Judah. The prophet had shown that Johanan son of Kareah and the rest of the army officers and all the people had not inquired of the prophet about God's will in good faith. For when they saw that God's counsel did not coincide with their wicked and foolish desires, they rose up against the prophet.

5-7. Instead, Johanan son of Kareah and all the army officers led away all the remnant of Judah who had come back to live in the land of Judah from all the nations where they had been scattered. They also led away all the men, women and children and the king's daughters whom Nebuzaradan commander of the imperial guard had left with Gedaliah son of Ahikam, the son of Shaphan, and Jeremiah the prophet and Baruch son of Neriah. So they entered Egypt in disobedience to the LORD and went as far as Tahpanhes. The prophet now gives more details about what he had just briefly touched on. He says that Johanan son of Kareah and all the army officers led away the remnant of the people and those who had returned from various countries. Then they entered Egypt in disobedience to the Lord.

8-10. In Tahpanhes the word of the LORD came to Jeremiah: "While the Jews are watching, take some large stones with you and bury them in clay in the brick pavement at the entrance to Pharaoh's palace in Tahpanhes. Then say to them, 'This is what the LORD Almighty, the God of Israel, says: I will send for my servant Nebuchadnezzar king of Babylon, and I will set his throne over these stones I have buried here; he will spread his royal canopy above them.'" This passage shows that Jeremiah was taken by force along with the others, so that he became an exile in Egypt against his wishes. He was compelled to go there, as if he had been put in chains.

11. "'He [Nebuchadnezzar] will come and attack Egypt, bringing death to those destined for death, captivity to those destined for captivity, and the sword to those destined for the sword.'" In other words, "Even if Egypt was heavily populated, the immense number of people would benefit nobody, for they will be conquered by their enemy. Some will die by the sword, and some will be driven into exile. Egypt will be destroyed as if no one stood up to defend her." The prophet adds this to shake the false confidence of the Jews.

12. "'He [Nebuchadnezzar] will set fire to the temples of the gods of Egypt; he will burn their temples and take their gods captive. As a shepherd wraps his garment around him, so will he wrap Egypt around himself and depart from there unscathed.'" Jeremiah mentions **the temples** so the Jews will understand that no part of the land will be safe from destruction. It often happens that when enemies take over a country the temples are spared, for religion commands respect, and thus even temples given over to idols have often remained untouched when enemies have destroyed everything else. But it is probable that the Babylonians had such presumption and pride that they wanted to destroy all the temples so that no religion existed anywhere except among themselves.

13. "'There in the temple of the sun in Egypt he [Nebuchadnezzar] will demolish the sacred pillars and will burn down the temples of the gods of Egypt.'" If sanctity and religion would not preserve the temples, what would become of private houses? God's prophet intimates that the ruin of Egypt will be so great that nothing in it will escape.

Jeremiah
Chapter 44

1-7. This word came to Jeremiah concerning all the Jews living in Lower Egypt—in Migdol, Tahpanhes and Memphis—and in Upper Egypt: "This is what the LORD Almighty, the God of Israel, says: You saw the great disaster I brought on Jerusalem and on all the towns of Judah. Today they lie deserted and in ruins because of the evil they have done. They provoked me to anger by burning incense and by worshiping other gods that neither they nor you nor your fathers ever knew. Again and again I sent my servants the prophets, who said, 'Do not do this detestable thing that I hate!' But they did not listen or pay attention; they did not turn from their wickedness or stop burning incense to other gods. Therefore, my fierce anger was poured out; it raged against the towns of Judah and the streets of Jerusalem and made them the desolate ruins they are today. Now this is what the LORD God Almighty, the God of Israel, says: Why bring such great disaster on yourselves by cutting off from Judah the men and women, the children and infants, and so leave yourselves without a remnant?"

Jeremiah had already prophesied against the Jews who had taken refuge in Egypt, as though there would be a safe and quiet retreat for them in that rich and almost unassailable land. But he now speaks against them for another reason. They had not only gone to Egypt against God's will, but while they were there they polluted themselves with all kinds of superstition. Doubtless God aimed to prevent this when he told them not to go to Egypt, for he knew how prone they were to idolatry and to false and adulterous ways of worship. He did not want them to live in that land where they might learn to pervert his worship. And this had happened, as is clear from this present prophecy. As they had thrown off all shame and given themselves up to the superstitions of the ungodly, the prophet again testified that God would take vengeance on them. The Jews who lived in Egypt did not deserve to be pardoned because they had deliberately rejected God's favor.

8. "Why provoke me to anger with what your hands have made, burning incense to other gods in Egypt, where you have come to live? You will destroy yourselves and make yourselves an object of cursing and reproach among all the nations on earth." This verse should be read with the previous verse. The prophet asked why the Jews willingly cut themselves off from every hope of safety and were seeking their own ruin. He now states this more fully: They were provoking God with their superstitions. He then points out the reason for all the evils that came upon them—the pollution of God's true worship by engaging in idolatry.

9-10. "Have you forgotten the wickedness committed by your fathers and by the kings and queens of Judah and the wickedness committed by you and your wives in the land of Judah and the streets of Jerusalem? To this day they have not humbled themselves or shown reverence, nor have they followed my law and the decrees I set before you and your fathers." The prophet now states the disgrace of the Jews in not acknowledging that God had most severely punished the superstitions to which they had previously been addicted.

The more clearly God reveals himself to us, the more grievously we sin if we turn away from serving and worshiping him. He has left nothing out of his Word that is necessary for us to worship him acceptably. Since we have in front of us the rule of a godly life, we will deserve reproof if we do not obey God's statutes.

11-12. "Therefore, this is what the LORD Almighty, the God of Israel, says: I am determined to bring disaster on you and to destroy all Judah. I will take away the remnant of Judah who were determined to go to Egypt to settle there. They will all perish in Egypt; they will fall by the sword or die from famine. From the least to the greatest, they will die by sword or famine. They will become an object of cursing and horror, of condemnation and reproach." God through the prophet again pronounces punishment on the obstinate. As the people Jeremiah has to deal with are so stubborn in their wickedness, it is little wonder that he repeats these warnings so often.

13-14. "I will punish those who live in Egypt with the sword, famine and plague, as I punished Jerusalem. None of the remnant of Judah who have gone to live in Egypt will escape or survive to return to the land of Judah, to which they long to return and live; none will return except a few fugitives." God said that only those few to whom he gave permission would be allowed to return to Judah.

15-16. Then all the men who knew that their wives were burning incense to other gods, along with all the women who were present—a large assembly—and all the people living in Lower and Upper Egypt, said to Jeremiah, "We will not listen to the message you have spoken to us in the name of the LORD!" He says that all the men who knew about the godless ways of their wives spoke to him. Jeremiah makes it clear here that the idolatry started with these women, but the men readily indulged them.

17. "We will certainly do everything we said we would: We will burn incense to the Queen of Heaven and will pour out drink offerings to her just as we and our fathers, our kings and our officials did in the towns of Judah and in the streets of Jerusalem. At that time we had plenty of food and were well off and suffered no harm." They now reveal their obstinacy. Having said that they had no faith in Jeremiah, as he had not been sent by God, they now add that they would be worshipers but only in their own way. We see here the source of all superstitions. People's pride lies behind all idolatry. When people arrogate so much to themselves and even decide how or what God (or god) should be worshiped, everything will go wrong.

18. "But ever since we stopped burning incense to the Queen of Heaven and pouring out drink offerings to her, we have had nothing and have been perishing by sword and famine." Here he emphasizes their ingratitude in blaming God for all their calamities. These punishments should have restored them to their right minds, but they only made them more and more obstinate.

19. The women added, "When we burned incense to the Queen of Heaven and poured out drink offerings to her, did not our husbands know that we were making cakes like her image and pouring out drink offerings to her?" The women said they were not the only ones who took part in this superstition, for a large number of men joined in.

20-23. Then Jeremiah said to all the people, both men and women, who were answering him, "Did not the LORD remember and think about the incense burned in the towns of Judah and the streets of Jerusalem by you and your fathers, your kings and your officials and the people of the land? When the LORD could no longer endure your wicked actions and the detestable things you did, your land became an object of cursing and a desolate waste without inhabitants, as it is today. Because you have burned incense and have sinned against the LORD and have not obeyed him or followed his law or his decrees or his stipulations, this disaster has come upon you, as you now see." The prophet refutes the impious objections the Jews used to try to undermine his teaching. He rejects all their boasting. At the beginning they had said, "Our kings, our princes, and our fathers used these rites before, and they have been given to us, as it were, by their hands." To this Jeremiah answers in essence, "This is certainly true, and for this reason God severely judged their impiety, destroying the kingdom and demolishing the city. If your kings and fathers and princes had not been so impious, God would not have punished them so severely, for he had promised to be a Father to the children of Abraham. God, then, must have been very seriously offended with you and your fathers and your kings."

24-26. Then Jeremiah said to all the people, including the women, "Hear the word of the LORD, all you people of Judah in Egypt. This is what the LORD Almighty, the God of Israel, says: You and your wives have shown by your actions what you promised when you said, 'We will certainly carry out the vows we made to burn incense and pour out drink offerings to the Queen of Heaven.' Go ahead then, do what you promised! Keep your vows! But hear the word of the LORD, all Jews living in Egypt: 'I swear by my great name,' says the LORD, 'that no one from Judah living anywhere in Egypt will ever again invoke my name or swear, "As surely as the Sovereign LORD lives."'"

Jeremiah continues with the same subject. He not only bitterly reproves the ungodly who despised his teaching, but he also shows that they can gain nothing by their audacity because they will at length be broken down, since they cannot bear to be corrected. He says at the beginning, **"You and your wives have . . . said."** The men are included. That is, "You have spoken, both men and women, and have shown **by your actions** how evil you are." They deliberately provoked God.

27. "'For I am watching over them for harm, not for good; the Jews in Egypt will perish by sword and famine until they are all destroyed.'" Here he repeats what he had said in the previous verses: None of the Jews except a **very few** (verse 28; cf. verse 14) would remain alive in Egypt.

28. "'Those who escape the sword and return to the land of Judah from Egypt will be very few. Then the whole remnant of Judah who came to live in Egypt will know whose word will stand—mine or theirs.'" Here he adds that a **few** people will escape. In verse 14 he said that nobody would escape, but he added at the end of that verse, **except a few fugitives.**

29-30. "'This will be the sign to you that I will punish you in this place,' declares the LORD, 'so that you will know that my threats of harm against you will surely stand.' This is what the LORD says: 'I am going to hand Pharaoh Hophra king of Egypt over to his enemies who seek his life, just as I handed Zedekiah king of Judah over to Nebuchadnezzar king of Babylon, the enemy who was seeking his life.'" Jeremiah seals his prophecy by adding a sign that would take place at that time. Although the Jews were unworthy to receive any sign, it was given so that they might know they had trusted in vain in the protection of Egypt, so they would be without any excuse.

Jeremiah
Chapter 45

1-5. This is what Jeremiah the prophet told Baruch son of Neriah in the fourth year of Jehoiakim son of Josiah king of Judah, after Baruch had written on a scroll the words Jeremiah was then dictating: "This is what the LORD, the God of Israel, says to you, Baruch: You said, 'Woe to me! The LORD has added sorrow to my pain; I am worn out with groaning and find no rest.'" The LORD said, "Say this to him: 'This is what the LORD says: I will overthrow what I have built and uproot what I have planted, throughout the land. Should you then seek great things for yourself? Seek them not. For I will bring disaster on all people, declares the LORD, but wherever you go I will let you escape with your life.'"

We have said that prophetic books were not written by their authors in the order in which they are now read. When a prophet had preached and committed to writing a summary of his teaching, he fixed it on the doors of the temple. Scribes collected the summaries, and the volumes we now have were made from these. I repeat this now in case someone may think Jeremiah took no notice of chronological order. For he will soon prophesy about the ungodly nations, and it is certain that these prophecies were given, in part, before the start of Jehoiakim's reign, some during his reign, and some in the time of Zedekiah. So you must bear in mind that the book we now have in our hands was not in a sense written by Jeremiah himself but contains collected summaries that were later made into one volume.

We are given here a special prophecy about Baruch, who, as we know, was the prophet's scribe, and not only his scribe or amanuensis but also his disciple. Here Jeremiah relates that Baruch was severely reproved for not having a resolute mind when the document in chapter 36 came to be written.

The LORD says: "I will overthrow what I have built and uproot what I have planted, throughout the land." In other words, "I have until now adorned this people with singular endowments. For I chose them as a heritage for myself, to be a holy people and a priestly kingdom. I live in the midst of them, I have undertaken to care for them, I am their Father, and they are to me not just a son but a firstborn son. This land is holy because I have set my name in it. I have therefore built and planted this people and this land. But now," he says, "I am pulling down and uprooting."

Jeremiah
Chapter 46

1-2. This is the word of the LORD that came to Jeremiah the prophet concerning the nations: Concerning Egypt: This is the message against the army of Pharaoh Neco king of Egypt, which was defeated at Carchemish on the Euphrates River by Nebuchadnezzar king of Babylon in the fourth year of Jehoiakim son of Josiah king of Judah.
Here Jeremiah starts to prophesy against foreign nations; he continues to do so until the penultimate chapter. This was not the first time he announced these oracles, but as I have explained, a book was eventually compiled that included his prophecies, and strict chronological order was not observed. In chapter 25 we see that he warned the ungodly nations about the punishment they deserved before Jehoiakim became king. But as I have said, the prophecies about ungodly nations have been collected together here.

3-5. "Prepare your shields, both large and small, and march out for battle! Harness the horses, mount the steeds! Take your positions with helmets on! Polish your spears, put on your armor! What do I see? They are terrified, they are retreating, their warriors are defeated. They flee in haste without looking back, and there is terror on every side," declares the LORD. Jeremiah now speaks in a way that was often used by the prophets but is not familiar to us. When the prophets pronounced God's judgments and punishments on the ungodly, they did not speak in simple language, as though they were describing a narrative. Rather, they used figurative expressions and introduced various people so that their teaching might penetrate more effectively into men's hearts. At one time they introduced God as speaking, and at another time they pronounced this or that as if someone else was speaking. And at other times they themselves proclaimed God's commands.

6. "The swift cannot flee nor the strong escape. In the north by the River Euphrates they stumble and fall." We must observe that whatever men use to make them safe does no good if God opposes them. The prophet means that although men may excel in many things and possess many gifts, they will still perish if that is God's will. Fleeing will not save the swift, and strength will not save the bold.

7-8. "Who is this that rises like the Nile, like rivers of surging waters? Egypt rises like the Nile, like rivers of surging waters. She says, 'I will rise and cover the earth; I will destroy cities and their people.'" The prophet again meets those doubts that might have been entertained by the godly, which would have prevented them from receiving this prophecy with faith and due reverence. When our thoughts are full of external things, God's power is disregarded. When, therefore, we speak of some impregnable kingdom, it does not enter our minds that no stronghold is of any account with God. So it was necessary to extol God's power highly when the prophets spoke about his judgments. If they had not done this, people would have said, "Those who are behind strong fortifications must be free from evils and, as it were, beyond the reach of weapons, and so there is nothing to fear."

9. "Charge, O horses! Drive furiously, O charioteers! March on, O warriors—men of Cush and Put who carry shields, men of Lydia who draw the bow." He continues with the same subject, dealing with whatever might discredit his prophecy. When the faithful saw that the Egyptians on that expedition not only had immense forces but also had alliances with the Ethiopians and the Libyans, it seemed hardly possible that such an army could be defeated. So the prophet says here that despite all this power and despite the strong alliances, all these forces would be defeated.

10. "But that day belongs to the LORD, the LORD Almighty [the Lord GOD of hosts, KJV]—a day of vengeance, for vengeance on his foes. The sword will devour till it is satisfied, till it has quenched its thirst with blood. For the Lord, the LORD Almighty, will offer sacrifice in the land of the north by the River Euphrates." The prophet has described the powerful forces of Pharaoh in which the people trusted; they thought victory was certain. Then he says the event will end in a very different way. He says that Pharaoh will only look on his chariots and horsemen, his hired soldiers and their weapons, but he will not look to God, **the Lord GOD of hosts.** Although this name is often used for God in Scripture, it is used here as a special title. The prophet is deriding Pharaoh's folly in thinking that the outcome of the war is in his own hand, as if God did not overrule everything. So the prophet says that the victory depends on God alone.

11. "Go up to Gilead and get balm, O Virgin Daughter of Egypt. But you multiply remedies in vain; there is no healing for you." The prophet says that the slaughter will be like a fatal plague, as if God wanted to deny the Egyptians all hope. We know that the kingdom of Egypt did not perish at that time. But the Egyptians were so depressed that they kept themselves shut up inside their own borders. So the prophet says that they have an incurable wound and that they will not recover their former power. After this time the kingdom of Egypt never flourished; and after a few years it was brought under Babylon's power.

12. "The nations will hear of your shame; your cries will fill the earth. One warrior will stumble over another; both will fall down together." He concludes this prophecy by saying that news of this slaughter will be reported among all the nations.

13. This is the message the LORD spoke to Jeremiah the prophet about the coming of Nebuchadnezzar king of Babylon to attack Egypt. The previous prophecy concerned slaughter by the Egyptian army, when Pharaoh went to help the Assyrians, with whom he had an alliance. But in this prophecy Jeremiah says that God's punishment will also fall on the people of Egypt. God was punishing them for their own evil actions and also because they had corrupted the Jews.

14-15. "Announce this in Egypt, and proclaim it in Migdol; proclaim it also in Memphis and Tahpanhes: 'Take your positions and get ready, for the sword devours those around you.' Why will your warriors be laid low? They cannot stand, for the LORD will push them down." Public speeches may be applauded, but they only fill people with a hollow fear or joy. But the prophets spoke with another purpose in mind—to teach, to exhort, to reprove, to warn in a way that was calculated to be effective.

16. "They will stumble repeatedly; they will fall over each other. They will say, 'Get up, let us go back to our own people and our native lands, away from the sword of the oppressor.'" Before they are struck by the enemy, they will be falling all over each other.

17. They did cry there, Pharaoh king of Egypt is but a noise; he hath passed the time appointed (kjv). The prophet prophesies what will happen in the future, but he speaks, as was the custom, in the past tense. The prophets announce future things as if people could see them, to give more credence to their prophecies.

18. "As surely as I live," declares the King, whose name is the LORD Almighty, "one will come who is like Tabor among the mountains, like Carmel by the sea." Why did the prophet say this? It was because the Egyptians thought they had escaped because there had been a delay.

19. "Pack your belongings for exile, you who live in Egypt, for Memphis will be laid waste and lie in ruins without inhabitant." The prophet exults over the Egyptians, so that he might confirm his teaching more and more. As we have said, and as experience teaches, unbelievers are hardly moved when God summons them to his tribunal. They remain in their folly unless their torpor is shaken out of them. This is why the prophet attacks the wicked so strongly—that he may wake them up from their drowsy state.

20. "Egypt is a beautiful heifer, but a gadfly is coming against her from the north." Jeremiah intimates here that although Egypt indulged in pleasures, it could not escape God's vengeance. The prophet undermines that nation's false confidence. It is as if he said, "The Egyptians trust in their prosperity like a heifer frisking in the fields, but calamity is coming from the north, from the Babylonians."

21. "The mercenaries in her ranks are like fattened calves. They too will turn and flee together, they will not stand their ground, for the day of disaster is coming upon them, the time for them to be punished." Here the prophet refers to the **mercenaries** in the Egyptian army who had come from countries as far away as Lydia.

22. "Egypt will hiss like a fleeing serpent as the enemy advances in force; they will come against her with axes, like men who cut down trees." Snakes hiss as they creep along, and Jeremiah says that the defeated Egyptians will be so shattered that they will not dare to grumble openly but will be reduced to muttering like hissing snakes.

23. "They will chop down her forest," declares the LORD, "dense though it be. They are more numerous than locusts, they cannot be counted." He compares the people of Egypt to a forest, for he had said that individual men would be like trees (verse 22). To confirm this he ascribes the words to God; he predicted nothing but what God had determined to do.

24. "The Daughter of Egypt will be put to shame, handed over to the people of the north." He says Egypt will be brought to the greatest disgrace, for her enemies will treat her dreadfully.

25. The LORD Almighty, the God of Israel, says: "I am about to bring punishment on Amon god of Thebes, on Pharaoh, on Egypt and her gods and her kings, and on those who rely on Pharaoh." The prophet speaks again in God's name and contrasts God's glory with the perversity of Egypt and of his own nation, for his warnings had little effect.

26. "I will hand them over to those who seek their lives, to Nebuchadnezzar king of Babylon and his officers. Later, however, Egypt will be inhabited as in times past," declares the LORD. Jeremiah declares that Nebuchadnezzar will be victorious over Egypt.

27. "Do not fear, O Jacob my servant; do not be dismayed, O Israel. I will surely save you out of a distant place, your descendants from the land of their exile. Jacob will again have peace and security, and no one will make him afraid." The prophet now speaks to the Israelites, for he was not appointed a teacher to ungodly nations. Whatever he said to ungodly nations was for the benefit of his people. The prophets extended their prophecies about God's judgments to all nations, for otherwise the Israelites would have been disheartened, thinking their condition was worse than that of other people. "What can this mean? God has chosen us

as his special people, but we are the most miserable of people. God judges us but spares the unbelieving nations. It would have been better for us if we had been rejected completely by God."

28. "Do not fear, O Jacob my servant, for I am with you," declares the LORD. "Though I completely destroy all the nations among which I scatter you, I will not completely destroy you. I will discipline you but only with justice; I will not let you go entirely unpunished." He repeats the thoughts of the previous verse—and little wonder, for under such hopeless circumstances it was not easy to sustain the people so they would wait patiently for their redemption.

Jeremiah
Chapter 47

1. **This is the word of the LORD that came to Jeremiah the prophet concerning the Philistines before Pharaoh attacked Gaza.** Jeremiah prophesies here against the Philistines, who were the Israelites' enemies and were very cruel to them. It is clear that God wanted to show through this prophecy his love for the Israelites, for he supported their cause and avenged the wrongs done to them. God predicted the ruin of the Philistines so the Israelites would know God's fatherly love for them as he set himself against their enemies.

2-3. **This is what the LORD says: "See how the waters are rising in the north; they will become an overflowing torrent. They will overflow the land and everything in it, the towns and those who live in them. The people will cry out; all who dwell in the land will wail at the sound of the hoofs of galloping steeds, at the noise of enemy chariots and the rumble of their wheels. Fathers will not turn to help their children; their hands will hang limp."** The prophet wanted to remind the Jews that it would only be the start of what God would do when Gaza was plundered, and that a much worse punishment hung over the ungodly nation that had so wronged God's people.

4. **"For the day has come to destroy all the Philistines and to cut off all survivors who could help Tyre and Sidon. The LORD is about to destroy the Philistines, the remnant from the coasts of Caphtor."** Jeremiah shows now more clearly and without any metaphor what he means: Destruction will come upon the Philistines.

5. **"Gaza will shave her head in mourning; Ashkelon will be silenced. O remnant on the plain, how long will you cut yourselves?"** The prophet returns to figurative language so that he might illustrate his prophecy more graphically and so influence the Jews. Shaved heads indicated mourning; in desperation they scratched their faces with their nails and pulled out their hair. He adds, **"Ashkelon will be silenced."** This city had a great name in the land of the Philistines and was close to Gaza.

6-7. "'Ah, sword of the LORD,' you cry, 'how long till you rest? Return to your scabbard; cease and be still.' But how can it rest when the LORD has commanded it, when he has ordered it to attack Ashkelon and the seacoast?"** Here Jeremiah turns to address God's **sword.** It is very striking and forceful when the prophet at one time addresses the land of the Philistines and at another time the **sword** of God. He is confirming his prophecy, which the Jews might have otherwise doubted.

Jeremiah
Chapter 48

1. **Concerning Moab: This is what the LORD Almighty, the God of Israel, says: "Woe to Nebo, for it will be ruined. Kiriathaim will be disgraced and captured; the stronghold will be disgraced and shattered."** This prophecy is against the Moabites. It would be of no interest if we did not remember the history on which the application of what is said depends. The Moabites originated from Lot, but they were of the same blood as the Israelites. They should have remembered their brotherhood and should have been kind to the Israelites, for God had spared them when the people of Israel went into Canaan. The Israelites passed through the borders of Moab without doing them any harm because God planned to preserve them for a time, out of regard for Lot. But the Moabites kept plotting against God's people. So here God prophesies against them, so that the Israelites might know he has not overlooked their miserable condition.

2. **"Moab will be praised no more; in Heshbon men will plot her downfall: 'Come, let us put an end to that nation.' You too, O Madmen, will be silenced; the sword will pursue you."** The prophet does not speak in an ordinary way but declares in lofty terms what God has committed to him. Not that the Moabites heard these warnings, but it was necessary that he should pronounce vengeance in this forceful way, so that the Jews would know that the cruelty of the Moabites would not go unpunished.

3. **"Listen to the cries from Horonaim, cries of great havoc and destruction."** By mentioning many cities, the prophet shows that the whole land is doomed to ruin; no corner of it will be exempt from destruction.

4. **"Moab will be broken; her little ones will cry out."** The prophet again speaks generally of the whole country, saying that the land of Moab is afflicted. This did not happen at this time; but to confirm the prophecy, he speaks as if the event has already taken place. The prophets, of course,

spoke as though God was speaking, describing things that were hidden as if they had already happened.

5-6. "**They go up the way to Luhith, weeping bitterly as they go; on the road down to Horonaim anguished cries over the destruction are heard. Flee! Run for your lives; become like a bush in the desert.**" Here Jeremiah uses imagery again, saying that **weeping** will be heard everywhere on the way to **Luhith.** This city was probably on high ground.

7. "**Since you trust in your deeds and riches, you too will be taken captive, and Chemosh will go into exile, together with his priests and officials.**" Jeremiah says why God will punish the Moabites, though later on we will see there were also other reasons why God was so displeased with them. Only one reason why God decided to destroy the land of Moab is given here; others, such as the Moabites' conspiring against the Israelites, are not mentioned.

8. "**The destroyer will come against every town, and not a town will escape. The valley will be ruined and the plateau destroyed, because the LORD has spoken.**" The Israelites had to depend on this promise for many years.

9. "**Put salt on Moab, for she will be laid waste; her towns will become desolate, with no one to live in them.**" Here is an instance of bitter derision. The Moabites' pride needed to be pierced.

10. "**A curse on him who is lax in doing the LORD's work! A curse on him who keeps his sword from bloodshed!**" The prophet here encourages the Babylonians to be so severe that they destroy the whole nation of Moab. As we have seen, the prophets assumed different characters, so that what they said might be more impressive.

11. "**Moab has been at rest from youth, like wine left on its dregs, not poured from one jar to another—she has not gone into exile. So she tastes as she did, and her aroma is unchanged.**" Here he says more clearly something we have seen before: It is no good for Moab to promise himself everlasting impunity on the grounds that he has prospered for such a long time. The prophet says he will be suddenly destroyed when God occupies the seat of judgment.

12. "**But days are coming,**" declares the LORD, "**when I will send men who pour from jars, and they will pour her out; they will empty her jars and smash her jugs.**" The prophet now adds that **days are coming** when God will suddenly punish them.

13. "**Then Moab will be ashamed of Chemosh, as the house of Israel was ashamed when they trusted in Bethel.**" We can see more clearly from this verse that the prophet is speaking not so much to the Moabites as to his own people. He is not teaching the Moabites in order to promote their safety. On the contrary, he means his teaching to benefit the Jews.

14-15. "**How can you say, 'We are warriors, men valiant in battle'?**

Moab will be destroyed and her towns invaded; her finest young men will go down in the slaughter," declares the King, whose name is the LORD Almighty. Here the prophet condemns the Moabites' pride. They trusted in their own strength and derided God and what the prophets announced.

16. "The fall of Moab is at hand; her calamity will come quickly." Here the prophet says something more: The vengeance he is talking about will come soon.

17. All ye that are about him, bemoan him; and all ye that know his name, say, How is the strong staff broken, and the beautiful rod! (kjv). The prophet seems to urge all the neighbors to show sympathy. But he was not saying that the Moabites deserved pity and that their neighbors should feel sorry for them and console (niv) them. In this figurative way of speaking he exaggerated the dreadful evils that were about to fall on the Moabites. It is as if he said, "God's judgment will be so terrible that all their neighbors will tremble, groan, and mourn for them."

18. "Come down from your glory and sit on the parched ground, O inhabitants of the Daughter of Dibon, for he who destroys Moab will come up against you and ruin your fortified cities." The prophet derides the presumption of the Moabites because the Babylonians will destroy their fortified cities.

19. "Stand by the road and watch, you who live in Aroer. Ask the man fleeing and the woman escaping, ask them, 'What has happened?'" The prophets spoke in this kind of lofty style in order to penetrate the hardness of people's hearts.

20-24. "Moab is disgraced, for she is shattered. Wail and cry out! Announce by the Arnon that Moab is destroyed. Judgment has come to the plateau—to Holon, Jahzah and Mephaath, to Dibon, Nebo and Beth Diblathaim, to Kiriathaim, Beth Gamul and Beth Meon, to Kerioth and Bozrah—to all the towns of Moab, far and near." The Lord says through Jeremiah that no part of the land will be exempt from destruction.

25. "Moab's horn is cut off; her arm is broken," declares the LORD. The prophet uses another metaphor to say the same thing. By horn he means power, as everyone who is at all familiar with Scripture knows. This word indicates strength or any defense for the protection of a nation. He says that Moab's horn is cut off. And then he adds that her arm is broken. The second clause clarifies the meaning of the first one.

26-27. "Make her drunk, for she has defied the LORD. Let Moab wallow in her vomit; let her be an object of ridicule. Was not Israel the object of your ridicule? Was she caught among thieves, that you shake your head in scorn whenever you speak of her?" The prophet now speaks to the Babylonians, who are to carry out God's punishment. So he says, "Make her drunk, for she has defied the LORD." That is, she has raised herself up in her pride against God.

28. "Abandon your towns and dwell among the rocks, you who live in Moab. Be like a dove that makes its nest at the mouth of a cave." Here Jeremiah pronounces exile on the Moabites.

29. "We have heard of Moab's pride—her overweening pride and conceit, her pride and arrogance and the haughtiness of her heart." Here the prophet anticipates that no matter how much the Moabites boast, God will be their Judge.

30. "I know her insolence but it is futile," declares the LORD, "and her boasts accomplish nothing." Whenever the ungodly boast, we should not be afraid, bearing in mind what the prophet teaches here. He says that this pride stems from their derision of God, but that it will not help them at all in their lives.

31. "Therefore I wail over Moab, for all Moab I cry out, I moan for the men of Kir Hareseth." The Lord says he will wail and cry out and moan as would someone who is oppressed by evil.

32. "I weep for you, as Jazer weeps, O vines of Sibmah. Your branches spread as far as the sea; they reached as far as the sea of Jazer. The destroyer has fallen on your ripened fruit and grapes." Here the prophet shows more clearly what he said in a general way before, that Sibmah will weep for her vines, as Jazer had for hers. These were cities in the land of Moab.

33. "Joy and gladness are gone from the orchards and fields of Moab. I have stopped the flow of wine from the presses; no one treads them with shouts of joy. Although there are shouts, they are not shouts of joy." He pursues the same metaphor or comparison, saying that all places that were previously fruitful will be made desolate.

34. "The sound of their cry rises from Heshbon to Elealeh and Jahaz, from Zoar as far as Horonaim and Eglath Shelishiyah, for even the waters of Nimrim are dried up." He means there will be continual howls and tears coming from different parts of the land and spreading to every corner.

35. "In Moab I will put an end to those who make offerings on the high places and burn incense to their gods," declares the LORD. In this verse the prophet says something he had referred to before—God will come to avenge the pride and cruelty of the Moabites.

36. "So my heart laments for Moab like a flute; it laments like a flute for the men of Kir Hareseth. The wealth they acquired is gone." The wealth of the Moabites was so great at that time that it dazzled everyone, but God would punish them severely.

37-39. "Every head is shaved and every beard cut off; every hand is cut and every waist is covered with sackcloth. On all the roofs in Moab and in the public squares there is nothing but mourning, for I have broken Moab like a jar that no one wants," declares the LORD. "How shattered she is! How they wail! How Moab turns her back in shame! Moab has become an object of ridicule, an object of horror to all those around her." The prophet gives a general description of very great mourning. In their great sorrow, people used to tear out their hair, shave their beard, put on sackcloth, and cut their hands with a knife or with their nails. Jeremiah puts them all together to show that Moab's grief will not be like normal mourning; the people will lament in an extreme way.

40. **This is what the LORD says: "Look! An eagle is swooping down, spreading its wings over Moab."** Here again he introduces God as the speaker, in order to confirm a seemingly impossible prophecy with divine authority. "God is he," the prophet says, "who declares that enemies will come who will fly through all the land of Moab." He compares the Babylonians to eagles.

41. **"The cities will be captured and the strongholds taken. In that day the hearts of Moab's warriors will be like the heart of a woman in labor."** He mentions these things because the country of Moab thought that it was invincibly defended by its cities and strongholds. They reasoned, "Should the Babylonians come and attack, many cities will resist them, and they will have to spend much time in overcoming these obstacles. It may happen, then, that they will become so tired that they will return to their own country, and we can recover what we have lost."

42. **"Moab will be destroyed as a nation because she defied the LORD."** God through the prophet says that although God's punishment might seem severe, it is just, because the Moabites have not only been cruel to their neighbors but have **defied** God.

43-44. **"Terror and pit and snare await you, O people of Moab," declares the LORD. "Whoever flees from the terror will fall into a pit, whoever climbs out of the pit will be caught in a snare; for I will bring upon Moab the year of her punishment," declares the LORD.** By these words the prophet shows that although the Moabites will try to escape in many ways, they will still be captured, for God's hand will trap them everywhere.

45. **"In the shadow of Heshbon the fugitives stand helpless, for a fire has gone out from Heshbon, a blaze from the midst of Sihon; it burns the foreheads of Moab, the skulls of the noisy boasters."** The Lord through the prophet Jeremiah confirms what he had said in the previous verse, that it will be no good for the Moabites to retreat to their strongest cities, to **Heshbon** and **Sihon**, for fire will envelop the whole land.

46. **"Woe to you, O Moab! The people of Chemosh are destroyed; your sons are taken into exile and your daughters into captivity."**

He adds that it will be no good for the Moabites to trust in their idol **Chemosh,** for people and idol will perish together.

47. "Yet I will restore the fortunes of Moab in days to come," declares the LORD. **Here ends the judgment on Moab.** God extends mercy, so that the Moabites will not be totally destroyed.

Jeremiah
Chapter 49

1. Concerning the Ammonites: This is what the LORD says: "Has Israel no sons? Has she no heirs? Why then has Molech taken possession of Gad? Why do his people live in its towns?" God had spared the Ammonites when he rescued his people from Egypt, but they were so ungrateful, they even harassed the children of Abraham. For this reason God through Jeremiah now prophesies against them.

2. "But the days are coming," declares the LORD, "when I will sound the battle cry against Rabbah of the Ammonites; it will become a mound of ruins, and its surrounding villages will be set on fire. Then Israel will drive out those who drove her out," says the LORD. Here God plainly testifies that he will not allow the Ammonites to enjoy their unjust plunder.

3. "Wail, O Heshbon, for Ai is destroyed! Cry out, O inhabitants of Rabbah! Put on sackcloth and mourn; rush here and there inside the walls, for Molech will go into exile, together with his priests and officials." God now expresses through the prophet triumph over the land of Ammon.

4. "Why do you boast of your valleys, boast of your valleys so fruitful? O unfaithful daughter, you trust in your riches and say, 'Who will attack me?'" People's minds continually vacillate because they do not ponder God's power enough, and so the prophet now declares that it was no good for the Ammonites to glory in their **valleys**. He wanted to get rid of anything that might keep people from believing his prophecy.

5. "I will bring terror on you from all those around you," declares the Lord, the LORD Almighty. "Every one of you will be driven away, and no one will gather the fugitives." Jeremiah concludes his prophecy by saying that God will undermine the confidence of the Ammonites and **bring terror** on them.

6. "Yet afterward, I will restore the fortunes of the Ammonites,"

declares the LORD. He now says the same thing that he had said to the Moabites. Some hope remained for the Ammonites.

7. **Concerning Edom: This is what the LORD Almighty says: "Is there no longer wisdom in Teman? Has counsel perished from the prudent? Has their wisdom decayed?"** Here Jeremiah turns to the Edomites, who were inveterate enemies of the chosen people although they should have been kindly disposed to them, for both had Abraham as their ancestor. The Edomites gloried in their holy descent and also had circumcision in common with the Jews. It was a most impious cruelty for the Edomites to show such bitter hatred toward their blood relatives. Our prophet reproves them most severely, as did Ezekiel and Obadiah (see Ezekiel 25:12-14; Obadiah 1, 8).

8. **"Turn and flee, hide in deep caves, you who live in Dedan, for I will bring disaster on Esau at the time I punish him."** The prophet reveals the extent of their pride. "Flee," he says. The language is abrupt, but the meaning is unambiguous. But when warned to flee, none of them moved, for they thought they were always safe in their own country.

9. **"If grape pickers came to you, would they not leave a few grapes? If thieves came during the night, would they not steal only as much as they wanted?"** The prophet says here that the destruction of the nation will be so great that it will be worse than any kind of plundering, for when you harvest your vines you leave some grapes, and when a thief enters a house, he does not take away everything with him but is satisfied with his booty. But with the Edomites, the Lord says, nothing will be left.

10-11. **"But I will strip Esau bare; I will uncover his hiding places, so that he cannot conceal himself. His children, relatives and neighbors will perish, and he will be no more. Leave your orphans; I will protect their lives. Your widows too can trust in me."** The prophet goads the Edomites when God says, mockingly, that he will protect their **orphans** and **widows**.

12. This is what the LORD says: **"If those who do not deserve to drink the cup must drink it, why should you go unpunished? You will not go unpunished, but must drink it."** In speaking of a **cup**, the prophet uses a phrase that often appears in Scripture. Scripture calls punishment inflicted on people for their sins a cup, of which God gives each person a fair measure. So calamities do not happen by chance but come from God's hand, as if he were giving men and women a cup to drink. When God afflicts his own people, they are forced to drink, as it were, his wrath. This is referred to as a sour or bitter cup.

13. **"I swear by myself,"** declares the LORD, **"that Bozrah will become a ruin and an object of horror, of reproach and of cursing; and all its towns will be in ruins forever."** Jeremiah declares that God has sworn an oath concerning the destruction of **Bozrah**. He uses a particular

to mean something more general, including the whole nation under the name of this city.

14. I have heard a message from the LORD: An envoy was sent to the nations to say, "Assemble yourselves to attack it! Rise up for battle!" The prophet again shows that God will bring about this calamity. Nobody would have thought the Edomites could be destroyed. The faithful needed to be taught about this. And this the prophet does when he says that all this will be done by God.

15. "Now I will make you small among the nations, despised among men." The prophet describes the state of that nation and compares it with that of the chosen people and even other nations. Although they were rich, they lived among mountains that were not fertile.

16. "The terror you inspire and the pride of your heart have deceived you, you who live in the clefts of the rocks, who occupy the heights of the hill. Though you build your nest as high as the eagle's, from there I will bring you down," declares the LORD. In other words, "How is it that God has made you contemptible? You have not succeeded in frightening your neighbors. You are swollen with pride, but this is mere delusion. You are greatly mistaken and deceive yourself about your strength; your condition should make you humble."

17. "Edom will become an object of horror; all who pass by will be appalled and will scoff because of all its wounds." The prophet did not repeat what he had said in order to explain more clearly what would have otherwise remained obscure, but to drive home the point in the hearts of the faithful when it seemed to them incredible.

18. "As Sodom and Gomorrah were overthrown, along with their neighboring towns," says the LORD, **"so no one will live there; no man will dwell in it."** He expands on what he has just said. He had said Edom would **become an object of horror,** and now he describes this in more detail. They will be like **Sodom and Gomorrah** when they **were overthrown.**

19. "Like a lion coming up from Jordan's thickets to a rich pastureland, I will chase Edom from its land in an instant. Who is the chosen one I will appoint for this? Who is like me and who can challenge me? And what shepherd can stand against me?" I think this means that as lions ascended to higher ground when the Jordan overflowed, so the Babylonians would come to the Edomites and invade their country like angry wild beasts.

20. Therefore, hear what the LORD has planned against Edom, what he has purposed against those who live in Teman: The young of the flock will be dragged away; he will completely destroy their pasture because of them. This means that whatever Jeremiah predicted about the Edomites could not be taken back, for it was a settled decree, as fixed as if God had thought about it for a hundred or a thousand years.

21. At the sound of their fall the earth will tremble; their cry will resound to the Red Sea. Even if the Jews thought this was impossible, God would overthrow that nation.

22. Look! An eagle will soar and swoop down, spreading its wings over Bozrah. In that day the hearts of Edom's warriors will be like the heart of a woman in labor. Again he speaks of the speedy coming of the Babylonians. It is as if he said, "When their nation seems to be at peace, when they rest secure in their own nest, the Babylonians will suddenly come."

23. Concerning Damascus: "Hamath and Arpad are dismayed, for they have heard bad news. They are disheartened, troubled like the restless sea." Jeremiah speaks about the kingdom of Syria here, referring to it as **Damascus**, which was where their kings lived. The Syrians had from the beginning been very hostile to the Israelites and had often attacked them. The kings of Israel then made a treaty with the Syrians in order to attack their fellow Jews in Judah. In this way the Syrians caused great trouble to the Jews and were friends to the Israelites until both kingdoms were attacked by the Babylonians. So it is probable that this prophecy was announced while the kingdom of Syria still stood, or at least before its final overthrow, for it became very weak before it was totally defeated.

24-26. "Damascus has become feeble, she has turned to flee and panic has gripped her; anguish and pain have seized her, pain like that of a woman in labor. Why has the city of renown not been abandoned, the town in which I delight? Surely, her young men will fall in the streets; all her soldiers will be silenced in that day," declares the LORD Almighty. The prophet continues with the same theme. As the kingdom of Syria had flourished and had become wealthy and powerful, it was hardly credible that it could be overthrown. The prophet describes in detail the fall of that kingdom in order to confirm what he had said.

27. "I will set fire to the walls of Damascus; it will consume the fortresses of Ben-Hadad." Here God himself speaks and declares that he himself will bring about the destruction that Jeremiah prophesied. He uses the illustration of **fire** because there is nothing so dreadful as burning, and we know that even the greatest cities are reduced to ashes by fire.

28. Concerning Kedar and the kingdoms of Hazor, which Nebuchadnezzar king of Babylon attacked: This is what the LORD says: "Arise, and attack Kedar and destroy the people of the East." The people of Kedar lived in a part of Arabia. It is not said why God punished these people. It may be that they had previously harmed the Israelites.

29. "Their tents and their flocks will be taken; their shelters will be carried off with all their goods and camels. Men will shout to them, 'Terror on every side!'" The prophet mentions **tents . . . flocks . . . shel-**

ters ... camels. The people of Kedar did not live in a fertile country, and they possessed no arable land. They had little wealth and no cities or palaces. The prophet says they are doomed to destruction and therefore will be exposed to their enemies.

30. "Flee quickly away! Stay in deep caves, you who live in Hazor," declares the LORD. "Nebuchadnezzar king of Babylon has plotted against you; he has devised a plan against you." Since these shepherds lived securely on their mountains, Nebuchadnezzar prepared his forces and divided them. Thus the people of Kedar were defeated not so much by strength as by counsel and craft.

31. "Arise and attack a nation at ease, which lives in confidence," declares the LORD, "a nation that has neither gates nor bars; its people live alone." They were so confident of their safety that they did not need gates or bars, and they lived alone. As they were shepherds and nobody envied them, they thought no enemy would ever attack them.

32. "Their camels will become plunder, and their large herds will be booty. I will scatter to the winds those who are in distant places and will bring disaster on them from every side," declares the LORD. The prophet again repeats that the people of Kedar will be so plundered by their enemies that nothing will remain for them.

33. "Hazor will become a haunt of jackals, a desolate place forever. No one will live there; no man will dwell in it." Here Jeremiah concludes his prophecy about the people of Kedar. He says their land will be deserted.

34-35. This is the word of the LORD that came to Jeremiah the prophet concerning Elam, early in the reign of Zedekiah king of Judah. This is what the LORD Almighty says: "See, I will break the bow of Elam, the mainstay of their might." When Jeremiah speaks about the Elamites, he is referring to a particular nation, one that is near to but distinct from the Persians. The Elamites helped the Babylonians oppress the Jews.

36. "I will bring against Elam the four winds from the four quarters of the heavens; I will scatter them to the four winds, and there will not be a nation where Elam's exiles do not go." The four winds will come to disperse all the people. God himself speaks here to lend more weight to this prophecy. When Scripture extols God's power it often refers to the winds, and it is a great miracle when the whole world is suddenly windswept.

37. "I will shatter Elam before their foes, before those who seek their lives; I will bring disaster upon them, even my fierce anger," declares the LORD. "I will pursue them with the sword until I have made an end of them." This verse shows that the Elamites were particularly cruel to God's people, for God surely had reason to punish them so severely.

38. "I will set my throne in Elam and destroy her king and offi-

cials," declares the LORD. The name of the people will not survive, for the whole race will become extinct, even though some individuals will not be killed.

39. **"Yet I will restore the fortunes of Elam in days to come,"** **declares the LORD.** Here God moderates the severity of the prediction because he will at length gather some of the Elamites and restore them, so that they might again obtain some place of honor.

Jeremiah
Chapter 50

1. **This is the word the LORD spoke through Jeremiah the prophet concerning Babylon and the land of the Babylonians.** So far our prophet has been speaking about neighboring nations that cruelly harassed the chosen people. It was some consolation when the children of Abraham understood that God took up their cause and avenged the wrongs they had suffered. Yet this of itself would have been of no great consolation. Many people might have been seen it as nothing unless there was some hope of restoration as well. So it was necessary that what we read in chapters 50—51 be predicted, for without these events there could be no restoration. Although this is the last prophecy to be given, we should note that the prophet had spoken about the destruction of Babylon from the beginning. But this prophecy is given as the conclusion of the book to lessen the sorrow of the exiles, for it was no small comfort to them to hear that the tyranny that had oppressed them would not last forever.

2. **"Announce and proclaim among the nations, lift up a banner and proclaim it; keep nothing back, but say, 'Babylon will be captured; Bel will be put to shame, Marduk filled with terror. Her images will be put to shame and her idols filled with terror.'"** He predicts the ruin of Babylon not in simple words, for nothing seemed then more unreasonable than to announce the things that God at length brought about. The sum of the whole is that although Babylon thought it was safe and secure through the help of its idol and through its wealth and military power, this confidence would become empty.

3. **"A nation from the north will attack her and lay waste her land. No one will live in it; both men and animals will flee away."** Having spoken about the power of Babylon and its idols, the prophet now indicates how Babylon will be destroyed. A nation will come **from the north**—that is, from north of Babylon.

4. **"In those days, at that time,"** declares the LORD, **"the people of Israel and the people of Judah together will go in tears to seek the**

LORD their God." The prophet now explains more clearly God's purpose in punishing the Babylonians so severely. His aim was to provide for the safety of his church.

5. "They will ask the way to Zion and turn their faces toward it. They will come and bind themselves to the LORD in an everlasting covenant that will not be forgotten." They will exhort one another to seek God and to link themselves to him through an everlasting covenant.

6. "My people have been lost sheep; their shepherds have led them astray and caused them to roam on the mountains. They wandered over mountain and hill and forgot their own resting place." The prophet compares God's people to lost sheep. He says they roamed on the mountains and forgot their own resting place. He throws the blame on the shepherds, through whom these miserable people had been led astray.

7. "Whoever found them devoured them; their enemies said, 'We are not guilty, for they sinned against the LORD, their true pasture, the LORD, the hope of their fathers.'" Jeremiah continues with the same subject, telling us about the miserable condition of the people before God relieved them from their evils. This shows God's goodness as he raised up his people, as it were, from hell when they despaired.

8. "Flee out of Babylon; leave the land of the Babylonians, and be like the goats that lead the flock." He tells them to become like the goats that lead the flock. By this he means that they should act with all possible speed. It is as if God said they should fear no more, for it was a capital offense to speak of their return as long as the Babylonians ruled over the Jews.

9. "For I will stir up and bring against Babylon an alliance of great nations from the land of the north. They will take up their positions against her, and from the north she will be captured. Their arrows will be like skilled warriors who do not return empty-handed." Here again God declares that enemies will come and overthrow the Babylonians.

10. "So Babylonia will be plundered; all who plunder her will have their fill," declares the LORD. Here the prophet mentions the effect of the victory. The country is laid waste, and the enemies depart with the spoils. In other words, "The enemies will not only take what is at hand but will gather together all the treasures of Babylon, until they become satiated."

11-12. "Because you rejoice and are glad, you who pillage my inheritance, because you frolic like a heifer threshing grain and neigh like stallions, your mother will be greatly ashamed; she who gave you birth will be disgraced. She will be the least of the nations—a wilderness, a dry land, a desert." God shows here that although the Babylonians insolently exulted for a time, their joy would be short-lived. He also points out that they faced ruin because of their arrogance toward God's people.

13. "Because of the LORD's anger she will not be inhabited but will be completely desolate. All who pass Babylon will be horrified and scoff because of all her wounds." It will become completely desolate, and everyone passing through will be astonished and yet will show no pity. The prophets often speak like this when they want to describe a dreadful desolation.

14. "Take up your positions around Babylon, all you who draw the bow. Shoot at her! Spare no arrows, for she has sinned against the LORD." The prophet now turns to address the Medes and Persians and incites them, in God's name, to destroy Babylon.

15. "Shout against her on every side! She surrenders, her towers fall, her walls are torn down. Since this is the vengeance of the LORD, take vengeance on her; do to her as she has done to others." Jeremiah continues to exhort the Persians and Medes, although he did not actually speak to them. This way of speaking encouraged the godly to be assured that what Jeremiah said would take place.

16. "Cut off from Babylon the sower, and the reaper with his sickle at harvest. Because of the sword of the oppressor let everyone return to his own people, let everyone flee to his own land." He still addresses the Medes and Persians and tells them to cut off from Babylon the sower, and the reaper; but his manner of speech means to include everyone else also. Farmers preserve people's lives; if there were no sowing and no reaping, everyone would die. So the prophet's telling them to take away the sowers and reapers is like saying, "Strike with the sword and kill all the inhabitants, so that nothing may remain but the land reduced to solitude." God commands the Babylonians to be killed, so that no farmer should remain to sow and reap.

17. "Israel is a scattered flock that lions have chased away. The first to devour him was the king of Assyria; the last to crush his bones was Nebuchadnezzar king of Babylon." In sum, whatever punishments God inflicts on his church are temporary and are useful for salvation, for they are remedies against their perishing in their vices.

18. Therefore this is what the LORD Almighty, the God of Israel, says: "I will punish the king of Babylon and his land as I punished the king of Assyria." He shows that he will avenge the cruelty of the Babylonians just as he had already avenged all the evils the Assyrians inflicted on his people.

19. "But I will bring Israel back to his own pasture and he will graze on Carmel and Bashan; his appetite will be satisfied on the hills of Ephraim and Gilead." After the people have been gathered, they will inhabit rich and fertile mountains, the hills of Ephraim and Gilead. After gathering his chosen people, God will be their faithful shepherd, so that they will feel assured that not only will they be allowed to return to their country, but that God will guard their safety.

20. "In those days, at that time," declares the LORD, "search will be made for Israel's guilt, but there will be none, and for the sins of Judah, but none will be found, for I will forgive the remnant I spare." The prophet now gives the primary reason why God intended to deal so kindly with his people: He would forgive their sins. This passage is remarkable, and from it we learn the valuable truth that when God punishes us severely, we should look beyond the punishment and look at the cause of all evils—namely, our sins.

21-22. "Attack the land of Merathaim and those who live in Pekod. Pursue, kill and completely destroy them," declares the LORD. "Do everything I have commanded you. The noise of battle is in the land, the noise of great destruction!" The prophet now assumes the role of a herald and encourages the Persians and the Medes to declare war on Babylon.

23-24. "How broken and shattered is the hammer of the whole earth! How desolate is Babylon among the nations! I set a trap for you, O Babylon, and you were caught before you knew it; you were found and captured because you opposed the LORD." Jeremiah exclaims in astonishment, "How broken and shattered is the hammer of the whole earth!" For it had previously broken all other nations. Then God says in effect, "I am he who has defeated Babylon." We neglect God's judgments or are blind to them because we do not carefully consider them; little things often excite us, while God's great actions are ignored.

25-26. "The LORD has opened his arsenal and brought out the weapons of his wrath, for the Sovereign LORD Almighty has work to do in the land of the Babylonians. Come against her from afar. Break open her granaries; pile her up like heaps of grain. Completely destroy her and leave her no remnant." The prophet says even more clearly than before that the war will not come about because of the Persians but because of God himself.

27. "Kill all her young bulls; let them go down to the slaughter! Woe to them! For their day has come, the time for them to be punished." By all her young bulls he means whatever is most valued in Babylon. When the day of vengeance came, such things would perish.

28. "Listen to the fugitives and refugees from Babylon declaring in Zion how the LORD our God has taken vengeance, vengeance for his temple." In other words, "Babylon on many accounts deserves to be destroyed, but God in destroying it will care for his own people and will demonstrate that he is the Father of the people he has adopted."

29. "Summon archers against Babylon, all those who draw the bow. Encamp all around her; let no one escape. Repay her for her deeds; do to her as she has done. For she has defied the LORD, the Holy One of Israel." The prophet tells the strong and warlike to come together, and then he mentions them specifically: all those who draw the bow—that is, all skilled archers. The Persians excelled in this art and were archers of the first order.

30. "Therefore, her young men will fall in the streets; all her soldiers will be silenced in that day," declares the LORD. He confirms what he had already stated and shows that in the defeat of Babylon everything of value will be destroyed.

31. "See, I am against you, O arrogant one," declares the LORD, the LORD Almighty, "for your day has come, the time for you to be punished." He again calls Babylon **arrogant** not because they had declared war out of folly or vain ambition but because they wanted to attack God and men without any reverence and without any regard for humanity.

32. "The arrogant one will stumble and fall and no one will help her up; I will kindle a fire in her towns that will consume all who are around her." God uses the metaphor of **fire** to describe the slaughter. And indeed slaughter, like a fire, consumed the whole kingdom—not only the city, but also all the neighboring nations, for the war reached as far as Asia.

33-34. This is what the LORD Almighty says: "The people of Israel are oppressed, and the people of Judah as well. All their captors hold them fast, refusing to let them go. Yet their Redeemer is strong; the LORD Almighty is his name. He will vigorously defend their cause so that he may bring rest to their land, but unrest to those who live in Babylon." Our prophet returns to his previous subject: God, in destroying the Babylonians, will take care of his people.

35. "A sword against the Babylonians!" declares the LORD—"against those who live in Babylon and against her officials and wise men!" The prophet means that neither power, nor military skill, nor knowledge of any kind will defend the Babylonians.

36-37. "A sword against her false prophets! They will become fools. A sword against her warriors! They will be filled with terror. A sword against her horses and chariots and all the foreigners in her ranks! They will become women. A sword against her treasures! They will be plundered." God says through the prophet that the bravest will not be able to resist the sword coming against them, for they will become, as it were, lifeless, or at least they will become so unmanly that they will think nothing of fleeing.

38. "A drought on her waters! They will dry up. For it is a land of idols, idols that will go mad with terror." The prophet had good reason to reproach the Babylonians. They gloried in their idols and so robbed God of his honor. What is ascribed to idols detracts from God.

39. "So desert creatures and hyenas will live there, and there the owl will dwell. It will never again be inhabited or lived in from generation to generation." The prophets usually speak like this when they give no hope.

40. **"As God overthrew Sodom and Gomorrah along with their neighboring towns," declares the** LORD, **"so no one will live there; no man will dwell in it."** This verse explains the previous one. We must remember, as Jude says in his letter (see Jude 7), that the destruction of Sodom is like a special mirror in which we see God's punishment of all the ungodly.

41. **"Look! An army is coming from the north; a great nation and many kings are being stirred up from the ends of the earth."** The prophet again shows where the destruction of Babylon will come from.

42. **"They are armed with bows and spears; they are cruel and without mercy. They sound like the roaring sea as they ride on their horses; they come like men in battle formation to attack you, O Daughter of Babylon."** Jeremiah speaks especially of formidable weapons to show that the Babylonians will not be able to sustain the assault of their enemies.

43. **"The king of Babylon has heard reports about them, and his hands hang limp. Anguish has gripped him, pain like that of a woman in labor."** The prophet means here that as soon as the report of the war reaches the Babylonians, they will be so disheartened through fear that they will be like a conquered people.

44. **"Like a lion coming up from Jordan's thickets to a rich pastureland, I will chase Babylon from its land in an instant. Who is the chosen one I will appoint for this? Who is like me and who can challenge me? And what shepherd can stand against me?"** The Babylonians will have to fight not against an idle enemy but against a terrible one, one who will surmount all obstacles, like an angry lion.

45. **Therefore, hear what the** LORD **has planned against Babylon, what he has purposed against the land of the Babylonians: The young of the flock will be dragged away; he will completely destroy their pasture because of them.** The prophet has good reason to mention the plans or counsel of the Lord, for the people thought something might happen that was different from what Jeremiah said. This verse shows that God had good reason for pronouncing Babylon's punishment.

46. **At the sound of Babylon's capture the earth will tremble; its cry will resound among the nations.** The prophet shows how great the calamity will be, for its noise will make the whole world **tremble.**

Jeremiah
Chapter 51

1. This is what the LORD says: "See, I will stir up the spirit of a destroyer against Babylon and the people of Leb Kamai." God says he will stir up the spirit of a destroyer against them because they had treated his people so cruelly and nearly destroyed them. We know that God upheld the cause of his church and therefore said that war was waged on it by the ungodly whenever they attacked the faithful.

2. "I will send foreigners to Babylon to winnow her and to devastate her land; they will oppose her on every side in the day of her disaster." He adds in the day of her disaster to show again that God had already destined the Babylonians to be destroyed.

3-4. "Let not the archer string his bow, nor let him put on his armor. Do not spare her young men; completely destroy her army. They will fall down slain in Babylon, fatally wounded in her streets." The prophet tells the Persians and Medes not to spare the young men among the Babylonians but to destroy the whole army, so that no part of it remains.

5. "For Israel and Judah have not been forsaken by their God, the LORD Almighty, though their land is full of guilt before the Holy One of Israel." From the beginning God had united the church to himself by a sort of marriage bond. The people had been received into this covenant so that they were contracted, as it were, into a spiritual marriage. The prophet now says they will not become widows. This is a reference to the hope of deliverance.

6. "Flee from Babylon! Run for your lives! Do not be destroyed because of her sins. It is time for the LORD's vengeance; he will pay her what she deserves." These words were spoken to strangers and visitors in Babylon. This passage is not telling the faithful to leave Babylon—that is, to withdraw from the superstitions and defilements of the world. That is not what the prophet is saying here.

7. "Babylon was a gold cup in the LORD's hand; she made the whole

earth drunk. The nations drank her wine; therefore they have now gone mad." The prophet is anticipating an objection: "How is it that this city, which you say is cursed, has flourished so much until now? Not only has all Assyria come under its power, but also the kingdom of Israel and the kingdom of Judah are not far from their final ruin." To this objection the prophet answers, **"Babylon was a gold cup in the LORD's hand; she made the whole earth drunk."** It is as if he said that God was not at all inconsistent to use the Babylonians to inflict his punishment, for he now punishes them.

8. **"Babylon will suddenly fall and be broken. Wail over her! Get balm for her pain; perhaps she can be healed."** The prophet now declares that Babylon's fall will be sudden, so that the faithful will see that God can accomplish in a moment what he has decreed.

9. **"We would have healed Babylon, but she cannot be healed; let us leave her and each go to his own land, for her judgment reaches to the skies, it rises as high as the clouds."** The prophet now assumes a different character. He speaks as if he is one of those who assisted the Babylonians. He compares the nations subject to Babylon and the hired and foreign soldiers to doctors.

10. **"The LORD has vindicated us; come, let us tell in Zion what the LORD our God has done."** The prophet now addresses the faithful, showing in particular that the ruin of Babylon will demonstrate God's fatherly favor toward his church.

11. **"Sharpen the arrows, take up the shields! The LORD has stirred up the kings of the Medes, because his purpose is to destroy Babylon. The LORD will take vengeance, vengeance for his temple."** The prophet encourages the Jews by declaring that God will vindicate his own worship. This also shows that worship according to the law, which had been taught by Moses, was the only worship of which God approved.

12. **"Lift up a banner against the walls of Babylon! Reinforce the guard, station the watchmen, prepare an ambush! The LORD will carry out his purpose, his decree against the people of Babylon."** The prophet said nothing except what God had decreed. He testifies that what he announced, he had taken from the hidden and immutable counsel of God.

13. **"You who live by many waters and are rich in treasures, your end has come, the time for you to be cut off."** He says that Babylon lived **"by many waters"** because the Euphrates not only flowed by the city but surrounded it. Above Babylon it divided into many streams, so that it formed, as it were, islands, and so access to the city was difficult. And yet...

14. **"The LORD Almighty has sworn by himself: I will surely fill you with men, as with a swarm of locusts, and they will shout in triumph over you."** He speaks about God in human language when he says that

God **has sworn by himself**; it is a solemn declaration when people swear by their own souls, as if laying down or pledging their own life.

15-16. "He made the earth by his power; he founded the world by his wisdom and stretched out the heavens by his understanding. When he thunders, the waters in the heavens roar; he makes clouds rise from the ends of the earth. He sends lightning with the rain and brings out the wind from his storehouses." The prophet here commends God's power. His aim is to encourage the Jews so they will be hopeful. They were not to judge Babylon according to its splendor, which dazzled everyone's eyes.

17-18. "Every man is senseless and without knowledge; every goldsmith is shamed by his idols. His images are a fraud; they have no breath in them. They are worthless, the objects of mockery; when their judgment comes, they will perish." Nothing is more transient than man, but while he is alive he possesses something divine. But what is there about a dead body that is like God? So the prophet rightly condemns this madness of the ungodly in Babylon—they worshiped gods who had no spirit in them.

19. "He who is the Portion of Jacob is not like these, for he is the maker of all things, including the tribe of his inheritance—the LORD Almighty is his name." The prophet had just said that the idols were mere impostors. But this part of his teaching would have been cold and uninteresting if he had not also proclaimed the glory of the one and only true God. In this passage the true God himself is presented to us, and we are taught to direct all our thoughts to him.

20-23. "You are my war club, my weapon for battle—with you I shatter nations, with you I destroy kingdoms, with you I shatter horse and rider, with you I shatter chariot and driver, with you I shatter man and woman, with you I shatter old man and youth, with you I shatter young man and maiden, with you I shatter shepherd and flock, with you I shatter farmer and oxen, with you I shatter governors and officials." The prophet here dispels the doubts of many people. He had spoken about the destruction of Babylon, whose defenses were thought to be impregnable; and now he shows that the wealth and power of Babylon did not stop God from destroying it completely whenever he wanted.

24. "Before your eyes I will repay Babylon and all who live in Babylonia for all the wrong they have done in Zion," declares the **LORD.** The prophet has reminded the Jews that all they had suffered from the Babylonians had been justly inflicted on them because of their sins. Now he adds this further thought.

25. "I am against you, O destroying mountain, you who destroy the whole earth," declares the **LORD. "I will stretch out my hand against you, roll you off the cliffs, and make you a burned-out mountain."**

Now God himself declares war on Babylon, so that this prophecy would be given more credit. The prophet had no regard for the Babylonians but only for his own nation, and especially for its godly remnant.

26. "No rock will be taken from you for a cornerstone, nor any stone for a foundation, for you will be desolate forever," declares the LORD. By **cornerstone** and **foundation** he means the strength of the buildings. So he says there was no hope that the stones would be built up again: Babylon would be an everlasting waste.

27. "Lift up a banner in the land! Blow the trumpet among the nations! Prepare the nations for battle against her; summon against her these kingdoms: Ararat, Minni and Ashkenaz. Appoint a commander against her; send up horses like a swarm of locusts." The prophet confirms that Babylon, no matter how proud it might be about its own strength, will not be able to escape God's hand of judgment.

28. "Prepare the nations for battle against her—the kings of the Medes, their governors and all their officials, and all the countries they rule." This prophecy was greatly confirmed by Jeremiah's declaring, before Cyrus or Darius were even born, that the Medes would come.

29. "The land trembles and writhes, for the LORD'**s purposes against Babylon stand—to lay waste the land of Babylon so that no one will live there."** There is a striking contrast here between the movement of the earth and the stability of God's purposes.

30-31. "Babylon's warriors have stopped fighting; they remain in their strongholds. Their strength is exhausted; they have become like women. Her dwellings are set on fire; the bars of her gates are broken. One courier follows another and messenger follows messenger to announce to the king of Babylon that his entire city is captured. . . ." The prophet here describes the destruction of Babylon in the same way that it is described by secular authors.

32. ". . . the river crossings seized, the marshes set on fire, and the soldiers terrified." This verse shows clearly that Jeremiah was God's herald and that his language was under the guidance of the heavenly Spirit, for he sets out how Babylon was taken as if he had witnessed this himself.

33. This is what the LORD **Almighty, the God of Israel, says: "The Daughter of Babylon is like a threshing floor at the time it is trampled; the time to harvest her will soon come."** By this metaphor the prophet confirms what he has just said: God will avenge his church and will punish the Babylonians at the right time. In Scripture this is usually called the time of God's visitation.

34. "Nebuchadnezzar king of Babylon has devoured us, he has thrown us into confusion, he has made us an empty jar. Like a serpent he has swallowed us and filled his stomach with our delicacies, and then has spewed us out." The prophet places the Israelites in God's presence (verse 36, etc.) so they may be sure that God has not deserted them and that he is not indifferent to the unjust and cruel treatment they received from their enemies.

35-36. **"May the violence done to our flesh be upon Babylon," say the inhabitants of Zion. "May our blood be on those who live in Babylonia," says Jerusalem. Therefore, this is what the LORD says: "See, I will defend your cause and avenge you; I will dry up her sea and make her springs dry."** Jeremiah has shown that the calamities of the people were not unknown to God, and now, in an indirect way, he urges the faithful to appeal to God as their defender. The prophet's aim is to show that their only remedy is to flee to God and to plead their cause before him.

37. **"Babylon will be a heap of ruins, a haunt of jackals, an object of horror and scorn, a place where no one lives."** He says that after God has raised his hand against Babylon, its destruction will be such that its splendor, which had previously astonished all nations, will be reduced to nothing.

38. **"Her people all roar like young lions, they growl like lion cubs."** Here, using another simile, Jeremiah repeats what he said about Babylon: In the midst of the slaughter, they will have no strength to resist.

39. **"But while they are aroused, I will set out a feast for them and make them drunk, so that they shout with laughter—then sleep forever and not awake," declares the LORD.** God through the prophet now describes how Babylon will be taken. From this we learn that the prophet did not speak in dark or ambiguous terms but showed that God's judgment would be known by their descendants, so that they would understand that God's Spirit had revealed these things through what the prophet said.

40. **"I will bring them down like lambs to the slaughter, like rams and goats."** He now says how easy it will be for God to destroy the Babylonians.

41. **"How Sheshach will be captured, the boast of the whole earth seized! What a horror Babylon will be among the nations!"** In other words, "Although the world will be astonished at Babylon's destruction, what I predict is still certain to happen."

42. **"The sea will rise over Babylon; its roaring waves will cover her."** The prophet makes a comparison here to confirm his prophecy about Babylon's destruction. It was incredible to think it could be subdued by human power, and he compares the calamity through which God would overwhelm it to a deluge.

43. **"Her towns will be desolate, a dry and desert land, a land where no one lives, through which no man travels."** He now says that the **towns** of Babylon will become **desolate**. Previously he seems to have directed his warnings against the city of Babylon itself; now he declares that God's punishments will extend to all the cities under the power of the Babylonians.

44. **"I will punish Bel in Babylon and make him spew out what he has swallowed. The nations will no longer stream to him. And the wall of Babylon will fall."** God again declares that he will take vengeance on the idols of Babylon. He speaks about **Bel** as if it were his enemy; yet God has no quarrel with a dead figure that is devoid of reason and feeling. Such a contest would be ridiculous.

45. **"Come out of her, my people! Run for your lives! Run from the fierce anger of the LORD."** Here the prophet urges the Israelites to flee from Babylonia and Assyria. Yet this exhortation was meant for another purpose—to encourage them to be hopeful about their deliverance. It was hardly believable that they could ever leave Babylon freely, for Babylon was like a tomb to them.

46. **"Do not lose heart or be afraid when rumors are heard in the land; one rumor comes this year, another the next, rumors of violence in the land and of ruler against ruler."** Here the prophet anticipates a danger. The Jews might be disturbed when they saw these dreadful upsets taking place later on. For when they began to expect to return from Babylon, there was great commotion there.

47. **"For the time will surely come when I will punish the idols of Babylon; her whole land will be disgraced and her slain will all lie fallen within her."** He repeats something he had stated previously: God will visit the idols of Babylon. He is not speaking only about Bel but includes all the false gods.

48. **"Then heaven and earth and all that is in them will shout for joy over Babylon, for out of the north destroyers will attack her,"** declares the LORD. As long as Babylon stood, heaven and earth sighed. But when God appeared as an avenger, heaven and earth and everything in them shouted for joy.

49. **"Babylon must fall because of Israel's slain, just as the slain in all the earth have fallen because of Babylon."** The prophet means that although God may allow the ungodly to oppose his church for a while, he will act for them at the right time, so that all those who have been cruel will be slain.

50. **"You who have escaped the sword, leave and do not linger! Remember the LORD in a distant land, and think on Jerusalem."** The prophet again tells the faithful to flee from Babylonia.

51. **"We are disgraced, for we have been insulted and shame covers our faces, because foreigners have entered the holy places of the LORD's house."** The chief glory of the chosen people was that they had a temple where they called on God, and not in vain; see Psalm 132:13-14. God chose to dwell with them, and that was their main dignity. But when

the temple was overthrown, what remained for them? It seemed as if all their hope of divine help and of salvation had been taken from them.

52-54. "But days are coming," declares the LORD, "when I will punish her idols, and throughout her land the wounded will groan. Even if Babylon reaches the sky and fortifies her lofty stronghold, I will send destroyers against her," declares the LORD. "The sound of a cry comes from Babylon, the sound of great destruction from the land of the Babylonians." The prophet wanted to raise the thinking of the godly so they would not give in when tested, since they were exposed to such shame and were devoid of all honor.

55. "The LORD will destroy Babylon; he will silence her noisy din. Waves of enemies will rage like great waters; the roar of their voices will resound." The prophet calls the faithful to consider God's power, for God had resolved to destroy Babylon completely. God through the prophet then says this will not be man's work but God's.

56. "A destroyer will come against Babylon; her warriors will be captured, and their bows will be broken. For the LORD is a God of retribution; he will repay in full." We now see how forcefully the prophet confirms what he has been saying. It is as if he said that the fall of Babylon was beyond doubt because God is the God of retribution. It was impossible for Babylon to escape unpunished since there were so many ways in which it had sought its own ruin.

57. "I will make her officials and wise men drunk, her governors, officers and warriors as well; they will sleep forever and not awake," declares the King, whose name is the LORD Almighty. The prophet uses here a way of speaking that often occurs in Scripture—namely, saying that lack of awareness is a kind of drunkenness through which God punishes people as he judges them.

58. This is what the LORD Almighty says: "Babylon's thick wall will be leveled and her high gates set on fire; the peoples exhaust themselves for nothing, the nations' labor is only fuel for the flames." The prophet repeats the name of God so that the Jews might reverently receive what he has promised. **Babylon's thick wall** was so wide that horses could walk along it four abreast. Its walls were so thick that the people thought they could disregard whatever the prophet had predicted.

59. This is the message Jeremiah gave to the staff officer Seraiah son of Neriah, the son of Mahseiah, when he went to Babylon with Zedekiah king of Judah in the fourth year of his reign. This is a remarkable sealing of everything we have said so far about the destruction of Babylon. The prophet not only spoke and promulgated what the Spirit of God had dictated but also put it down in a book. And not content with this, he delivered the book to Seraiah the son of Neriah when he went to Babylon at Zedekiah's command. It was read there, before being thrown into the Euphrates (verse 63). He strengthened his hope in everything that it had divinely predicted.

60-64. Jeremiah had written on a scroll about all the disasters that would come upon Babylon—all that had been recorded concerning Babylon. He said to Seraiah, "When you get to Babylon, see that you read all these words aloud. Then say, 'O LORD, you have said you will destroy this place, so that neither man nor animal will live in it; it will be desolate forever.' When you finish reading this scroll, tie a stone to it and throw it into the Euphrates. Then say, 'So will Babylon sink to rise no more because of the disaster I will bring upon her. And her people will fall.'" The words of Jeremiah end here. We see here the prophet's great courage as he dared to command the king's messenger. We see that he was endued with a spirit of invincible courage as he carried out his work.

Notice also the meekness and piety of Seraiah. He was submissive and feared no danger; so it is clear that the fear of God was in his soul.

Jeremiah
Chapter 52

[Editor's note: Since Calvin handled this last chapter, which is largely historical, in his discussion on Jeremiah 39, he did not comment on it here. However, we include Jeremiah 52:1-34 here, without comment, for your study and thought.]

Zedekiah was twenty-one years old when he became king, and he reigned in Jerusalem eleven years. His mother's name was Hamutal daughter of Jeremiah; she was from Libnah. He did evil in the eyes of the Lord, just as Jehoiakim had done. It was because of the Lord's anger that all this happened to Jerusalem and Judah, and in the end he thrust them from his presence.

Now Zedekiah rebelled against the king of Babylon.

So in the ninth year of Zedekiah's reign, on the tenth day of the tenth month, Nebuchadnezzar king of Babylon marched against Jerusalem with his whole army. They camped outside the city and built siege works all around it. The city was kept under siege until the eleventh year of King Zedekiah.

By the ninth day of the fourth month the famine in the city had become so severe that there was no food for the people to eat. Then the city wall was broken through, and the whole army fled. They left the city at night through the gate between the two walls near the king's garden, though the Babylonians were surrounding the city. They fled toward the Arabah, but the Babylonian army pursued King Zedekiah and overtook him in the plains of Jericho. All his soldiers were separated from him and scattered, and he was captured.

He was taken to the king of Babylon at Riblah in the land of Hamath, where he pronounced sentence on him. There at Riblah the king of Babylon slaughtered the sons of Zedekiah before his eyes; he also killed all the officials of Judah. Then he put out Zedekiah's eyes, bound him with bronze shackles and took him to Babylon, where he put him in prison till the day of his death.

On the tenth day of the fifth month, in the nineteenth year of Nebuchadnezzar king of Babylon, Nebuzaradan commander of the imperial guard, who served the king of Babylon, came to Jerusalem. He set fire to the temple of the Lord, the royal palace and all the houses of Jerusalem. Every important building he burned down. The whole Babylonian army under the commander of the imperial guard broke down all the walls around Jerusalem. Nebuzaradan the commander of the guard carried into exile some of the poorest people and those who remained in the city, along with the rest of the craftsmen and those who had gone over to the king of Babylon. But Nebuzaradan left behind the rest of the poorest people of the land to work the vineyards and fields.

The Babylonians broke up the bronze pillars, the movable stands and the bronze Sea that were at the temple of the LORD and they carried all the bronze to Babylon. They also took away the pots, shovels, wick trimmers, sprinkling bowls, dishes and all the bronze articles used in the temple service. The commander of the imperial guard took away the basins, censers, sprinkling bowls, pots, lampstands, dishes and bowls used for drink offerings—all that were made of pure gold or silver.

The bronze from the two pillars, the Sea and the twelve bronze bulls under it, and the movable stands, which King Solomon had made for the temple of the LORD, was more than could be weighed. Each of the pillars was eighteen cubits high and twelve cubits in circumference; each was four fingers thick, and hollow. The bronze capital on top of the one pillar was five cubits high and was decorated with a network and pomegranates of bronze all around. The other pillar, with its pomegranates, was similar. There were ninety-six pomegranates on the sides; the total number of pomegranates above the surrounding network was a hundred.

The commander of the guard took as prisoners Seraiah the chief priest, Zephaniah the priest next in rank and the three doorkeepers. Of those still in the city, he took the officer in charge of the fighting men, and seven royal advisers. He also took the secretary who was chief officer in charge of conscripting the people of the land and sixty of his men who were found in the city. Nebuzaradan the commander took them all and brought them to the king of Babylon at Riblah. There at Riblah, in the land of Hamath, the king had them executed.

So Judah went into captivity, away from her land. This is the number of the people Nebuchadnezzar carried into exile:

in the seventh year, 3,023 Jews;

in Nebuchadnezzar's eighteenth year, 832 people from Jerusalem;

in his twenty-third year, 745 Jews taken into exile by Nebuzaradan the commander of the imperial guard.

There were 4,600 people in all.

In the thirty-seventh year of the exile of Jehoiachin king of Judah, in the year Evil-Merodach became king of Babylon, he released Jehoiachin king of Judah and freed him from prison on the twenty-fifth day of the twelfth month. He spoke kindly to him and gave him a seat of honor higher than those of the other kings who were with him in Babylon. So Jehoiachin put aside his prison clothes and for the rest of his life ate regularly at the king's table. Day by day the king of Babylon gave Jehoiachin a regular allowance as long as he lived, till the day of his death.

Lamentations

Introduction to Lamentations

By John Calvin

I now undertake to explain the lamentations of Jeremiah. Jeremiah sets before everyone things that they knew were true. We will quickly see that this way of stating things is quite different from other prophetic writings. There is no doubt that Jeremiah, after the city of Jerusalem had been destroyed and the temple burned, bewailed the miserable state of his own nation, so that he might show that even in such a disastrous state some benefit might be derived from what he says. This should be carefully noted, for if we do not bear this in mind, the book will lose its special interest.

When Jeremiah saw that his teaching would bear fruit, he first spoke about God's judgments; second, he exhorted the people to repent; third, he encouraged them to hope in God; and lastly, he showed them the open door for prayer, so that they might flee to God and his mercy in times of extremity. None of this could have happened without faith.

Now to a certain extent we understand the purpose behind Jeremiah's writing. His aim was to show that although nothing but desolation existed in the land, although the temple was destroyed and God's covenant seemed to have finished, and so all hope of salvation was at an end, yet hope still remained, provided that the people sought God in repentance and faith. So Jeremiah continued with his calling and made it plain that his teaching could benefit them.

He grieves over the extreme calamity of his people, but he mingles with his lamentations the teaching of repentance and faith. On the one hand he shows that the people suffered just punishment for their many sins; but on the other hand he shows them God's mercy, that under the threat of death itself the Jews might seek life. By his own example he stimulates them to pray, and this prayer was founded on faith. It follows that Jeremiah, after the people had become completely alienated from worshiping God, spent his time collecting together the remnant. So though the church was in total disarray and reduced to almost nothing, Jeremiah constructed some kind of building out of the ruins. That is the substance of this book.

Lamentations
Chapter 1

1. **How deserted lies the city, once so full of people! How like a widow is she, who once was great among the nations! She who was queen among the provinces has now become a slave.** The prophet could only express the greatness of the calamity by expressing his astonishment. He then assumes the person of one who sees something new and unexpected and is filled with amazement. It was indeed an incredible thing. A place chosen for God to live in, the city Jerusalem was not only the royal throne of God but also his earthly sanctuary, as it were, and so the city might have been thought to be exempt from all danger. When the city fell, therefore, and was uprooted from its foundations, when the temple was disgracefully plundered and then burnt by enemies, when the king was driven into exile, his children killed in his presence, and the people scattered—was this not a horrible and monstrous thing?

The prophet had good reason, then, for this exclamation. No one would have ever thought that such a thing would happen. Everyone's faith must have been upset. "What does God mean? How is it that he has promised that this city would last forever? And now the city has disappeared without any hope of future restoration." This spectacle made them sink into the depths of despair. The prophet exclaims, **How deserted lies the city, once so full of people!** Here, by making a comparison, he amplifies the indignity of the situation. On the one hand he refers to the flourishing state of Jerusalem before the calamity, and on the other he shows how it has now been turned into darkness. This change was like the sun falling from heaven. He says that this city had many people, but that it was now deserted.

How like a widow is she, who once was great among the nations! He says that Jerusalem had not only been full of citizens but had also extended her power through many nations. It is well known that many nations were under her power during the reigns of David and Solomon. **She who was queen among the provinces has now become a slave.**

The prophet wonders at the destruction of the city of Jerusalem, regarding it as a marvel that not only disturbed people but confounded them. The prophet did not just speak about his own feelings, but also about those of other people. Speaking on behalf of everyone, he deplores the calamity.

2. Bitterly she weeps at night, tears are upon her cheeks. The weeping of Jerusalem is constant. She never stops crying.

Among all her lovers there is none to comfort her. Note this carefully. Nothing is more helpful in grief than to have friends near us to show us kindness, to share our sorrow, and to console us. The prophet says here that there was no one seeking to soothe their sorrow.

All her friends have betrayed her; they have become her enemies. Jerusalem has been forsaken by her friends, which only increases the pain of her sorrow.

3. After affliction and harsh labor, Judah has gone into exile. She dwells among the nations; she finds no resting place. All who pursue her have overtaken her in the midst of her distress. The prophet says that the Jews had migrated—that is, they left their own country and fled to other countries—because they were subjected to miseries and cruel slavery.

4. The roads to Zion mourn, for no one comes to her appointed feasts. All her gateways are desolate, her priests groan, her maidens grieve, and she is in bitter anguish. Jeremiah refers here to another reason for their sorrow: The worship of God had ceased. It had stopped for so long that it seemed as if it had become extinct forever. He says that **the roads to Zion mourn** because no one came to the **feasts.** When the Jews saw God's worship neglected, it was more grievous than finding themselves bereaved of children or wives or plundered of their possessions. The more precious God's Word was to them, and the more they esteemed the religion in which eternal salvation consisted, the more severe and mournful was it to see the church so scattered that God could no longer be worshiped.

5. Her foes have become her masters; her enemies are at ease. The LORD has brought her grief because of her many sins. Her children have gone into exile, captive before the foe. The prophet says that the cause of all their trouble lay with God: God afflicted Jerusalem because of her great sins. He now starts to show that there is no reason why the Jews should be swallowed up with grief and despair, if only they would consider where this evil came from.

6. All the splendor has departed from the Daughter of Zion. Her princes are like deer that find no pasture; in weakness they have fled before the pursuer. He continues with the same subject, saying that the daughter of Zion was stripped of all her ornaments. We know what made up the honor and dignity of the people. Moses, in order to show the greatness of God's grace, exclaimed, "What other nation is so great as to have their gods near them the way the Lord our God is near us whenever we pray to him?" (Deuteronomy 4:7). But **all the splendor** was taken away from **the Daughter of Zion.**

7. In the days of her affliction and wandering Jerusalem remembers all the treasures that were hers in days of old. When her people fell into enemy hands, there was no one to help her. Her enemies looked at her and laughed at her destruction. He confirms the previous verse when he says that when she was afflicted by God's hand and reduced to extreme need, Jerusalem remembered **all the treasures.** By these words he intimates that when Jerusalem was in its splendor, it did not think enough about God's blessings. People who despise God fill themselves with whatever flows from his bounty, and yet do not acknowledge him. Ingratitude is like an abyss that absorbs all the fullness of God's blessings.

When her people fell into enemy hands. This was a terrible misery because they had flourished for so long.

8. Jerusalem has sinned greatly and so has become unclean. All who honored her despise her, for they have seen her nakedness; she herself groans and turns away. Here the prophet expresses more clearly and strongly what he has just stated: All the evil that the Jews suffered came from God's vengeance, and they deserved such punishment because they had not offended in minor ways but had heaped up for themselves a dreadful judgment by handing themselves over to godlessness in so many ways.

She herself groans and turns away. That is, she was so oppressed with grief that there was no hope of a remedy. To turn away is to deprive oneself of all hope of restoration.

9. Her filthiness clung to her skirts; she did not consider her future. Her fall was astounding; there was none to comfort her. "Look, O LORD, on my affliction, for the enemy has triumphed." At the end of the previous verse he said that the baseness of Jerusalem had been seen, and now he says that it was on her skirts. The prophet seems to be alluding to menstruating women who try to hide their uncleanness as much as they can; but their efforts do not work, for nature must have its course. In short, the prophet intimates that the Jews had become so filthy that their uncleanness could be seen on their skirts.

She did not consider her future. The Jews were so overwhelmed with despair that they did not elevate their thoughts to God's promises.

10. The enemy laid hands on all her treasures; she saw pagan nations enter her sanctuary—those you had forbidden to enter your assembly. The prophet again deplores that all sacred things have been profaned. This complaint comes from his bitter sorrow. It was a sad thing for the faithful to lose all their possessions, to wander in exile, and to suffer great hardships; but it was even more painful for them to see the temple desecrated and all religion exposed to shame. By **treasures** he does not mean riches or anything that belongs to this fading world, but those eternal treasures that God had deposited with the chosen people. The enemy, then, had laid hands on the altar, on the table, on the ark of the covenant, and on all the sacred vessels.

11. All her people groan as they search for bread; they barter their treasures for food to keep themselves alive. "Look, O LORD, and consider, for I am despised." The prophet here complains that all the citizens of Jerusalem are constantly groaning because of the famine. To seek bread is a universal desire. But he uses this word **bread** to indicate their extreme need. He compares them with beggars who go about here and there seeking bread.

12. "Is it nothing to you, all you who pass by? Look around and see. Is any suffering like my suffering that was inflicted on me, that the LORD brought on me in the day of his fierce anger?" Jerusalem addresses those who pass by, so that she might make it all the clearer how great is her calamity. Had she directed her words only to her neighbors, they would not have had such force. But when she spoke to strangers, she showed the depth of her calamity; it should have aroused the sympathy of people from the most distant countries as they traveled past Jerusalem.

13. "From on high he sent fire, sent it down into my bones. He spread a net for my feet and turned me back. He made me desolate, faint all the day long." The prophet continues with the same subject: God's vengeance had raged most dreadfully against Jerusalem. By using a metaphor he says that **fire** had been sent into her bones. It was as if God had penetrated into the inmost parts of the body.

"He spread a net for my feet." God had removed every means of escape. Jerusalem is speaking, saying she has been caught in God's judgments. It is also stated here that she was **desolate, faint all the day long**—continually.

14. "My sins have been bound into a yoke; by his hands they were woven together. They have come upon my neck and the Lord has sapped my strength. He has handed me over to those I cannot withstand." She says that according to human reasoning, she has no hope—there seemed to be no way of rising again. Yet she did not despair but trusted that God would at length, by his almighty power, make her rise from her fatal ruin. This manner of speaking should be noted, for hope sees things that are hidden.

15. "The Lord has rejected all the warriors in my midst; he has summoned an army against me to crush my young men. In his winepress the Lord has trampled the Virgin Daughter of Judah." She says that all her warriors have been trampled underfoot. We know how much the Jews put their trust in men, right up to the time when they were completely defeated. As, then, they had shown so much insolence and pride toward the prophets, it became a source of great sorrow when Jerusalem herself saw that she was devoid of all protection and that her warriors were trodden underfoot.

16. "This is why I weep and my eyes overflow with tears. No one is near to comfort me, no one to restore my spirit. My children are destitute because the enemy has prevailed." Throughout, he speaks in the person of a woman, for it is Jerusalem herself speaking, and not Jeremiah. Jerusalem says her eyes will be like fountains of water. She says she is fainting and, as it were, dying and that there is no one present to give her comfort, so that her soul might be revived.

17. Zion stretches out her hands, but there is no one to comfort her. The LORD has decreed for Jacob that his neighbors become his foes. The prophet says that Zion has stretched out her hands as a token of sorrow, or to seek friends from every side. When we want to move people to pity, we stretch out our arms.

Jerusalem has become an unclean thing among them. He says that Jerusalem has become like a menstruating woman. Jerusalem was thought of as being unclean, as if the prophet said there was no humanity or moderation among the enemies of the Jews, because they were not thought of as people but as abominable filth.

18. "The LORD is righteous, yet I rebelled against his command." The greatness of her sorrow is again deplored. What follows is addressed to all nations.

"Listen, all you peoples; look upon my suffering." What was the cause for this great sorrow? **"My young men and maidens have gone into exile."** The Jews lived in that foreign land as if they had been placed there by God's hand. Jerusalem was meant to be their permanent residence, given to them from above. In short, it was, as it were, a pledge of the eternal inheritance. When they were driven into captivity, it was the same as being thrown out of heaven and banished from God's kingdom.

19. "I called to my allies but they betrayed me. My priests and my elders perished in the city while they searched for food to keep themselves alive." Here the people of God complain, in the person of a woman, that in their calamity they are left devoid of every comfort. Grief is increased if no one is present to show any kindness. For it is a great comfort when friends show their kindness and endeavor to mitigate the severity of the evil.

20. "See, O LORD, how distressed I am! I am in torment within, and in my heart I am disturbed, for I have been most rebellious." Jeremiah refers to the severity of their punishment.

"Outside, the sword bereaves; inside, there is only death." That is, "When we travel, the sword meets us; and when we hide ourselves at home, many deaths surround us."

21. "People have heard my groaning, but there is no one to com-

fort me. **All my enemies have heard of my distress; they rejoice at what you have done. May you bring the day you have announced so they may become like me.**" In short, the faithful now confess not only that they were afflicted by God's hand, but also that what the prophets had so often warned, and what they had despised, was now fulfilled. And so they confessed not only that they deserved punishment, but that it was the right time for them to be punished, for they had not repented despite all the warnings.

22. **"Let all their wickedness come before you; deal with them as you have dealt with me because of all my sins. My groans are many and my heart is faint."** We see that the faithful lay their prayers humbly before God and at the same time confess that they were now receiving what they deserved. Now they set before God their extreme sorrow, grief, tears, and sighs. This is the correct way to behave in God's presence—to confess that they are being punished justly, and also to lie down, as it were, confounded, and at the same time to venture to look up to him and to rely on his mercy with confidence.

Lamentations
Chapter 2

1. How the Lord has covered the Daughter of Zion with the cloud of his anger! He has hurled down the splendor of Israel from heaven to earth; he has not remembered his footstool in the day of his anger. The second elegy now starts. The prophet again explains in wonder that an incredible thing has happened. At first sight it seemed very unreasonable that a people upon whom God had not only lavished his favor but with whom he had made a perpetual covenant should be forsaken by him in this way.

When Jerusalem was reduced to desolation, there was, or so it seemed, an abolition of God's covenant. It is therefore not surprising that the prophet exclaims here, **How the Lord has covered the Daughter of Zion with the cloud of his anger!**

2. **Without pity the Lord has swallowed up all the dwellings of Jacob; in his wrath he has torn down the strongholds of the Daughter of Judah. He has brought her kingdom and its princes down to the ground in dishonor.** The prophet pursues the same subject but in other words. He says that **without pity the Lord has swallowed up all the dwellings of Jacob.**

3. **In fierce anger he has cut off every horn of Israel. He has withdrawn his right hand at the approach of the enemy. He has burned in Jacob like a flaming fire that consumes everything around it.** Jeremiah expresses the same thing in various ways; but all that he says tends to show that it was evidence of God's extreme vengeance when the people, the city, and the temple were destroyed. Note that God is here represented as the author of that calamity. Otherwise it would have been no good for the prophet to lament the ruin of his own country. But since in all adversities he acknowledged the hand of God, he afterwards adds that God had good reason for being so displeased with his own people.

He then says that **every horn** has been **cut off** by God. We know that by **horn** is meant strength as well as excellence or dignity.

4. Like an enemy he has strung his bow; his right hand is ready. Like a foe he has slain all who were pleasing to the eye; he has poured out his wrath like fire on the tent of the Daughter of Zion. Now he uses another metaphor, saying that God, who usually defended his people, now takes up arms against them. Naming a part to mean the whole, he includes in the **bow** every other weapon. Therefore, saying that God **has strung his bow** is the same as saying he was fully armed.

5. The Lord is like an enemy; he has swallowed up Israel. He has swallowed up all her palaces and destroyed her strongholds. He has multiplied mourning and lamentation for the Daughter of Judah. He says that God himself is like an enemy, in case the Israelites should focus on the Babylonians and think that they were the main cause of the war.

6. He has laid waste his dwelling like a garden; he has destroyed his place of meeting. The LORD has made Zion forget her appointed feasts and her Sabbaths; in his fierce anger he has spurned both king and priest. Jeremiah says that the king and the priest have been rejected by God. They were meant to be pledges of God's fatherly favor. On the one hand, he who reigned as a descendant of David was a living image of Christ; and on the other hand, there was always a high priest from among the descendants of Aaron to reconcile people to God.

7. The Lord has rejected his altar and abandoned his sanctuary. He has handed over to the enemy the walls of her palaces; they have raised a shout in the house of the LORD as on the day of an appointed feast. In other words, the city has not been taken by the bravery of enemies; rather, the Babylonians fought under the authority and banner of God. In short, the prophet is saying that the Jews perished miserably through their own fault. The Babylonians were victorious in battle and took the city not through their own courage or skill, but because God had resolved to punish that ungodly and wicked people.

8. The LORD determined to tear down the wall around the Daughter of Zion. He stretched out a measuring line and did not withhold his hand from destroying. He made ramparts and walls lament; together they wasted away. It is indeed true that the Babylonians had actively carried on the war and lacked no military skill to capture the city. But the prophet directs the attention of the Jews to a different thought here, so that they might acknowledge that they were suffering justly for their sins and that God was the chief author of that war and that the Babylonians were to be seen as hired soldiers.

9. Her gates have sunk into the ground; their bars he has broken and destroyed. Her king and her princes are exiled among the nations, the law is no more, and her prophets no longer find visions from the LORD. The prophet relates, in different words, what he has already said: The walls of Jerusalem have fallen. But he now speaks also of the **gates** and says they have sunk into the ground or become fixed in the ground (it may be translated either way). In other words, the gates had been no hindrance to the enemies as they entered the city. He thus derides the foolish confidence of the people, who relied on their defenses and thought the city was impregnable.

10. The elders of the Daughter of Zion sit on the ground in silence; they have sprinkled dust on their heads and put on sackcloth. The young women of Jerusalem have bowed their heads to the ground. The prophet here depicts the people's terrible calamity in a striking way. He says that the elders, as if full of hopeless despair, are lying on the ground, that they sprinkle dust on their heads, that they are clothed in sackcloth (as usual in times of great sorrow), and that the young women bow their heads to the ground. This means that the elders did not know what to do and encouraged others to join them in acts of fruitless and abject lamentation. We know that young women take great care about their beauty and indulge themselves in pleasure; so when they sit with their face and hair on the ground, it is a token of extreme mourning.

11. My eyes fail from weeping, I am in torment within, my heart is poured out on the ground because my people are destroyed, because children and infants faint in the streets of the city. The prophet himself now speaks, saying that his eyes **fail from weeping** as he weeps for the calamities of the people. Even in the deepest grief tears eventually dry up. But when there is no end to weeping, the sorrow must become very bitter.

12. They say to their mothers, "Where is bread and wine?" as they faint like wounded men in the streets of the city, as their lives ebb away in their mothers' arms. The prophet shows that food was so scarce that children died **in their mothers' arms** and in vain sought food and cried out that they were without help or provision.

13. What can I say for you? With what can I compare you, O Daughter of Jerusalem? To what can I liken you, that I may comfort you, O Virgin Daughter of Zion? Your wound is as deep as the sea. Who can heal you? That is, "Your calamity is like the deepest abyss. I cannot find anyone in the world with whom I can compare you, for your calamity exceeds all calamities."

14. The visions of your prophets were false and worthless; they did not expose your sin to ward off your captivity. The oracles they gave you were false and misleading. This verse should be noted carefully. Jeremiah spoke about the false prophecies of the false prophets, which he said were empty. He now shows how they had deceived the people because they did not expose their sin. From this we see that nothing is more important than to be warned about our sins and made aware of them, so that we may repent.

15. All who pass your way clap their hands at you; they scoff and shake their heads at the Daughter of Jerusalem: "Is this the city that was called the perfection of beauty, the joy of the whole earth?" He says that Jerusalem was called **the perfection of beauty** because God had adorned it with special gifts. He had especially favored it with the incomparable honor of being called by his name. Jerusalem was in a way the earthly palace of God, on account of the temple. In addition to this, the doctrine of salvation was to be found there (see Isaiah 2:3; Ezekiel 47:1-12). Since Jerusalem had been adorned with such remarkable gifts, the prophet introduces here strangers who ask in effect, "Can it be that a city so celebrated for beauty has become a desolation?"

16. All your enemies open their mouths wide against you; they scoff and gnash their teeth and say, "We have swallowed her up. This is the day we have waited for; we have lived to see it." He doubtless means they were being taunted, for he immediately adds that they **gnash their teeth.** In other words, enemies not only blamed and condemned them but had also given tokens of extreme hatred. People who **gnash their teeth** are showing the bitterness of their minds, as well as great anger; wild animals gnash their teeth. So the prophet is saying that their enemies had not only harassed the people with taunts and scoffing but had treated them cruelly.

17. The LORD has done what he planned; he has fulfilled his word, which he decreed long ago. He has overthrown you without pity, he has let the enemy gloat over you, he has exalted the horn of your foes. Jeremiah concludes that God had **let the enemy gloat** and that God had **exalted the horn** of their foes. By these words he confirms that we should turn our eyes to God when men are insolent to us and exult over our miseries. Otherwise we may be totally overwhelmed.

18. The hearts of the people cry out to the Lord. O wall of the Daughter of Zion, let your tears flow like a river day and night; give yourself no relief, your eyes no rest. There will be—no, there already is—a reason for constant lamentation. So he exhorts them to weep day and night. But we must bear in mind what we have said before—the prophet did not speak like this to make the people bitter. As they had not genuinely repented, the prophet sets before them the punishment that God had inflicted, so that they might think about their sins.

19. Arise, cry out in the night, as the watches of the night begin; pour out your heart like water in the presence of the Lord. Lift up your hands to him for the lives of your children, who faint from hunger at the head of every street. As I have said, the prophet does not just want the Jews to cry, but he urges them to **pour out** their hearts **like water** and then adds, **in the presence of the Lord.** Unbelievers make themselves almost hoarse by crying, but they are only like brute beasts. Here the prophet distinguishes between God's elect and the reprobate as he tells his people to weep in the presence of God, seeking alleviation from him; they could not have done this if they were not convinced that he was the author of all their calamities.

20. "Look, O LORD, and consider: Whom have you ever treated like this? Should women eat their offspring, the children they have cared for? Should priest and prophet be killed in the sanctuary of the Lord?" This way of praying was very common; see Psalm 79:6; Jeremiah 10:25. The sum of what is said is that there was a just reason why God should turn to mercy and thus be reconciled to his people, because he was not dealing with strangers but with his own family, whom he had been happy to adopt.

21. "Young and old lie together in the dust of the streets; my young men and maidens have fallen by the sword. You have slain them in the day of your anger; you have slaughtered them without pity." Here he relates another calamity—the young and the aged were lying prostrate in the streets. He links the children to the old men to show that there all ages were affected—the sword had killed young men and young women. The enemies had not spared the old and had also killed the flower of the people.

22. "As you summon to a feast day, so you summoned against me terrors on every side. In the day of the LORD's anger no one escaped or survived; those I cared for and reared, my enemy has destroyed." Many groups of people came to Jerusalem on feast days, for when the trumpets sounded, all were called. So the prophet says that God has sent terrors from all directions to afflict the people.

Lamentations
Chapter 3

1. I am the man who has seen affliction by the rod of his wrath. The prophet says he is an afflicted man, or a **man who has seen affliction.** This is a common expression in Scripture. Similar expressions are also common—to see affliction, to see good, to see evil, to see life, to see death. He says here he has experienced many afflictions and that he has, as it were, been given over to miseries. How? By the **rod** of God's **wrath.**

2. He has driven me away and made me walk in darkness rather than light. The letters of the Hebrew alphabet are repeated three times in this chapter. In the first two chapters the verses begin with the successive letters of the alphabet. But in this chapter each letter comes three times. So verse 1, verse 2, and verse 3 start with the letter *aleph;* the fourth, fifth, and sixth verses start with the letter *beth;* and so on until the end of the chapter.

Darkness. We know that in Scripture *darkness* stands for every kind of lamentation.

3. Indeed, he has turned his hand against me again and again, all day long. The prophet says God had become an enemy to him. The **hand** of God was **against** him.

4. He has made my skin and my flesh grow old and has broken my bones. He is speaking metaphorically here. Illness often makes people look old, for leanness can be a result of pain. In this way the skin contracts and the wrinkles of old age appear even in young people. As sorrow saps the strength, so a person is said to grow old when he or she pines away in mourning. This is what the prophet means here. God, he says, **has made my skin and flesh grow old;** that is, "he has worn me out, inside and outside, so that I am almost wasted away."

5. He has besieged me and surrounded me with bitterness and hardship. "God," he says in essence, "holds me confined on every side, so that I have no way of escape."

6. He has made me dwell in darkness like those long dead. This is hyperbole, but we must always remember that it is not possible to depict the depth of the sorrow that the faithful feel when terrified by God's wrath.

7. He has walled me in so I cannot escape; he has weighed me down with chains. He means that he was not only bound with chains but was bound in such a way that he could not lift up his feet.

8. Even when I call out or cry for help, he shuts out my prayer. This verse should be especially noted. Unless God immediately meets us, we become languid; not only is the ardor of our prayers cooled, but it becomes almost extinguished.

9. He has barred my way with blocks of stone; he has made my paths crooked. The prophet could find no success in all his efforts and actions because God was opposing him.

10. Like a bear lying in wait, like a lion in hiding. Harsh is the complaint when Jeremiah compares God to **a bear** and to **a lion.** I have already said that the apprehension of God's wrath terrified the faithful of that day so much that they could not sufficiently express the depth of their calamity. We must also bear in mind that they were expressing themselves in a human way. They did not always curb their feelings but said some things that they deserved to be rebuked for.

11. He dragged me from the path and mangled me and left me without help. In this verse the prophet shows how deeply the faithful are disturbed when they feel God is against them.

12-13. He drew his bow and made me the target for his arrows. He pierced my heart with arrows from his quiver. Here the prophet introduces another metaphor: God had shot him with arrows.

14. I became the laughingstock of all my people; they mock me in song all day long. They sang about him mockingly **all day long.** This constancy proved more clearly the depth of their evil.

15. He has filled me with bitter herbs and sated me with gall. Unbelievers feed their bitterness, for they do not unburden their souls to God. The best way to find comfort is not to flatter ourselves in our bitterness and grief, but to seek to purify our souls and to open them to God, no matter how bitter they are. Then God can remove our bitterness and feed us with the sweetness of his goodness.

16. He has broken my teeth with gravel; he has trampled me in the dust. The prophet was lying down or pulled along in the dust. The expression is taken from those who are dragged along the ground as a way of reproach, like a carcass or like some filthy thing that we despise.

17. I have been deprived of peace; I have forgotten what prosperity is. The Jews understood every kind of prosperity, including **peace.**

18-19. So I say, "My splendor is gone and all that I had hoped from the LORD." I remember my affliction and my wandering, the bitterness and the gall. We learn from this passage that the faithful are not free from despair, for it enters their souls. But this is no reason to indulge in despair. On the contrary, they should firmly resist it. For when the prophet said this, he did not mean that he had succumbed to this trial, but that he was overwhelmed for a short time.

20. I well remember them, and my soul is downcast within me. The prophet seems to be using different words to confirm what he had just said: The memory of afflictions overwhelmed his soul. The soul is said to be humbled in man when he lies down under the burden of despair. But it is also the soul that raises man up and, as it were, revives him. But when the soul is downcast, that is a most terrible thing.

21. Yet this I call to mind and therefore I have hope. When we call our evils to mind and see how ready we are to despair and how we are prone to succumb to it, hope can arise and help us, as the prophet says here.

22-23. Because of the LORD's great love we are not consumed, for his compassions never fail. They are new every morning; great is your faithfulness. God's mercies had not ended, and his compassions had not failed. How can this be? Because they are **new**, or renewed, **every morning**.

24. I say to myself, "The LORD is my portion; therefore I will wait for him." We must bear this truth in mind if we are not to fail in adversity. All our thoughts may wander and go astray until we are convinced that God alone is sufficient for us, so that he alone may become our heritage.

25. The LORD is good to those whose hope is in him, to the one who seeks him. The prophet reminds us here that God's blessings flow to us from his favor like a fountain. In other words, "As a perennial fountain sends out its water, so God's goodness reveals itself."

26. It is good to wait quietly for the salvation of the LORD. Our happiness is hidden in God. As Paul says, we are like the dead, and our life is hidden in Christ (see Colossians 3:3).

27. It is good for a man to bear the yoke while he is young. We bear God's **yoke** when we relinquish our own judgment and become wise through God's Word; when our affections are surrendered and subdued, we hear God's commands and obey them. As our dispositions when we are old are not easily changed, the prophet says it is good for us **to bear the yoke** while we are **young.**

28. Let him sit alone in silence, for the LORD has laid it on him. The prophet now says, "Whoever rests under God's yoke will be silent and not given to evil."

29. Let him bury his face in the dust—there may yet be hope. It is clear from the clause **there may yet be hope** that the prophet is speaking about severe trials. The faithful do not doubt that God will give them hope, for they are certain that God, who shines in darkness by his Word, will at length show that he is not unfaithful.

30. Let him offer his cheek to one who would strike him, and let him be filled with disgrace. Here he mentions another fruit of patience. The faithful, even when they are injured by the wicked, remain calm.

31. For men are not cast off by the Lord forever. There is no patience unless there is hope. As patience cherishes hope, so hope is the foundation of patience. Comfort too is linked to patience or endurance, as Paul says (Romans 15:4).

32. Though he brings grief, he will show compassion, so great is his unfailing love. When God gives us a glimpse of who he is, he shows us his mercy and patience. For unless his goodness and mercy meet us when we come to him, our hearts will be filled with dread. But when God comes dressed in mercy, we may have hope concerning our salvation. Though we are conscious of evil, we trust in God's mercy and so never lose the hope of salvation.

33. For he does not willingly bring affliction or grief to the children of men. This confirms the same truth: God does not delight in the evils or miseries of humankind.

34-36. To crush underfoot all prisoners in the land, to deny a man his rights before the Most High, to deprive a man of justice—would not the Lord see such things? In other words, "It is indeed true that the wicked imagine that God is blind to all evil deeds, but he is not." This madness is often attributed to the ungodly: They think they can sin with impunity because God, they suppose wrongly, does not care what people do.

37-38. Who can speak and have it happen if the Lord has not decreed it? Is it not from the mouth of the Most High that both calamities and good things come? God is not the author of evil, although nothing happens without his permission, for his purposes are quite different from ours. So it is absurd to implicate him in a crime of murder or theft or adultery. In a word, as far as the heavens are from the earth, so great is the difference between the deeds of God and the deeds of men. The goals are altogether different.

39. Why should any living man complain when punished for his sins? As long as people wallow in their own sins, they will never acknowledge God as the judge of the world. Thus they continually go astray through their own perverse imaginations.

40. Let us examine our ways and test them, and let us return to the LORD. The prophet tells us to do things in a certain order. We are to examine our whole life (this is to be influenced by the fear of God) and then return to him. Though he treats us severely, he still kindly invites us to come to him, always extending free pardon to sinners.

41. Let us lift up our hearts and our hands to God in heaven, and say . . . To conversion he adds prayer. We cannot be reconciled to God unless he buries our sins; nor can faith and repentance be separated. And to taste God's mercy opens to us the door of prayer. This should be carefully noted because the unbelieving sometimes appear to be very busy seeking God's favor, but they only concern themselves with an outward change of life. They are not concerned about being pardoned but go boldly before God, as if they were not exposed to his judgment.

42. "We have sinned and rebelled and you have not forgiven." The faithful are not here expostulating with God but are on the contrary acknowledging that God's severity is just. They know that their own sins caused God to deal with them severely. This is the substance of what is said here.

43. "You have covered yourself with anger and pursued us; you have slain without pity." To show the dreadful vengeance of God, the prophet says that God has punished the wicked in an implacable manner. But as I have said, he does not accuse God of cruelty, even when he says, **"You have covered yourself with anger."**

44. "You have covered yourself with a cloud so that no prayer can get through." The prophet confirms the same thing with different words. He repeats the word **covered**. To clarify the metaphor he adds, **with a cloud.** He simply means that a cloud interposed, so that God might punish the Jews without restraint, as they deserved. (See Isaiah 59:1-2.)

45-46. "You have made us scum and refuse among the nations. All our enemies have opened their mouths wide against us." The degradation of the people was not hidden but was open to all nations, as if God had built a theater in Judea and there exhibited a remarkable and unusual example of his vengeance. The prophet repeats that the people were offscourings, or scrapings or sweepings, rubbish.

47. "We have suffered terror and pitfalls, ruin and destruction." This means that the people had been so reduced and defeated that they had no escape. It is the same with us when we are full of dread and look here and there and see nothing but disaster everywhere. We are then at our wits' end.

48-49. Streams of tears flow from my eyes because my people are destroyed. My eyes will flow unceasingly, without relief. This means that his tears flowed like rivers. The prophet mentions his own groaning and tears to arouse himself to prayer and to lead others to pray.

50. Until the LORD looks down from heaven and sees. This is how we should weep, so that we might cherish hope while we wait for God to look down on us and see our miseries from heaven.

51. What I see brings grief to my soul because of all the women of my city. When we weep and our eyes are full of tears, and when the mind becomes exhausted, this is evidence of deepest grief. And Jeremiah wanted to express this great grief by saying that what he saw brought **grief** to his **soul.**

52. Those who were my enemies without cause hunted me like a bird. We will see at the end of this chapter the various complaints that the prophet used to deplore the miseries of his own nation, so that he might eventually receive God's mercy. He says here that the Babylonians were like men who hunted birds, comparing the Jews to birds.

53. They tried to end my life in a pit and threw stones at me. He was reduced to the last extremity because he was not only captured by his enemies but was also thrown into a pit.

54. The waters closed over my head, and I thought I was about to be cut off. Although this was the saying of a man in a hopeless state, it is evident from the context that the prophet still hoped in God's mercy. But he is here speaking according to the human way of seeing things.

55. I called on your name, O LORD, from the depths of the pit. This passage should be carefully noted. When Satan cannot turn us away from prayer in any other way, he implies that we are weak. "What do you mean, you miserable being? Will God listen to you? What can you do? You tremble, you are anxious—indeed, you despair. Do you still think God will take any notice of you?" Whenever Satan tries to shut the door against us and stop us from praying, we must recall what the prophet says here. Although he thought he was lost, he did not throw away the confidence he had in God's help.

56. You heard my plea: "Do not close your ears to my cry for relief." The prophet's saying that God **heard** is like saying he had prayed in such a way that God became a witness of his earnestness. The prophet summons God as a witness to his crying, as if he said that he was not so overwhelmed by his adversity that he failed to flee to God.

57. You came near when I called you, and you said, "Do not fear." Here the prophet tells us that he experienced the goodness of God because he was not rejected when he prayed.

58. O Lord, you took up my case; you redeemed my life. The prophet, who speaks in the name of all the faithful, had found God to be his Helper and Defender, not only once, but whenever he had been in trouble.

59. You have seen, O LORD, the wrong done to me. Uphold my cause! He asks God to undertake his cause and to appear as his defender.

60-61. You have seen the depth of their vengeance, all their plots against me. O LORD, you have heard their insults, all their plots against me. The saints often spoke like this because God, when he viewed their miseries, was always ready to come to their aid.

62-63. . . . what my enemies whisper and mutter against me all day long. Look at them! Sitting or standing, they mock me in their songs. The prophet means that whether his enemies consulted silently and quietly or tried to do things openly, nothing was hidden from God (**You have seen . . .**—verse 60).

64-65. Pay them back what they deserve, O LORD, for what their hands have done. Put a veil over their hearts, and may your curse be on them! The prophet did not pray for evil to descend on everyone indiscriminately but on the reprobates, who were constantly God's enemies and the enemies of his church.

66. Pursue them in anger and destroy them from under the heavens of the LORD. The prophet asks that their destruction will testify that God sits in heaven and is the judge of the world, the One to whom the ungodly must give an account of themselves.

Lamentations
Chapter 4

1. **How the gold has lost its luster, the fine gold become dull! The sacred gems are scattered at the head of every street.** By gold he means the splendor of the temple, for God had designed the temple to be built in a very magnificent way.

The sacred gems are scattered. This was indeed a sad spectacle, for God had consecrated the temple to himself, that he might dwell in it. When the stones of the sanctuary were thus disgracefully scattered, it must have deeply hurt the minds of all the godly, for they saw that God's name was thus exposed to people's reproaches.

2. **How the precious sons of Zion, once worth their weight in gold, are now considered as pots of clay, the work of a potter's hands!** The prophet now comes to the people, although he does not include all the people but only those who excelled in honor. He says they had become like **pots of clay** (see Jeremiah 18:2ff.; 19:11). When he now says that the leaders, **the precious sons of Zion,** were stripped of all dignity, he depicts God's judgment, which the Jews had for a time disregarded.

3. **Even jackals offer their breasts to nurse their young, but my people have become heartless like ostriches in the desert.** By this comparison the prophet amplifies the miseries of the people, saying that their condition is worse than jackals and ostriches. The people are without help; seeking the help of their mothers and others is in vain.

4. **Because of thirst the infant's tongue sticks to the roof of its mouth; the children beg for bread, but no one gives it to them.** The prophet describes the famine in the city, which he had predicted. He had said it would be better to be killed than to remain alive with these people. The people did not listen to the prophet, and now he rebukes them for their previous unbelief.

5. **Those who once ate delicacies are destitute in the streets. Those nurtured in purple now lie on ash heaps.** There is no doubt that the siege

drove the people to acts that are too degrading to mention, as is implied further in the next verse and portrayed clearly in verse 10.

6. The punishment of my people is greater than that of Sodom, which was overthrown in a moment without a hand turned to help her. The people of Jerusalem did not perish immediately like the Sodomites. In this sense their punishment was greater than that of Sodom. For God saw that they were so obstinate in their wickedness that he destroyed some by famine, some by disease, and some by the sword.

7-8. Their princes were brighter than snow and whiter than milk, their bodies more ruddy than rubies, their appearance like sapphires. But now they are blacker than soot; they are not recognized in the streets. Their skin has shriveled on their bones; it has become as dry as a stick. The prophet speaks here of the Nazirites, by whom we know the worship of God was honored; they not only observed the law but consecrated themselves to God. We learn that as God's favor had appeared to the Nazirites before, so now also his vengeance would be known, because they had been reduced to a degrading deformity.

9. Those killed by the sword are better off than those who die of famine; racked with hunger, they waste away for lack of food from the field. In other words, they have not been pierced by the sword but have been wounded by famine.

10. With their own hands compassionate women have cooked their own children, who became their food when my people were destroyed. As the prophet says these mothers were compassionate, no one should think they were devoid of all natural feeling. But the prophet also meant to show the blindness that comes from God's dreadful vengeance. The prophet's words would not have affected the people enough unless he testified that the mothers he refers to were not so brutal as not to have gladly given food to their children. They were supernaturally blinded by madness.

11. The LORD has given full vent to his wrath; he has poured out his fierce anger. He kindled a fire in Zion that consumed her foundations. To our ears, **given full vent to his wrath** seems a harsh expression, but it means that he executed his extreme judgment.

Fire rarely penetrates to the foundations of a building. But the prophet says here that this fire will not only destroy the roofs and what is above the ground but will consume Zion's **foundations.**

12. The kings of the earth did not believe, nor did any of the world's people, that enemies and foes could enter the gates of Jerusalem. The prophet says that **kings** and **people** alike did not believe their enemies could storm Jerusalem.

13. But it happened because of the sins of her prophets and the iniquities of her priests, who shed within her the blood of the righteous. Jeremiah denounces the sin of the **prophets** and the iniquity of the **priests**

and then mentions the savage cruelty that was, so to speak, the summit of all their vices. When those who despised God went so far as to give themselves over to shedding innocent **blood**, it revealed their diabolical obstinacy.

14. Now they grope through the streets like men who are blind. They are so defiled with blood that no one dares to touch their garments. We see that all of Jerusalem was so polluted that no one could pass through it without becoming unclean.

15. "Go away! You are unclean!" men cry to them. "Away! Away! Don't touch us!" When they flee and wander about, people among the nations say, "They can stay here no longer." Their evil was so great that they were gripped with fear. So they turned to devious paths and met darkness and had no hope of a return to their land.

16. The LORD himself has scattered them; he no longer watches over them. The priests are shown no honor, the elders no favor. The prophet views the desolation and says there is no other conclusion than that the Jews would be exiles. As all the ways were closed to them and they could not return, so God's eyes were shut, and he would not look on them.

17. Moreover, our eyes failed, looking in vain for help; from our towers we watched for a nation that could not save us. The prophet accuses the people of another sin—neglecting God and trusting in false and vain hopes. We know how much the prophet warned the people not to trust the Egyptians for deliverance. But the people never believed this until it was shown to be true through their own bitter experience.

18-19. Men stalked us at every step, so we could not walk in our streets. Our end was near, our days were numbered, for our end had come. Our pursuers were swifter than eagles in the sky; they chased us over the mountains and lay in wait for us in the desert. The Babylonians followed the Jews like hunters, watching every step they took.

We could not walk in our streets. It is as if he said, "We had no freedom in our own city; much less were we allowed to go out and ramble in the fields."

The prophet taunts them by saying that those who pursued them were **swifter than eagles.**

20. The LORD's anointed, our very life breath, was caught in their traps. We thought that under his shadow we would live among the nations. In other words, "Although we may be driven to foreign nations, yet the king will be able to gather us, and his shadow will extend far and wide to keep us safe." The Jews believed this wrongly because by their defection they had thrown off the yoke of Christ and of God, as it says in Psalm 2:3. Since they had shaken off the heavenly yoke, it was no good for them to trust in the shadow of an earthly king; they were totally unworthy of God's protection.

21. Rejoice and be glad, O Daughter of Edom, you who live in the land of Uz. But to you also the cup will be passed; you will be drunk and stripped naked. The prophet tries to lessen the sorrow of the godly, who saw that they were being insolently taunted by their neighbors. He says the people of Edom will be so confounded by the atrocity of their evils that they will be dead to all shame.

22. O Daughter of Zion, your punishment will end; he will not prolong your exile. But, O Daughter of Edom, he will punish your sin and expose your wickedness. The sorrow of the Jews would be very miserable, but the Edomites would also be punished. The prophet says in effect, "The punishment of your sin, daughter of Zion, has indeed been completed; but your sin, Daughter of Edom, will be uncovered." Jeremiah wanted to compare the Jews with the Edomites in order to reveal to the Jews that the Edomites would be overwhelmed, just as they had been.

Lamentations
Chapter 5

1. Remember, O LORD, what has happened to us; look, and see our disgrace. This is more of a complaint than a prayer. Jeremiah mentions what had happened to the people in their extreme calamity in order to turn God toward compassion and mercy.

2. Our inheritance has been turned over to aliens, our homes to foreigners. A listing of the many calamities is now given by the prophet so that he and his people may obtain God's favor. The Jews had been robbed of their fields and also of their **homes.**

3. We have become orphans and fatherless, our mothers like widows. Here the prophet not only speaks on behalf of all the people but utters complaints on behalf of each of them. So the verse does not apply only to the whole body but to individual members. It is not normal for a country to become full of orphans after a single battle, but the prophet says here that there will be orphans and widows because of God's continual vengeance.

4. We must buy the water we drink; our wood can be had only at a price. The prophet does not complain that they have been deprived of luxuries, but he mentions **water** and **wood,** common necessities of life. It is a terrible change when anyone who once cut wood of his own and harvested his own wine and corn can now not have even a drop of water without having to buy it.

5. Those who pursue us are at our heels; we are weary and find no rest. Here he says that the people are oppressed with a terrible bondage. We know how long the prophet warned them without any success. Here, however, he seeks God's favor, saying that the people are miserable without limit or end.

6. We submitted to Egypt and Assyria to get enough bread. It was evidence of a dreadful curse when the people were forced to beg for **bread.** Instead of feeding others out of their plenty, they were driven to beg bread from the Egyptians and Assyrians.

7. Our fathers sinned and are no more, and we bear their punishment. Our prophet wanted God to be merciful. To achieve this object he says in effect, "O Lord, you have indeed punished justly in the past when our ancestors abused your goodness and forbearance. But the time has come now for you to see if we are like our ancestors. They were punished in the past; may we receive your favor in the present."

8. Slaves rule over us, and there is none to free us from their hands. The Jews had been robbed of their freedom, but their condition was made far worse, for they had been made subject to servants.

9. We get our bread at the risk of our lives because of the sword in the desert. What has the sword to do with the desert? The Jews were exposed to death in the desert, where they had to go if they were to find any bread.

10. Our skin is hot as an oven, feverish from hunger. Food nourishes human life, but famine burns it up.

11. Women have been ravished in Zion, and virgins in the towns of Judah. He mentions here another kind of reproach. God had commanded chastity to be observed among his people. When therefore virgins and women were defiled, it was an extremely disgraceful thing.

12. Princes have been hung up by their hands; elders are shown no respect. When no respect is shown to the elderly, the worst kind of barbaric acts follow.

13. Young men toil at the millstones; boys stagger under loads of wood. Of all manual work, the lowest was grinding corn. This work was usually given to slaves or donkeys. This means that the Jews were treated most shamefully. Boys were forced to carry loads of wood too heavy for them.

14. The elders are gone from the city gate; the young men have stopped their music. Here the prophet briefly shows that the city was reduced to ruins, so that nothing but desolation could be seen there. When cities are lived in, judges sit at the gate. The picture the prophet gives is of a city where all civil order has been abolished.

15. Joy is gone from our hearts; our dancing has turned to mourning. We know that life is more bitter than death when people are in a constant state of mourning. Where there is no joy, life is worse than death.

16. The crown has fallen from our head. Woe to us, for we have sinned! Knowledge of our sins will tame our pride and check our grumbling, which the ungodly constantly indulge in as they oppose God. Our evils, then, should lead us to consider God's judgment and to confess our sins. This is what our prophet has in mind.

17-18. Because of this our hearts are faint, because of these things our eyes grow dim for Mount Zion, which lies desolate, with jackals prowling over it. It was a dreadful thing that Jerusalem had become

desolate, with jackals replacing God and his people. No wonder Jeremiah mentions this as one of the bitterest calamities.

19. You, O LORD, reign forever; your throne endures from generation to generation. The prophet now lifts his eyes up to God. By his example he encourages all godly people to turn toward God. When we concentrate on the present, nothing but adversity clouds our eyes; the remedy is to raise our eyes to God, for no matter how terrible things are in this world, he remains the same. In short, were the world to change and perish a hundred times, nothing could ever affect the immutability of God.

20. Why do you always forget us? Why do you forsake us so long? The prophet here seems to be expostulating with God. The faithful, even when they patiently submit to God's scourges, place their complaints at his feet as they unburden themselves (see Psalm 13:1ff.). Jeremiah saw the situation according to the evils then being endured. Doubtless he believed that God had not forsaken his own people and that he had not forgotten them, but he complains in this way because of his human frailty. He did not grumble so that people might indulge themselves in their own thoughts, but so they might ascend by degrees to God and overcome all these temptations.

21. Restore us to yourself, O LORD, that we may return; renew our days as of old. The prophet shows that the remedy is in God's hand whenever he decided to help his people. So he exults in God's power, as if he were saying that God is not without power but can help his people whenever he pleases.

Note that he grounds his hope on the ancient benefits of God. As God had previously redeemed his people, so the prophet encourages himself to entertain hope and suggests to others the same ground of confidence.

22. . . . unless you have utterly rejected us and are angry with us beyond measure. God cannot reject his people, remain angry with them, and never be reconciled. We see from this that the prophet does not simply set down a condition, as if he said, "O God, if you are to be angry forever with us and we will never be reconciled, we have no hope of salvation. But if you will be reconciled to us, we will then entertain good hope." The prophet did not think in this way but had a sure confidence in God's favor. For God will never forsake those whom he has chosen (see Romans 11).